The Game Maker's Manual - Atari ST and STOS BASIC

Stephen Hill

SIGMA PRESS – Wilmslow, United Kingdom

First published in 1990 Reprinted 1990

Sigma Press, 1 South Oak Lane, Wilmslow, Cheshire SK9 6AR, England.

British Library Cataloguing in Publication Data

A CIP catalogue record for this book is available from the British Library.

ISBN: 1-85058-158-4

Typesetting and design by

Sigma Hi-Tech Services Ltd

Cover design and layout by

Ellis, Ives and Sprowell, and Professional Graphics

Printed and Bound by:

Manchester Free Press, Paragon Mill, Jersey Street, Manchester M4 6FP.
Tel: 061-236 8822

Distributed by

John Wiley & Sons Ltd., Baffins Lane, Chichester, West Sussex, England.

Contents

1 First Steps 1
1.1 Planning a game 1
1.2 Initial ideas 2
1.3 Producing a game plan 3
    1.3.1 Understanding the problem 3
    1.3.2 Modular programming 7
    1.3.3 Pseudo-code 7
1.4 Critical phases 12
1.5 Designing the graphics 12
    1.5.1 Background screens 12
    1.5.2 Choosing the resolution 13
    1.5.3 Mock-ups 14
    1.5.4 Designing the sprites 15
1.6 Data structures 17
    1.6.1 Introduction to data structures 17
    1.6.2 Memory constraints 18
    1.6.3 Garbage collection 19
    1.6.4 Memory requirements of an array 19
1.7 Overview of the game plan 19
1.8 Using the game plan 20
    1.8.1 Collision detection 21
1.9 Documentation 22
1.10 Testing 23
    1.10.1 Syntax errors 23
    1.10.2 Logic errors 23
    1.10.3 Final testing 24
1.11 Optimization 25
    1.11.1 Look-up tables 25
    1.11.2 The shift instructions 26
    1.11.3 Optimization check-list 27
1.12 Conclusion 27

2 Shoot-em-ups 28
2.1 Space invaders 28
2.2 Basic techniques 29
    2.2.1 A brief look at Zoltar 29

2.3 Designing a shoot-em-up 30
2.3.1 Anatomy of a shoot-em-up 30
2.4 Moving the aliens 30
2.4.1 Moving the aliens in a straight line 32
2.4.2 Complex attack paths 32
2.4.3 Movement tables 34
2.5 Fire control 37
2.5.1 Controlling the gun 37
2.5.2 Firing a missile 38
2.6 Collision detection 39
2.6.1 Collisions between the player's ship and missile 40
2.6.2 Collision between attacker and a missile 40
2.7 Animating the background 41
2.8 Inside Zoltar 41
2.8.1 Initialisation 42
2.8.2 Control loop 42
2.8.3 The play game routine 43
2.8.4 The Magedon! 45
2.8.5 Possible enhancements 46

3 Rebound games 47
3.1 Introduction 47
3.2 Game plan of a rebound game 48
3.2.1 Critical routines for rebound 48
3.3 The game screen 50
3.3.1 Designing the screen 50
3.3.2 Creating a screen 50
3.3.3 Drawing the blocks on the screen 52
3.4 The bat 53
3.4.1 Controlling the bat 53
3.4.2 Positioning the bat 54
3.5 The ball 54
3.5.1 Initial conditions (gluing the ball to the bat) 54
3.5.2 Releasing the ball 54
3.5.3 Moving the ball 54
3.6 Collisions 56
3.6.1 Detecting a collision with the bat 56
3.6.2 Collisions between the ball and the block 57
3.6.3 Collisions between a ball and the walls 57
3.6.4 Collisions with the ball and an irregular object 58
3.7 Rebounds 59
3.7.1 Rebound tables 59
3.7.2 Rebounds with a wall 59
3.7.3 Rebounds with the bat 62
3.7.4 Rebounds with the block 63
3.8 Inside Orbiter 67

3.8.1 Initialisation 67
3.8.2 The control loop 69
3.8.3 Playing a game 70

4 Simulations 75
4.1 What is simulation? 75
4.2 Simulation games 76
4.2.1 The game world 76
4.2.2 Game tie 77
4.3 Simulating movement in space 77
4.3.1 The equations of motion 77
4.3.2 Motion in two dimensions 82
4.3.3 3D Movements 86
4.4 Flight simulators 88
4.4.1 Game plan of a flight simulator 89
4.4.2 Reading the controls 89
4.4.3 Control panels 90
4.5 Space simulations 91
4.6 Other simulations 92
4.6.1 Creating a simulation 92
4.6.2 Economic simulation 92
4.7 Conclusions 98

5 Role-playing games 99
5.1 History 99
5.2 Anatomy of a role-playing game 100
5.2.1 Character classes 101
5.2.1 Attributes 101
5.2.3 Experience 103
5.3 Scenarios 104
5.3.1 What is a scenario? 104
5.3.2 Practical considerations 104
5.3.3 Some basic scenario ideas 105
5.3.4 The game map 106
5.4 Game plan of a role-playing game 108
5.5 Creating a character 109
5.5.1 Selecting the attributes 109
5.5.2 Generating a character 110
5.6 Drawing the map 115
5.6.1 Displaying a map from above 115
5.6.2 Displaying part of a map 116
5.6.3 3D effects 125
5.7 Controlling the character 125
5.7.1 Using the keyboard 125
5.7.2 Joystick input 126
5.7.3 Using the mouse 127

5.8 Multiple characters 127
5.8.1 The leading character 128
5.8.2 Individual control 128
5.9 Combat 128
5.9.1 Mêlée rounds 129
5.10 Magic 135
5.11 Conclusion 136

6 Adventure games 137
6.1 A little history 137
6.2 Adventurers start here 138
6.2.1 Sample transcript from Colossal cave 138
6.2.2 Why STOS Basic? 139
6.3 Scenario design 139
6.3.1 Creating a map 140
6.4 Game plan of an adventure 141
6.4.1 Standard routines 143
6.5 Understanding text 143
6.5.1 The text parser 143
6.5.2 The verb noun parser 144
6.5.3 Expanding the parser 148
6.6 Picturing the scene 152
6.6.1 Choosing the graphics 152
6.6.2 The screen compactor 152
6.7 Graphic adventures 153
6.8 The rooms 155
6.8.1 The long room description 155
6.8.2 The short room description 156
6.8.3 Storing the room descriptions 156
6.8.4 Displaying your descriptions 157
6.8.5 Moving between rooms 158
6.9 The objects 161
6.9.1 Choosing the objects 161
6.9.2 The current location 162
6.9.3 The inventory 163
6.10 Handling the events 163
6.11 Acting on the user's commands 165
6.11.1 Global commands 165
6.11.2 Local commands 167
6.11.3 System commands 168
6.11.4 Movement commands 169
6.12 Conclusions 170

7 3D Techniques 171
7.1 Introduction 171
7.2 Creating an object in 3D 171

7.2.1 Coordinate systems 171
7.3 General techniques 174
7.3.1 Moving the origin 174
7.3.2 Scaling an object 175
7.4 Displaying an object in 3D 177
7.4.1 Perspective 177
7.4.2 Clipping 184
7.5 3D rotation 186
7.5.1 Rotation directions 186
7.5.2 The 3D rotation formulae 187
7.6 Checking for visibility 194
7.7 Flight simulators 196
7.8 practical considerations 199
7.8.1 Sine tables 199
7.9 Conclusions 200

8 Animation Techniques 201
8.1 Colour scrolling 201
8.1.1 Basic principles 201
8.1.2 FLASH 203
8.1.3 SHIFT 203
8.1.4 The FADE instruction 204
8.2 The ANIM command 205
8.3 Screen animation 206
8.3.1 SCREEN$ 207
8.3.2 Screen flipping 208
8.4 Conclusion 209

9 Sampled sound 211
9.1 Introduction 211
9.2 The STOS MAESTRO system 212
9.3 Special effects 213
9.3.1 Choosing the recording speed 213
9.3.2 Getting the most out of your sampler 214
9.4 Potential sound sources 214
9.4.1 The MAESTRO samples disk 214
9.4.2 The public domain 215
9.4.3 Films and tapes 215
9.4.4 Television 215
9.4.5 Other sources 216
9.4.6 Creating an alien 216
9.4.7 Direct synthesis 217
9.5 Possible applications 218
9.5.1 Arcade games 218
9.5.2 Simulations 218
9.5.3 RPGs 218

9.5.4 Adventures 218
9.6 Conclusion 219

10 Scrolling techniques 221
10.1 Introduction 221
10.2 Basic principles 222
10.3 The SCROLL command 224
10.4 A window to the world 228
10.4.1 The game map 229
10.4.2 The MAP definer 229
10.4.3 Storing the map 230
10.4.5 Scrolling through a map 230
10.4.6 Initialising the game map 231
10.4.7 Redrawing the fringe 232
10.5 Screen flipping 236
10.6 Using sprites with a screen scrolling game 238
10.6.1 Difference between UPDATE and SYNCHRO 238
10.7 Conclusion 239

11 Assembly language programming techniques 241
11.1 Why program in assembly language? 241
11.2 Choosing an assembler 242
11.2.1 The STOS Basic assembler 242
11.2.2 Other assemblers 242
11.3 Free standing assembly language programs 243
11.4 STOS Basic extensions 244
11.5 Interpreter extensions 245
11.5.1 The header 245
11.5.2 Initialisation section 247
11.5.3 Syntax checking 248
11.5.4 Function definitions 253
11.5.5 System support routines 254
11.5.6 Interpreter extension checklist 259
11.5.7 B is for BUG! 259
11.6 The compiler extensions 261
11.6.1 The header for compiler extension 261
11.6.2 The compiler library 264
11.6.3 Creating a compiler library 265
11.6.4 Retrieving the parameters entered by the user 266
11.6.5 Using a data area 266
11.6.6 System variables 267
11.6.7 Compiler extension checklist 270
11.7 Conclusions 270

Glossary 271
Index 277

1

First Steps

1.1 Planning a game

It's a well known fact that the journey of a thousand miles begins with just a single step. This is especially true if you're trying to write a computer game, as it's all too easy to fall flat on your face before you have really started. Wouldn't it be nice if there was someone out there to help you on your way? Well, that's the aim of this chapter. I can't promise to solve all your problems for you, but I can try to signpost some of the danger signs you will encounter during your journey.

Many people think that the difficult part of games programming is actually writing the code. But if you were to ask a professional programmer about this, the answer would probably surprise you. Programming is easy, they would say, it's only the initial planning phases that are complicated. Commercial software houses often employ separate people especially to make up the initial plans. These **systems analysts** don't produce a single line of code. But they are usually paid several times the salary of even the best computer programmer.

If you want to write a computer game successfully, you need to combine the skills of both the programmer and the systems analyst. Sometimes the temptation to start programming immediately can be almost irresistible. This temptation should be avoided at all costs! Any mistakes you make early on in your program will be propagated through your code like a horde of locusts, and will eat away at it until it is stone dead. After you've invested a great deal of time and energy into a particular program, it can be heartbreaking to discover that the basic concept of the program is completely unworkable. Writing a game without a plan is as silly as visiting a strange city without bothering to take a map. In both situations you would probably get totally lost before you reached halfway to your intended destination. Planning is one of the most crucial phases of games creation. Good programmers plan each step of their programs carefully before writing a single line. So when they write their programs they always know precisely what they are trying to achieve, and have already solved most of the potential problems well in advance.

If you plan your game scrupulously, the programming will suddenly seem incredibly easy. A day's worth of planning can often save you several weeks of difficult programming. So any effort involved in the planning process will usually be rewarded many times over.

The real beauty of the planning stage, is that enables you to discover any potential difficulties in your program well in advance. If some of these problems prove to be insoluble, it's then usually possible to adapt your game to avoid them completely. You can also perform simple experiments to check how the mechanics of your game will work out in practice. This lets you explore many possible ideas before committing yourself to anything concrete.

1.2 Initial ideas

Few computer games are written in isolation. Nowadays, most games can be placed into one of a small number of basic types. These categories include arcade games, adventures, platform games, and war-games. Some formats have been developed from just a single success story, whilst others are the latest developments of ideas which hark back to the very earliest days of computing.

You start off by choosing one of the type of games which particularly interest you. You should then try to think of any ways one of these games could be improved. Obviously, it's pointless to attempt to write an exact duplicate of someone else's program in STOS Basic. Not only is this almost certainly illegal, but it's also completely futile. If people want to play the original ARKANOID, they will invariably prefer to buy the official version rather than yours. At least that way they will be rewarding the people who did the actual work on the project.

Furthermore, if you wish to sell your program to either a commercial software house or a magazine, you will need to add something new and innovative to make your game stand out from the crowd.

A good source of inspiration is to look at as many existing examples of your chosen format as possible. You can then make out a complete list of the various things you like and dislike about these games. Hopefully, this process should give you a number of useful ideas about how the game might be expanded. Think of different modifications to the game, and try to work out the consequences of these changes in terms of the final game play. But don't get too carried away with any single idea. Inevitably, as your plans progress, some notions will prove to be unworkable, and other possibilities will occur to you instead.

In order to illustrate this technique, I'll list a few of the plus and minus points from MEGAMAX'S MEGAROIDS game. I've chosen this program incidentally, because it's one of the few games which are owned by the majority of ST users.

Likes:

- ❏ Nice graphics;
- ❏ GEM based;
- ❏ Action fast and furious;
- ❏ Good implementation of the game "ASTEROIDS";
- ❏ High score table;
- ❏ Works equally well on colour or monochrome systems.

Dislikes:

- ❏ Poor use of colour;
- ❏ No support for low resolution;
- ❏ Keyboard used to control ship rather than joystick;
- ❏ Lack of variety;
- ❏ Poor use of sound.

On the whole, MEGAROIDS is quite a reasonable game. It's certainly an excellent demonstration of MEGAMAX's C compiler. But these comments do suggest a number of possible improvements. These could form the basis of a new version of MEGAROIDS written in STOS Basic.

1.3 Producing a game plan

I'll now go into the precise details of how one of these game plans can be created. The first stage is to produce a detailed specification. This should consist of a complete written description of the game in standard English. The aim of the specification is to list all the important features of your program, and to attempt to isolate any potential problems. You can also use this process as an opportunity to work out the detailed mechanics of the game play. What's the aim of the game? How will it eventually be achieved by the player?

Failure to concentrate sufficiently on this problem can have potentially disastrous results. It's quite possible to spend a great deal of time and energy to produce a game which looks and sounds absolutely brilliant, but which is completely unplayable. This is an area that even the experts can occasionally get wrong. So even if you already have a fairly good idea about the sort of game you wish to create, it's still worth while drawing out a detailed game plan.

It's amazing how many improvements can arise from the simple transition of an idea onto paper.

1.3.1 Understanding the problem

I'll now show you how a complete specification can be produced for the MEGAROIDS type game I mentioned earlier. I'll start off with a brief description of the game in English. If you've got a version of MEGAROIDS on your ST, it might be a good idea to play around with it for a while before you read any further.

The first decision I'll take is to choose a name for my new game. The selection on a name is often quite difficult, since you need to find something which hasn't already been used. I'll provisionally call my game PATHFINDER, keeping the option to change it later if it proves necessary.

Specification for PATHFINDER

Description:

This is a game based on the old arcade favourite ASTEROIDS. The player is given control of a space ship which can be moved around on the screen. The ship is initially placed at the centre of the playing area. During the game, a number of large rocks slowly creep up from the edges. If one of these rocks hits the players ship then the player will lose a life. The object of the game is simply to zap the rocks with the gun before they collide with the space ship.

Alongside this verbal description, you can also add rough sketches of the various graphical elements which make up the game. A mock-up of a typical screen might look rather like the one shown in Figure 1.1.

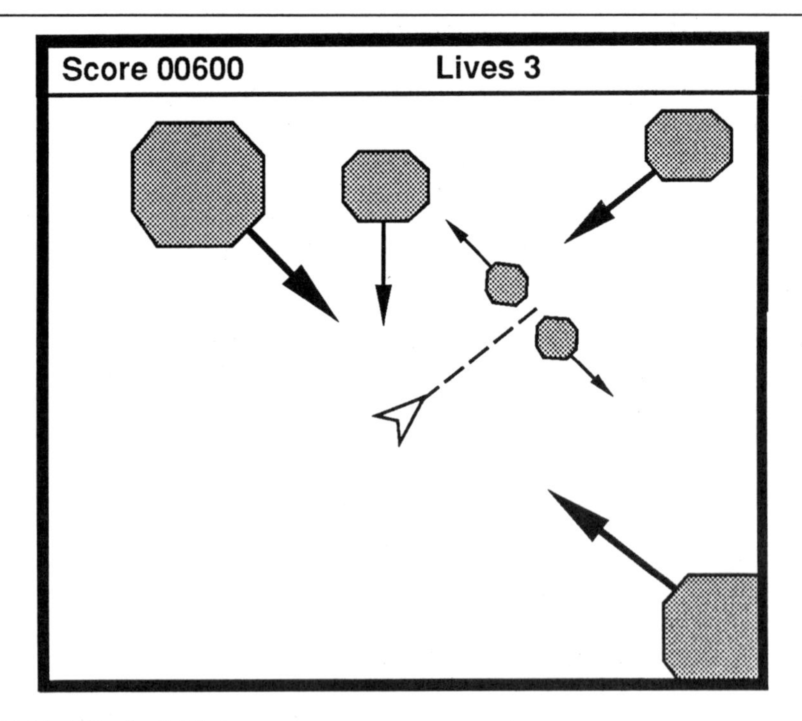

Figure 1.1 Mock-Up of a Pathfinder screen

You can now jot down a list of the various actions which will take place when the game is played, along with any initial thoughts about how these might be implemented in the final program.

Actions:

1 The rocks will move in straight lines from a random point on the edge of the screen.

Note: Move using STOS MOVE command.

2 Shooting a large rock will split it into two medium sized ones which will move apart at right angles to the rocks original course.

Note: Large rock uses 32 by 40 sprite?
Medium rock uses 16 by 20 sprite?

3 Shooting a medium sized rock will split it into two smaller ones. These rocks will move away from each other after they are created.

Note: Small rock uses 16 by 8 sprite?

4 Shooting a small rock will destroy it.

5 The smaller the rock, the faster it will move and the higher the points which will be scored when it is hit.

6 The player controls a small space ship using the joystick.

Note: implement ship as 16 by 16 sprite.

7 Pulling the left hand joystick will move the player's ship around on the screen.

8 If the ship is hit by a rock, both ship and the rocks are destroyed.

9 Pressing the fire button releases a missile. This takes the form of a moving dot.

10 The player will be allowed to fire as many shots as he likes on the screen.

11 If a shot hits a rock, the rock will be either split or destroyed depending on its size. The players score will increased appropriately.

If you examine these actions carefully, a couple of significant questions should arise:

STOS Basic only allows you to use fifteen sprites at any one time. Since each rock will spawn up to four smaller rocks during the game, you will need to restrict the initial number of rocks accordingly. The maximum number of asteroids at the start of the game can be calculated by simply dividing the number of sprites by four. This results in a initial maximum of 3.75 rocks. Obviously, it's impossible to split a sprite into pieces, so the initial number of asteroids will be three or less. This will use up 12 of the 15 sprites, leaving you with three spares. As the rocks are successively destroyed, your program can then add new ones from the sides of the screen.

There's also a question of speed. STOS Basic works best when there are just a limited number of sprites on the screen. So how will it cope with these 12 sprites? Luckily, the original specification required only the smallest rocks to be moved at high speed. Providing you keep these sprites as small as possible, you should still be able to produce a game which plays reasonably smoothly.

The final problem, posed by the specification, is the nature of the dot used for the missile. How will this be generated? You can't use a sprite, as there are only a couple spare. Could you use the STOS Basic PLOT command in some way? Or will you have to work around this problem by changing the specification? You might find that the only way to beat this problem would be to remove requirement number 10 completely. This was the line which allowed the player to fire multiple missiles. You would now be able to implement your missile using a single sprite.

Alternatively, you could also attempt to generate the missile using PLOT. Before continuing with your game plan, you could check whether this approach was feasible by writing a small program as an experiment. If this was successful, you could then design your game, secure in the knowledge that the solution to the problem was actually achievable. This situation is typical of the type of difficulty which is commonly thrown up during the planning stage. If you hadn't bothered with the game plan, you would only have discovered the problem well into writing the program. The only feasible solution might even have involved completely rewriting your game from scratch!

Of course, the specification I have shown you is only intended as a rough demonstration, and would probably need expanding before it was ready to proceed any further. The game play in particular, would currently appear to be rather repetitive. Here are a few suggestions for possible improvements:

12 Different types of rocks have separate colours.

13 Red boulders explode violently and score higher points.

14 Yellow boulders need several hits before they explode, and score maximum points.

15 If the player hits the <SPACE> bar, the ship jumps to a random location. (Hyperspace option)

16 An enemy ship appears at random intervals and fires at the player. Killing this ship scores extra points.

The key thing to remember about these game plans, is that they should never be set in concrete. Even the best plan can be improved, and you will probably think up a number of potentially interesting ideas during the development process. It's recommended that you only treat the game plan as a flexible framework which can be fleshed out in the course of time.

1.3.2 Modular programming

The next stage in the development process is to group the various activities into separate tasks. These will eventually form the basis for the subroutines which are used in the final STOS Basic program. Experience has shown that any large program can be simplified enormously if it is split up into a number of smaller, more manageable chunks. This approach is known as **modular programming**.

Modular programming has proved phenomenally successful in the world of computing. STOS Basic itself was produced using a similar technique, as were all the pieces of associated software. Modular programs are both easy to write and easy to change. So you can start off with something extremely basic, and steadily expand it into a polished and attractive game.

You begin by listing the individual activities which are to be performed by the program. These can be grouped together into the following way:

1 Initialise the screen
2 Move the rocks
3 Move the ship
4 Test the joystick
5 Fire the bullet
6 Detect collisions

Each of these five activities represents the execution of a specific section of the program. Unfortunately, this list only gives you a very crude picture of the program, as there is no information specifying the particular order in which an activity will be performed. Before you can include this in your descriptions, it's necessary to extend the current notation so as to allow you to make decisions. The easiest way to achieve this, is to use something called **pseudo-code** (pronounced soo-doe-code).

1.3.3 Pseudo-code

Pseudo-code enables us to completely describe the action of any computer program using a limited form of English.

The fundamental unit of this pseudo-code notation is the statement. Statements are represented by a few words which explain concisely what each operation is supposed to achieve.

The following English phrases are all valid pseudo-code statements:

```
Move the ship
Update score
```

Like Basic, you can control your activities using statements such as IF...THEN, and loops like REPEAT...UNTIL. But since we are working on paper, there is no complicated syntax to remember.

Pseudo-code is not limited to just describing a computer program, and can be applied to any activity. The best way to understand pseudo-code is to attempt to write some yourself. Try to produce a pseudo-code description of the activities you would need to perform in order to make a cup of black coffee. Assume you are giving instructions to an intelligent, but literal-minded person who has no initiative whatsoever. If you have a little experience with adventure games, you should have a good idea of the sort of words you will need to use.

After a little work, you should have written something like:

```
get coffee jar
get coffee mug
get spoon
grab top of coffee jar
grasp top of the jar
repeat
     turn top
until top is removed
push spoon in coffee jar
scoop up some coffee
empty coffee from spoon into mug
put down coffee jar
put down spoon
put down mug
get kettle
fill kettle from sink
plug kettle's lead into power socket
turn on kettle
while kettle is turned on
If kettle boils
     then
          turn off kettle
          pour water into coffee mug
     endif
wend
```

As you can see, even simple activities need to be broken down into quite a long list of instructions. Fortunately, writing a computer game is MUCH easier than making a cup of coffee! (How many coffee machines do you know which can perform all these actions by themselves?)

The main intention of pseudo-code is to provide a sort of halfway house between a human language like English and a computer language like Basic. This allows you to produce a description of how an activity can be performed, without worrying about any boring implementation details.

Eventually each pseudo-code statement will be translated into Basic. After translation it may represent anything from one to several hundred actual instructions. Here are some small fragments of this pseudo-code applied to the pathfinder problem:

```
If rock is hit then destroy rock
If joystick has been moved
      then
            move the players ship
            check for collisions
      endif

Repeat
      Move rock
Until rock leaves screen

While missile is moving
      Check for collisions
Wend
```

It should be apparent that the statement between the IF and THEN represents a comparison of some sort. If this comparison is fairly complex, each test may involve a separate module in the resulting program.

This will be called before the check occurs, and will normally set a Basic variable which can be tested using the STOS Basic IF instruction.

See how I've used indentation to highlight groups of associated statements. Also note the WEND and ENDIF instructions, which indicates the outer limits of the list of statements which are to be performed by the WHILE and the IF operations respectively.

It is important to realise that there is nothing particularly sacred about the precise details of the notation I've just been discussing. You can therefore chop and change this notation as much as you like, without robbing the technique of any of its power. So if you would prefer to invent your own pseudo-code system instead of using mine, go ahead. The only thing that really matters is how easy it is for you to understand. Anything else is irrelevant.

A larger example of this pseudo-code, which concisely describes the action of the Pathfinder game is given in Figure 1.2 on the next page.

This code is not supposed to be complete by any means, and would need to be extended for the finished game plan. It is however, more than adequate to enable you to isolate a few more of the game's more important components. Have a brief look at this code, and try to jot down a list of crucial activities.

Hint: Each activity will be associated with a single pseudo-code statement.

```
Initialise the screen.
Repeat
    Move the rocks
    Check for collisions
    If a rock hits the ship
        then
            destroy ship
        endif
    If a bullet hits a large rock
        then
            split rock
            update score
        endif
    If a bullet hits a medium rock
        then
            split rock
            update score
        endif
    If a bullet hits a small rock
        then
            remove rock from the screen
            update score
            add new rock from edge of the screen
        endif
    Test the joystick
    If joystick has been pulled
        then
            move the ship
        endif
    If the fire button is pressed
        then
            activate bullet
        endif
    If bullet is activated
        then
            move bullet
        endif
Until ship is destroyed
```

Figure 1.2 Pseudo-Code description of Pathfinder

The main activities will be:

- ❑ Initialise the screen;
- ❑ Move rocks;
- ❑ Detect collisions;
- ❑ Destroy ship;
- ❑ Split rock;
- ❑ Update score;
- ❑ Remove rock from screen;
- ❑ Place new rock at edge of screen;
- ❑ Test the joystick;
- ❑ Move ship;
- ❑ Activate bullet;
- ❑ Move bullet.

These activities can also be expanded into pseudo-code. So the "Check for Collisions" activity could be expressed as:

Description of Check for Collisions:

```
Check for collision between a rock and the ship
    If bullet activated
        then
            check for collision between rock and bullet
            check for collision between ship and bullet
        endif
    If ship collides with bullet then destroy ship
```

By expanding all of the procedures using the same systematic method, you can refine the game plan still further. You should then isolate any new activities which will be required, and describe each of them with their own fragment of pseudo-code.

If you repeat this process, you will finally be left with a list of pseudo-code definitions representing each of the Basic procedures. These can then be translated directly into a small number of STOS Basic instructions. Normally, this point will be reached within approximately three or four loops. The game plan will now be complete, and you will have a complete description of the workings of your game.

Think of the planning process like the peeling of an onion, layer by layer. As the method progresses, the precise workings of the program will slowly be unravelled.

My own example has practically reached this point. Only the "destroy ship" activity will need to be developed any further. The various "check for collision" routines could be performed using a single "COLLIDE" instruction from STOS Basic.

Sometimes your original plan will prove slightly impractical. If for instance, you had added a check for the collision between two rocks, you would have encountered a problem. This is because the STOS Basic "COLLIDE" command has to include the number of a specific sprite. You would therefore need test the status each individual sprite of the screen in turn, before a collision would be detected. In practice, this process could slow down the action of your game significantly.

You could avoid this complication completely by simply jumping back to the original specification, and making the appropriate changes. Remember that the specification can easily be altered at any point during the development process.

1.4 Critical phases

The execution of any game can be split into three critical phases:

- ❑ Initialisation;
- ❑ Control loop;
- ❑ Termination.

The initialisation stage corresponds to the "Initialise screen" activity from Pathfinder. Its aim is to prepare all the various screens and load your variables with their initial values.

The Control loop forms the heart the game, and controls the action of the entire program. A typical example of this type of procedure can be seen in the pseudo-code I showed you earlier for the pathfinder program. (See Figure 1.2)

The Termination phase performs a simple cleaning-up operation after the game has concluded. This normally includes the following activities:

- ❑ Close any currently open files;
- ❑ Update the high score table on the disk;
- ❑ Present the player with the option of a further game.

1.5 Designing the graphics

1.5.1 Background screens

It's now time to design the various screens which will be appearing in your game. STOS Basic includes a range of facilities which make it especially easy to incorporate beautiful graphics directly into your Basic programs. Although STOS doesn't supply you with a built-in drawing utility, it's totally compatible with both the Neochrome and DEGAS graphics packages.

The single most important consideration when designing your graphics is to make them as easy to change as possible. The majority of software houses now employ different people to write their games, and to draw the screens. The latter include talented artists such as Mandarin's Dave McLachlan who drew most of the original artwork for STOS Basic. The employment of people of this calibre during the development of a game has contributed enormously to the vast improvement in the quality of such graphics over the past few years. If you wish to sell your game commercially, it is quite likely that your artwork will need to be re-drawn professionally at some stage. Even if your graphics are exceptional, there is always the possibility that the name will be have to be altered before publication. Most commercial games go through several name changes during development. This could have a significant affect on the final appearance of your game. Fortunately, STOS Basic is amazingly flexible in this respect.

All the sprite definitions are stored in a separate memory bank, and can be changed independently from the rest of your program. You can also load screen banks with an image in either DEGAS, or NEOCHROME format and compress them into just a fraction of their normal size using the compaction accessory. This format should generally be used for your background screens. Any other screens in your game are best created using the map definer, because these maps can be readily modified at any time without having to make major changes in the structure of your program.

1.5.2 Choosing the resolution

The most fundamental decision you must make when designing your game screens, is to decide which one of the ST's three resolutions you will be using. Unlike many other programming languages, STOS Basic is capable of performing equally well in all of the ST's three graphics modes. Since most ST users possess a colour system, your choice is really between medium or low resolution. Each of these modes has its own inherent set of advantages and disadvantages.

Low resolution is perfect for games which need a lot of colour. This includes the majority your arcade favourites such as Arkanoid and Xenon. Sometimes however, low resolution images simply can't contain all the information you wish to display on the screen, so medium resolution has to be used. Furthermore it's often quite easy to convert a medium resolution game into monochrome.

This widens your games appeal to all ST users, and is potentially a very useful selling point. (I'm reliably informed that 90% of Germans use ST's with a monochrome monitor!)

Certainly, if you're thinking of writing an adventure, it's well worth taking a little extra trouble to design your game for use with both mono and colour systems. Any built-in graphics can be easily restricted to low resolution without noticeably reducing the quality of the game. It's even possible to convert your colour pictures into monochrome inside the program. This technique is neatly used to add a touch of graphics to Rainbird's "The PAWN" when it is displayed on a monochrome monitor.

Obviously if you are restricted to a mono monitor, the decision will be effectively taken out of your hands. The market for high-resolution games may be fairly limited, but there is also very little competition in this area. The best idea is to write your game on a monochrome system initially, and then modify it for use in medium resolution colour. It is this approach which has been adopted by MINDSCAPE for their excellent BALANCE OF POWER.

1.5.3 Mock-ups

Before you begin drawing your final artwork, it is useful to sketch out the basic screen format on a piece of paper. Despite the undoubted power of drawing packages such as DEGAS and NEOCHROME, it's all too easy to get bogged down in extraneous details. You should initially concentrate on the overall structure of the screen, rather than producing a completely perfect rendition of the image. Many games require you to split the screen into a number of separate sections. It is therefore important to decide on the physical size of these areas, and work out exactly where they will be positioned.

Figure 1.3 shows an example of a typical mock-up of the screen for the ORBITER game supplied with STOS Basic.

Figure 1.3 Mock-Up of a background screen

After you have created your mock-ups on paper, you can then enter your sketches directly into Neochrome. These can be saved on the disk, and used for the preliminary versions of your game. It may be tempting to spend ages drawing the final artwork at this point. This is very dangerous idea, as it fixes the structure of the graphics at far too early a stage.

If you keep the initial screens simple, you can effortlessly make major modifications to your program as the game progresses.

This approach was used to great effect during the creation of the STOS Basic sprite definer. The author (Francois Lionet) originally based the program around a background screen which was supplied at the start of the assignment. The finished artwork was then added by Dave McLachlan, after the program itself had been completed.

Oddly enough, I never saw any of this artwork while I was writing the section on the sprite definer in the STOS Basic manual. This led to hilarious results when I first attempted to demonstrate the sprite definer to my friends, as I was thrown totally by the fancy icons. So despite having explained it to you in copious detail, I was sheepishly forced to refer back to my own manual before I could actually use it!

1.5.4 Designing the sprites

Any sprites which are to be used in your game need to be chosen with special care. Although STOS Basic is extremely good at moving your sprites around on the screen, some limitations are inevitable. The most important constraint is one of speed. As you would expect, the maximum speed of a sprite varies depending on its size. In general, the smaller the sprite, the faster it can be manipulated.

It's worth remembering that the more sprites you have on the screen, the slower they can be moved around.

This is particularly relevant to arcade games, such as space invaders, which often require you to restrict the size of your ships to 16 by 16 pixels in order to get the maximum speed.

Other programs, such as platform games, have comparatively few sprites on the screen. You therefore have the luxury of using sprites up to around 32 by 40. Finally, there are role-playing games which will often display less than three or four sprites at a time. These can easily utilise sprites up to the maximum of 64 by 64.

Of course, the previous discussion is only intended as a rough guide. Don't be afraid to experiment with larger sprites to see what happens. Providing you ruthlessly keep the number of objects on the screen to a bare minimum, it's still possible to envisage a perfectly playable arcade game using even the largest sprites.

Additionally, the movement speed of a sprite is also dependent on the screen resolution. Since the higher resolutions use less information to represent a single point on the screen, all sprite movements can be performed faster. This means a 32x32 sprite in medium resolution can be moved appreciably faster than the equivalent sprite in low resolution. So if your game requires particularly large objects, it might be worth considering writing the program to use medium resolution graphics.

Because the main sprite definer is compatible only with low resolution, you would be forced you to create your sprites using the SPRITE2 program, which can be found on the accessory disk.

You must keep track of the amount of memory which will be consumed by your sprites. On a 520 ST, STOS Basic leaves you with over 220k of memory to hold your programs and data. Normally, this will be more than adequate for the majority of your game ideas. If, however, you are contemplating using a very large number of game screens, you might find that memory starts to become rather tight. A single 64 by 64 sized sprite will take over 2k of the ST's memory in low resolution. So if you wanted to use dozens of these images, you could quickly run out of space.

The solution is to calculate your games memory requirements during the initial planning stage. This allows you tailor the size of your sprites precisely to the amount of available memory. But how can you compute the memory needs of a STOS Basic sprite? Fortunately, there a simple rule of thumb which can calculate the memory taken by any low resolution sprite:

```
MEMORY = WIDTH/2 * HEIGHT + 8
```

To work out the storage used by a 32x32 sprite, you could perform the following calculation:

```
MEMORY = 32/2 * 32 + 8
       = 16*32 + 8
       = 512 + 8
       = 520 bytes
```

This figure applies to each individual image you are using. So 10 of these images would use around 5k of the ST's memory.

Similarly, the equations for medium and high resolutions are:

```
MEMORY = WIDTH/4 * HEIGHT + 8 (Medium res)
MEMORY = WIDTH/8 * HEIGHT + 8 (High res)
```

The final size constraint is generated by your earlier decisions concerning the nature the background screen. If you are writing a platform game, you may have already decided to split the screen into three separate levels. This will inevitably determine the most appropriate size of your characters.

As with the background screens, it's sensible to produce a complete mock-up of all your sprites before you create them with the sprite definer. This is especially important if you wish to produce an animation sequence such as a walking man. By keeping the initial drawing extremely simple, you can work out the position of the various limbs relatively easily. You can then draw successive frames of the movement on separate pieces of paper, and animate the figure by simply flicking through the pages one after another.

This system may seem rather crude, but despite the availability of modern computers, it is still commonly used by many professional animators.

After you've animated the skeleton of the figure, you can then enter these frames directly into the STOS Basic sprite definer. It's wisest to leave these in their original state until the program is nearing completion. This will allow you to change the size or appearance of your sprites quickly, as your game evolves.

Figure 1.4 Mock-up of a sprite – the octopus from ANIMALS1.MBK (on STOS Basic accessory disk)

1.6 Data structures

1.6.1 Introduction to data structures

The last phase of the planning process, is to decide where the various pieces of information required in your game are to be stored. If you have written out your program in pseudo-code, some of this data will be fairly obvious. You can for instance, quickly list many of the simple variables which will occur in the pathfinder program. e.g.

```
score
number_of_rocks
lives_left
```

There will however, also be a need for far more complicated arrangements of data. These will be held in special data structures. "Data structure" is just a fancy name for a collection of items of similar information. There are a number of different types of data structures which can be used. These include arrays, lists, stacks and records. When writing a computer program, you are often faced with a bewildering range of storage methods.

By choosing the data structures most appropriate to the problem in hand, you can often speed up your game significantly. Supposing you wished to select the data structures required for the pathfinder program. In this case, the biggest requirement will be for a way of keeping track of the individual rocks. Every rock will be drawn using one of the 15 available sprites.

STOS Basic refers to each sprite using a number from 1 to 15. It's very important to keep track of the size of a rock, as this will be needed to decide whether the rock should be split in two or destroyed after a successful hit. You therefore need to create a table containing the size of each individual rock. This can be done using an array which can be defined at the start of the program in the following way:

```
10 DIM ROCK(12)
```

Each sprite will have a number specifying the size of the rock which it represents. If you have decided to have different sorts of rock in the game, you will also need separate arrays to hold this data. These can be defined in exactly the same way.

When you are defining your variables, you may be tempted combine many similar arrays in a single multi-dimensional array. However, it's recommended that you use a single dimension whenever possible, because STOS Basic does take slightly longer to retrieve information from an array with more than one dimension.

This means that a line like;

```
X=XARRAY(10):Y=YARRAY(10)
```

performs marginally faster than the equivalent;

```
X=ARRAY(10,1):Y=ARRAY(10,2)
```

The first line is also much easier to read.

1.6.2 Memory constraints

When you are choosing the data structures used by your game, it's important to keep an eye on the amount of memory they are taking up. The storage used by any variable depends on its type, as shown in the following table:

Type	*Size*	*Notes*
Integer	4 Bytes	Default variable type
Real	8 Bytes (even in v2.4)	Followed by a "#"
String	up to 65536	Followed by a "$"

1.6.3 Garbage collection

The STOS Basic SCREEN$ command often forces you to manipulate some very large strings indeed. Unfortunately, it can prove almost impossible to calculate in advance the amount of memory which will be used. This is particularly relevant if you are planning to swap information between several strings, because it can lead to an annoying problem known as **garbage collection**.

Garbage collection is a tidying-up operation which is invisibly performed by the STOS Basic system. It occurs at fairly irregular intervals, and can occasionally halt your entire game for several seconds.

The only reliable solution, is to use the STOS Basic FREE command to force this operation at a convenient point in your program. e.g.

```
10 X=FREE
```

Note that the garbage collection routine used for programs compiled using the STOS Compiler is much faster than the original interpreted one. This can lead to a dramatic improvement in the performance of certain games.

1.6.4 Memory requirements of an array

The amount of memory taken by an array can be calculated by simply multiplying the number of elements by the size of each one. In practice, the memory used can quickly mount up, especially when you are using arrays with more than a single dimension. This is particularly evident if your game utilises wireframe graphics. A single object in your game could easily need 30 or more coordinate pairs to describe it. If you wished to display this object from 10 different viewpoints, you would need to create a three dimensional array as follows:

```
10 dim object(10,30,2)
```

The total number of elements in this array would be 10*30*2 or 600. The memory used would therefore be 600*4 or 2400 bytes. This may not seem much, but it would still limit you to around 80 different objects on a standard 520 ST. If you tried to write a program which ignored this constraint, you could soon find yourself with a serious memory shortage.

1.7 Overview of the game plan

The planning stage of your game is now complete. Whew! If it all looks rather tedious, it is important to realise that the entire process can often be finished in less than a day.

Pseudo-code is especially useful; it is much easier to write than Basic, because you can leave out many of the fiddly implementation problems and concentrate on the overall structure of program. Even if you are only prepared to spend a couple of hours on your plan, you can still save yourself weeks of futile programming.

I'll conclude this section with a summary of the various steps in the planning process:

1 Choose a game type

2 Produce a written specification. This should include mock-ups of any screens used, and brief descriptions of the size and appearance of the sprites.

3 Isolate the various activities in your program.

4 Generate a pseudo-code description of each activity starting with the control loop.

5 Successively repeat steps 3-4 for each of the activities in your program.

6 Isolate the information needed by your program, and choose the appropriate data structures to contain it.

1.8 Using the game plan

Once you've finished your game plan, you are now ready to start generating the program lines which make up your game. Normally, this should be fairly easy, because much of the work will have already been done. It's best to write each section of your program on paper before typing it in. This is particularly important if you don't have a printer, as it can often prove almost impossible to debug large programs without a listing beside you.

As you write your program, it's sensible to make a note of all the different variables on a separate piece of paper. This will serve as a valuable memory jogger during the debugging process. Don't bother creating the finished artwork until the program is approaching completion. Try to concentrate on the game-play without the distractions of the graphics.

If you're writing an arcade game, most of the programming effort will need to be spent on producing the sections which will perform the sprite movements. Even if you have planned your game to perfection, there will inevitably be some problems which you simply cannot solve on paper. You then need to experiment with your program until you have achieved the desired effect.

Take the pathfinder program. In this case, you will have to concentrate on the sections of the program which move the rocks around on the screen. This will require you to create a list of movement strings which can be executed by the STOS Basic MOVE X and MOVE Y instructions.

Although you may have a very good idea about the approximate directions you will need, you will still need to experiment with a number of possibilities before you can generate the precise results you desire. It's therefore a good idea to start off with a simple test program which will enable you to play around with the various different options.

Here is a small example of a sprite experimenter program for you to type in.

Example 1.1 Sprite experimenter program

```
10 cls physic : cls back
20 input "Sprite Number";S
30 input "Image Number ";I
40 line input "Vertical moves";V$
50 line input "Horizontal moves";H$
60 sprite S,160,100,I
70  move x S,H$ : move y S,V$ : move on
80 input "Stop?";S$
90  move off : goto 10
```

This program expects to find some sprites in memory before it is run. If you've already created your sprites, you can enter these using a line like:

```
load "back.mbk"
```

Otherwise you should use the sprite definer accessory to produce a set of sprites with the appropriate sizes. These don't need to be anything fancy, as you are only interested in the speed and direction of the sprites rather than their appearance. Often a simple rectangular block is more than sufficient for this purpose. After you have experimented with this program, you should be left with a list of movement definitions which can be incorporated into your game.

Personally, I use this **prototyping** technique a great deal. By testing a bare-bones version of the code, you can quickly determine which approaches will actually work, and which can be safely discarded.

1.8.1 Collision detection

The most critical part of an arcade game is the collision detector. If this is badly written, your game will be virtually unplayable, no matter how good it looks. You should therefore endeavour to make this routine as fast and reliable as possible. STOS Basic includes two instructions for collision detection, COLLIDE and ZONE. COLLIDE is used to detect a collision between two or more sprites. Typical applications are in games such as ZOLTAR, or SPACE INVADERS.

The ZONE command allows you to check whether a specific rectangular area of the ST's screen currently contains a sprite. This command is extremely fast, and it is used to great effect by the game ORBITER, to discover when the ball hits one of the coloured blocks.

There is also a useful DETECT instruction, which enables you to test the colour of the point underneath the hot spot of a sprite. This could be very useful when creating games such as PINBALL.

Remember that the operation of these instructions is relative to a sprite's hot spot. So choose the position of this point very carefully.

For further information on the subject of collision detection, see Chapters 2 and 3.

1.9 Documentation

If you've ever attempted to modify one of your programs after a period of some months, you will already be aware of the vital importance of good documentation. This is especially true if you are hoping to sell your game. Frankly, a badly documented program is unlikely to be accepted by any of the ST magazines, as the workings will appear to be incomprehensible to their readers. Furthermore, software houses will often require substantial alterations to a game before accepting it. If the program is resistant to change, then it could easily be rejected out of hand.

Some people restrict their documentation to just the occasional REM statement. There is however, a great deal more to program documentation than this. Each subroutine in your program should begin with a couple of REM's explaining precisely what it does, and detailing any variables which it uses to communicate with the rest of the program. If you have made out a game plan, this will form a valuable part of your documentation. So tidy it up and update it to provide a full description of the program structure of your game.

If you try to add the remark statements after the program has been written, you can easily end up missing something crucial. You should also try to choose the names of your variables to indicate the nature of their contents. This considerably improves the readability of your listings. Look at the following lines of Basic code:

```
10 if SP=5 then S=S+100
10 if SHIP=5 then SC0RE=SC0RE+100
```

Both lines perform exactly the same action, but the second version is a great deal easier to read.

Note how I've neatly avoided using the keyword OR in the variable SC0RE by replacing the O's with zeros. This has little effect on the readabilty, but stops STOS from interpreting the line as:

```
10 if SHIP=5 then SC or E= SC or E+100
```

Remember that STOS Basic allows you to use variables with names up to 31 characters long. These names are stored in the ST's memory only once, no matter how many times they are used in your program. You have therefore no excuse for using complicated or confusing names in your routines.

1.10 Testing

1.10.1 Syntax errors

After you've written your game out on paper, it's time to enter it into your ST. Ideally your program will work perfectly the first time you run it, but unfortunately, this is very rarely the case. You can divide the various bugs in your game into two separate categories. The easiest problems to solve are caused by syntax errors. These generate STOS Basic error messages, and are usually produced by simple typing mistakes which can be quickly corrected.

1.10.2 Logic errors

The second type of bug is the dreaded logic error. This is created by an error in the design of the program. If you have planned your program properly, these logic errors should be rare. But since no-one is infallible, it is quite likely that the odd logic error will still creep into your program unnoticed.

Whenever possible, you should always try to test each section of your program separately. This removes the additional complication of debugging the entire program, and isolates any problems to one particular section of code. Obviously, this approach is only effective for some types of routines. These include subroutines for input; sprite movement; screen scrolling; screen generation; adventure parsing; and character generation. These can be entered into the ST one at a time, and saved to the disk in individual files. Other activities however, can only be tested within the context of the finished game. The classic example of this sort of procedure is the collision detection routine used in an arcade game.

Debugging a program is an art in itself. The standard technique involves working out the expected contents of your program's variables, and checking these against the actual values produced when the program runs. The easiest way to achieve this, is to insert the appropriate PRINT statements at various points in your program. These statements will need to be carefully removed from your program after the problem has been have solved. Any statements you miss, will corrupt your game screen at unexpected intervals. STOS Basic provides you with a useful command called FOLLOW, which is equivalent to the TRACE instructions found in other versions of the language. FOLLOW prints out the contents of any list of variables as and when they are changed. It also informs you of the line number at which this change has occurred. Unfortunately, the FOLLOW command generates an incredible amount of information, most of which is irrelevant to the problem in hand. It can also occasionally slow the action of your game down to a crawl. So it's usually a good idea to use a combination of both methods.

1.10.3 Final testing

This is normally the last stage in the creation of your game. It is also one of the most critical. There are two separate aspects of this testing process. The first involves checking every possible eventuality in your game for errors. If you are considering selling the game, this testing should be exhaustive.

Failure to do this can have potentially disastrous effects, as I know from painful experience. Try to do something really silly in your game, and see how it reacts. If there's any conceivable way a user can mess up your program, somebody will probably attempt to do it. The only safeguard against this, is to be unbelievably thorough in your testing. It's also a good idea to make use of the STOS Basic ON ERROR directive to allow your program to safely recover from any unavoidable errors, such as the player unexpectedly removing a disk, while your program is accessing the drive.

Don't assume that the player has any previous knowledge of the game at all. Remember that many people attempt to play a game straight from the box, without bothering to read the instructions. Such people include many professional software reviewers, who often have to work to very strict dead-lines.

If you're writing an arcade game, you should concentrate on the critical routines such as collision detection. These are almost impossible to test in isolation, and need to be checked very carefully indeed. The biggest problem with these routines is caused by the fact the sprite movement is performed independently of the rest of the program.

Unless you execute the collision detection command at exactly the same time as the collision occurs, an erroneous result may be returned. This means that your program needs to call the collision detection routine at frequent intervals during your game.

Fortunately, the range of the COLLIDE and ZONE instructions can be specified explicitly in your program. This allows you to tailor the accuracy of your routine to the particular circumstances of your game. The diagram on the next page (Figure 1.5) illustrates this technique.

Give the player the benefit of the doubt whenever possible, in the following way: set the detection range to be slightly larger than the attacking ships, to guarantee that any genuine collisions will be discovered by your program, but make the collision range smaller than the defender. This will ensure that the player's ship is only destroyed when it has definitely been hit.

The final aspect of your game which you should check is the quality of the game play. This is really a very subjective area indeed, and can only be checked by getting as many people to play the game as possible. In my experience, there is a very fine line between a game which is exciting and challenging, and a game which is impossibly difficult. Sometimes by reducing the speed and complexity of a game you can vastly improve its appeal. So don't be afraid to modify the game extensively to get the feel just right.

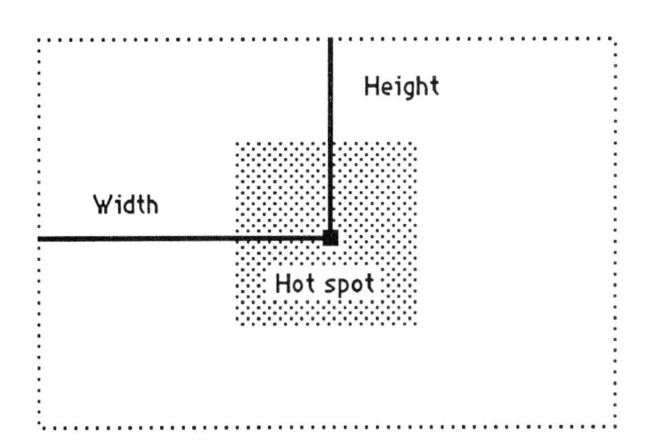

Figure 1.5 The Collision Zones

1.11 Optimization

I'll conclude this chapter with a brief look at a number of optimization techniques which can be used to improve the overall performance of your STOS Basic programs. Some types of game require your program to execute a large number of complicated calculations time and again. The worst offenders are 3D graphics programs which need to compute the appearance of an object from many different angles.

These calculations can take an extraordinarily long time to perform, and this can slow down the action of your game considerably. You should be especially wary of any mathematics involving the trigonometric functions because these are particularly slow in version 2.3 of STOS Basic. Luckily, this problem has been corrected by the latest update supplied with the STOS compiler.

1.11.1 Look-up tables

The solution to these problems, is work out the most commonly needed results in advance, and store them in a so called look-up table. This is just a list of pre-computed values which can be subsequently accessed practically instantaneously by your game. The best way to create one of these tables is to write a small Basic program. Here is a crude demonstration of how one of these tables could be produced.

Example 1.2 Table of sines

```
10 rem Table of SINE values
20 DIM SN#(360)
30 for i=0 to 360
40 SN#(i)=SIN(RAD(i))
50 NEXT I
```

You could now generate the SIN of 45 degrees with a line like:

```
x=SN#(45)
```

Look-up tables are often converted into data statements and inserted directly into your program. This approach has been used by the ORBITER program to hold its rebound tables.

1.11.2 The shift instructions

Another useful optimization technique, is to replace certain arithmetic operations with faster versions. You may already know that INC and DEC can be used to add or subtract one from a variable at high speed.

Replacing X=X+1 with INC X, and X=X-1 with DEC X can improve the performance of critical sections of your program by around 25%.

There are also versions of "*" and "/" which can speed up multiplication and division operations. These are provided by the ROL and ROR instructions.

ROL multiplies a variable by a power of 2.

i.e.

```
ROL.L 1,X is equivalent to X=X*2
```

and

```
ROL.L 2,X is the same as X=X*4
```

Similarly, ROR will divide a number by a power of 2:

```
ROR.L 1,X is identical to X=X/2
ROR.L 3,X can replace X=X/8
```

Typical speed improvements are up to 25% for ROL and over 80% for ROR. One minor limitation is that both of these operations will only work for positive numbers smaller than 1,073,741,824. This is unlikely to be a serious restriction!

1.11.3 Optimization Check-list

1. If your program performs many complex computations, work them out in advance and place them in a look-up table.

2. Replace statements such as A=A+1 and A=A-1 by INC A and DEC A respectively.

3. Replace divisions and multiplications by a power of two by ROR.L and ROL.L instructions.

4. Avoid Boolean algebra. This is often slower than the equivalent IF...THEN instructions in STOS Basic.

5. Use explicit constants in your assignments instead of variables. A=A+10 is marginally faster than A=A+TEN. This is exactly the opposite to the Basic used by the ATARI 800XL.

6. Graphics programmers should always place an AUTOBACK OFF statement at the beginning of their programs, even if the game uses sprites. If you need the sprite background to contain an exact copy of the screen under display, it's much faster to use an explicit call to SCREEN COPY after the graphics have been drawn. e.g

   ```
   screen copy physic to back
   ```

   Depending on your precise application, this will generally reduce the overall time taken by your drawing operations by between 10 and 80 percent.

7. Don't try to combine too many instructions which use interrupts in one program. There's only so much computer time for these routines to use, and the more you try to do, the slower things become. Avoid playing music during the speed critical parts of your game. When I removed the music statements from Zoltar and added some sampled sounds for the STOS Maestro project, I discovered that the game-play speeded up noticeably. Also, only activate your menus when they are actually needed by the user. Killing the menus frees valuable time for the rest of system.

If you still have speed problems, you will probably need to purchase the separate STOS Basic compiler. This is capable of significantly speeding up the execution of many STOS Basic programs (up to twice as fast), and can be highly recommended.

1.12 Conclusion

Well, that's the first step, what's next? In the next ten chapters, I'll be providing you with a host of cook-book solutions which cover most of your common programming problems. Read on, and discover the vast and exciting world of writing games with STOS Basic'.

2

Shoot-em-ups

2.1 Space invaders

The original Space Invaders was the direct ancestor of most modern arcade games. All subsequent space combat games from Galaxians up to and including Elite are descended in some small way from this single classic program.

The basic concept of the game was remarkably simple. The player was confronted with a fleet of attacking alien space ships which were steadily marching towards the bottom edge of the screen. As the game progressed, each alien would let off a salvo of deadly missiles which would gradually eat away at the players defences. The aim was to destroy all the invaders one at a time before they reached the bottom of the screen.

From our current perspective it's hard to fully comprehend the reason for this game's phenomenal success. But at the time, home computers were still in their infancy. Space invaders was the first computer game most people had ever seen, and it captured the public's imagination in a way which has never been successfully duplicated. For me, space invaders triumphed because of the compelling nature of the action. Anyone who wanted to achieve reach any respectable score would be unable to relax for a second along the way.

It's also true that space invaders had no real competition. It was quite literally the first game of its kind in existence.

There were of course, dozens of limitations with the original game. After you had played space invaders for some time, the movements of the alien ships started to become predictable. Later developments, such as Galaxians, were to incorporate a much-needed element of variety into the game-play. In order to complete one of these games, you had to successfully destroy a vast number of different screens, each with its own unique set of problems. Galaxians also moved the aliens in smoother and more realistic attack formations. This tremendously improved the overall quality of the game, as you now never knew precisely where the aliens were going to appear next.

Another of my favourites was Gorf, which included some surprisingly modern features. It was, for instance, the first arcade game to provide the player with a computer generated speech system. Gorf was effectively a clone of both Space Invaders and Galaxians, and it attempted to combine four entirely separate arcade games in one. This idea caught on quickly, and has now become a standard feature in many popular games.

It's absolutely essential for the action in one of these games to be both fast and furious.

Up until now, the only way of achieving this sort of speed was to write the entire game in 68000 machine code. But with the introduction of STOS Basic, it's now possible to produce a perfectly acceptable arcade game without having to concern yourself with any of these complications.

2.2 Basic techniques

In this section, I will be discussing a number of techniques which will enable you to produce your very own arcade games for fun and for profit. I'll also be giving you a fascinating glimpse inside the Zoltar program provided free with the STOS Basic system.

2.2.1 A brief look at Zoltar

The best way to learn about the workings of a game, is to examine one which has already been written. So it's a worthwhile exercise to load up Zoltar from the STOS games disk, and note down some of its features. Try to count the number of sprites on the screen at once, and think about the possible ways they could be moved using the STOS Basic SPRITE and MOVE instructions.

If you look carefully, you should be able to deduce the facts listed in Figure 2 below.

---

1 There are a maximum of 15 sprites on the screen at any one time. These consist of nine aliens, five missiles, and a single ship which is controlled by the player.

2 The sprites on the screen are relatively small. (Actually 16x16)

3 The alien ships move smoothly in complicated curved paths.

4 The player controls the defending ship using the ST's mouse cursor.

5 Only four missiles are fired by the aliens in any one salvo.

6 Once the player has fired a missile, it continues until it either hits something, or it reached to top of the screen.

7 There is a separate game screen containing a single, massive alien (inexplicably known as the MAGEDON).

Figure 2.1 Analysis of Zoltar

It's possible to draw a couple of interesting conclusions from this information. The first statement implies that all 15 available sprites are being used on the screen at once. This has clearly forced the programmer to restrict the sizes of the sprites to an absolute minimum (16x16).

Also, the movements of the aliens are extremely complex. This type of motion would be very hard to implement using the STOS Basic MOVE instruction, so it's likely that the programmer is animating them directly with the SPRITE command.

2.3 Designing a shoot-em-up

After you've produced a specification for your game, you'll need to isolate the critical activities in the program. Think about Zoltar, and try to name some of the main program sections. Don't worry about how these routines might be implemented, as I'll be discussing them in detail a little later. You should also ignore the features which are specific to Zoltar, such as the menu system, the Magedon, and the game creator. Hopefully, you will eventually be left with a list which looks rather like this:

- Initialisation;
- Load attack wave;
- Move aliens;
- Control player;
- Fire missile;
- Detect collisions;
- Animate background.

These activities will provide the backbone for any genuine shoot-em-up game.

2.3.1 Anatomy of a shoot-em-up

The next stage in the development process, is to produce a detailed description of the mechanics of your game. This is written in the pseudo-code which I introduced in Chapter 1. If you haven't familiarised yourself with this system, it's well worth making a brief detour before progressing any further. I've included such a description in Figure 2.2 on the next page.

Although the actual order of this code might vary slightly between different implementations, the overall format will remain pretty much the same. I'll now take each of these activities, and show you how they might be written using STOS Basic.

2.4 Moving the aliens

The animation of the attacking aliens is one of the most vital areas of your program. If you make a mistake in this section, then the game will be both ugly and unplayable. It's therefore well worth concentrating heavily on this section during the design of your game. This will reap real dividends when you begin to generate the final STOS Basic program.

```
Initialise background screen

Repeat

Load attack wave
Initialise attack wave

    Repeat

    Move attacking ships
    Check for a free missile
    If missile free for use
        then
            Choose one of the attacking ships
            Fire missile from ship
        endif

    Input player movement
    If fire pressed and missile is not already moving
        then
            Fire missile
        endif

    Move player's missile
    Move attacker's missiles
    Animate background screen
    Detect for a collision between player and a missile
    Detect for a collision between player and attacker
    If player is hit
        then
            Destroy player
            Lives=Lives-1
        endif

    Detect collision between player's missile and enemy
    If enemy hit
        then
            Destroy enemy
            Attackers=Attackers-1
            Increment score
        endif

    Until Lives=0 or Attackers=0

Until Lives=0

Another game?
```

Figure 2.2 Game Plan of a Shoto-em-up game

The optimum approach to this problem depends almost entirely on the type of motion which will be needed in your game. I'll now have a detailed look at several of the more likely possibilities.

2.4.1 Moving the aliens in a straight line

Some games only call for the attackers to proceed in simple straight lines. These movements are best produced using a matched pair of MOVE X and MOVE Y instructions. If you wanted to move your aliens in a zigzag pattern, for instance, you could use the following fragment of STOS Basic.

```
load "back.mbk"1:rem Load example sprites from STOS Games
disk
10 sprite 1,0,0,1:Rem Place sprite on screen
15 rem Sweep sprite 1 to and fro
20 move x 1,"(1,4,80)(1,-4,80)1
25 rem repeatedly move sprite up and down
30 move y 1,"0(1,4,50)(1,-4,50)1"
40 move on:rem activate movements
```

While this type of routine is certainly capable of generating some useful effects, it's not really applicable to modern games such as Galaxians. These generally expect you to rush your sprites through much more complex and intricate attack sequences.

2.4.2 Complex attack paths

There are effectively two ways of generating the smooth sprite animations found in a modern arcade game. One idea is to split any complicated manœuver into a number of simple components. These can then be generated by producing a couple of large movement strings for use with the STOS Basic MOVE commands.

Look at the pattern shown in Figure 2.3 below:

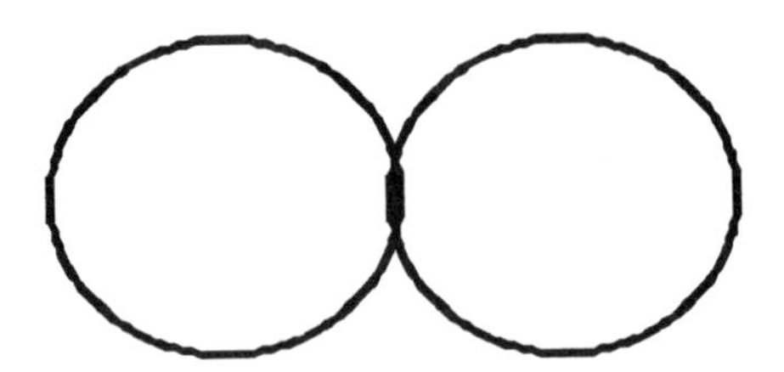

Figure 2.3 Moving the sprite in a double loop

This route can be approximated by the straight line segments in Figures 2.4a, and 2.4b. Each section of this course can be taken in turn, and the required movements initiated using an appropriate combination of MOVE X and MOVE Y instructions. The smoothness of the attack wave will depend entirely on the number of movement steps you are prepared to expend to produce the effect. So Figure 2.4b generates a far cleaner curve than the relatively crude Figure 2.4a.

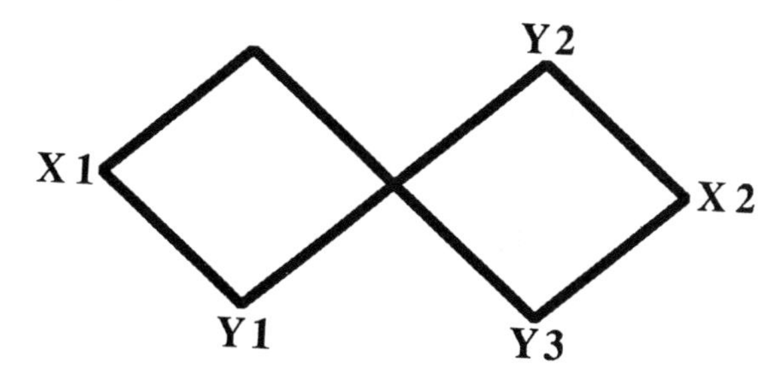

(a) a simple approximation to a loop

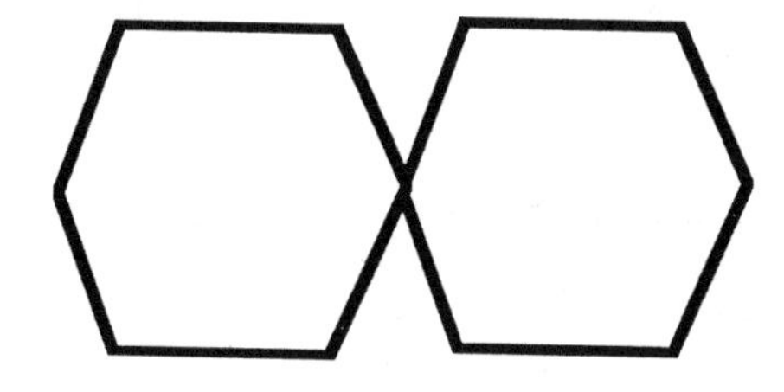

(b) a closer approximation to a loop

Figure 2.4 a and b Straight line approximations to a curve

In order to use this technique, you have to divide up each line into its separate vertical and horizontal components. These can be found by drawing the curve out on paper, and then running your finger along the required route.

Place your finger at point X1 on Figure 2.4a, and follow the curve until you reach your original starting point. Now make a note of your fingers movement from left to right. It should be apparent that the horizontal part of the motion is just a simple back and forth movement from X1 to X2. This could be generated with an instruction like:

```
MOVE X 1,"(1,1,100)(1,-1,100)1"
```

You can now repeat the same process for the vertical component, starting from the lowest point in the curve (Y1) and moving your finger right to Y2. As you trace the path from Y1 to Y3, your finger progresses up to Y2 and down to Y3. The journey from Y3 back to Y1 also involves a single up and down movement. This information is allows you to quickly create the movement string needed to reproduce the vertical part of the motion with MOVE Y. e.g.

```
MOVE Y,"(1,-1,50)(1,1,50)(1,-1,50)(1,1,50)1"
```

This could be reduced to:

```
MOVE Y,"(1,-1,50)(1,1,50)L"
```

You would of course, need to experiment very carefully before you could create the precise effect you wanted. But the technique I've just shown you does provide an efficient method of animating your sprites through relatively complex sequences of movements.

The problem, of course, is that the motion tends to jerk slightly between the separate movement steps. So although you can generate some impressive effects using this system, it will be impossible to attain genuinely fluid attack sequences .

2.4.3 Movement tables

If you wish to animate your sprites really smoothly, you should forget about the MOVE commands completely, and perform all sprite movements directly using the STOS Basic SPRITE instruction. This can be achieved using a **movement table**.

A movement table is just a simple list of coordinates, with one pair of numbers corresponding to each possible position of the sprite. Every time the sprites are moved, the appropriate entry in the movement table is accessed from memory to find the new screen positions of the aliens. These can then be moved into place with a series of instructions like:

```
SPRITE 1,X(I);Y(I),I
```

The arrays X(I) and Y(I) contain the coordinates of sprite position number I. Each attack wave in your game will have its own separate movement table. If you're feeling particularly adventurous, you can even specify different movements for each type of ship.

The only limits to the complexity of the attack sequence, are the size of the movement table, and the overall speed of the STOS Basic sprites. Because of sheer power of STOS Basic, and the massive amount of memory in your ST, you would be really hard pressed to exceed either of these restrictions in practice.

Example 2.1 Movement tables in action

```
10    rem example 2.1
20    mode 0 : cls physic : cls back : flash off : hide on :
curs off
30    gosub 110 : rem get sprite palette
40    rem load up movement table
50    read SIZE,SPEED,IMAGE : dim XPATH(SIZE),YPATH(SIZE)
60    for I=0 to SIZE : read XPATH(I),YPATH(I) : next I
70    rem animate sprite
```

```
80  for I=0 to SIZE-1 : sprite 1,XPATH(I),YPATH(I),IMAGE :
wait SPEED : next I
90  goto 80
100 goto 80
110 rem Get pallete from sprite bank
120 XP=hunt(start(1) to start(1)+length(1),"PALT") : if
XP=0 then return
130 XP=XP+4 : for I=0 to 15 : colour I,deek(I*2+XP) : next I :
return
19999rem movement data
20000data 24,5,25
20001data 125,97,98,84,83,82,51,86,47,95,70,118,83,127,
97,128,122,123,137,107
20002data 153,78,172,69,198,74,214,90,218,108,211,124,200,
127,187,126,167,115,151,105
20003data 137,100,135,99,133,98,133,98,221,125,204,129,
190,130,173,125,162,119,155,111
```

You'll probably be wondering how I produced all that impenetrable data at lines 2000-2003. Even the simplest movement sequence contains dozens of complicated coordinate pairs, and it would be unbelievably tedious to have to generate all this information by hand. Fortunately there's a clever trick you can use to avoid this difficulty completely. All you need to do, is to write a small program to enter the movement coordinates with the mouse cursor. You can now use this routine to generate a separate movement table for each wave in your game.

This was the approach adopted by the creators of Zoltar. So rather than being just an afterthought, the game creator was actually an integral part of the original game design. Here's a simple path definer for use in your own games:

```
10  rem Example
20  rem Path definer
30  rem load a sprite bank into memory
40  F$=file select$("*.mbk","Load some sprites",7) : if
F$="" then stop
50  if len(F$)<5 then boom : goto 40
60  if right$(F$,4)<>".MBK" then boom : goto 40
70  dim PAL(16) : rem dimension palette
80  dim XPATH(10000),YPATH(10000)
90  load F$
100 mode 0
110 rem set movement speed (1=very fast 10=very slow)
120 input "Movement speed (1-10)";SP
130 SPEED=11-SP
140 if SPEED<1 or SPEED>10 then boom : goto 120
150 rem choose a sprite
```

```
160 input "Which sprite do you wish to animate";IMAGE
170 rem initialise screen
180 print "Click left mouse key to start"
190 flash off : gosub 630 : rem get sprite colours
200 if XP<>0 then for I=0 to 15 : colour I,PAL(I) : next I
210 change mouse IMAGE+3
220 rem wait for a mouse button to be pressed
230 while mouse key=0 : wend : wait 10 : cls physic : cls back
240 curs off : locate 0,0 : centre "Creating a path"
250 rem create the movement table using the mouse
260 repeat
270 XPATH(P)=x mouse : YPATH(P)=y mouse
280 wait 5 : inc P : locate 10,20 : print "Position ";P;" ";
290 until P>10000 or mouse key<>0 : change mouse 1
300 rem animate the sprite using the table you have just
defined
310 for I=0 to P-1 : wait SPEED : sprite 1,XPATH(I),YPATH(I),
IMAGE : locate 10,20 : print "Position ";I;" "; : next I
320 rem save data to disc as a list of data statements
330 rem load using FLOAD "*.ASC"
340 sprite 1,-100,-100,0 : locate 0,20 : input "Do you want
to save this data (Y/N)";A$
350 if A$="Y" or A$="y" then gosub 300 : rem save data
360 input "Another go? (Y/N)";A$
370 if A$="Y" or A$="y" then P=0 : goto 120
380 stop
390 change mouse 1
400 rem choose filename
410 F$=file select$("*.asc","Save movement table",7)
420 if F$="" then return
430 if len(F$)<5 then boom : goto 410
440 rem choose start of data statements
450 input "Starting line";FIRST_LINE
460 if FIRST_LINE<1000 or FIRST_LINE>60000 then print
"Starting line must be in range 1000-60000." : print " Try
again" : goto 450
470 open out #1,F$ : rem open data file
480 rem save size of table, movement speed and image number
490 print #1,str$(FIRST_LINE)+" data "+str$(P)+","
+str$(SPEED)+","+str$(IMAGE)
500 rem generate data statements in D$
510 for I=0 to P/10
520 D$=str$(FIRST_LINE+I+1)+" data "
530 for J=0 to 9
540 rem add a movement position to the list
```

```
550 BIT$=str$(XPATH(I*10+J))+","+str$(YPATH(I*10+J))-" "
: D$=D$+BIT$
560 rem separate coordinates with a comma
570 if J<>9 then D$=D$+","
580 next J
590 print #1,D$ : rem write data to disc
600 next I
610 close #1 : rem close data file
620 return
630 rem Get sprite pallete
640 XP=hunt(start(1) to start(1)+length(1),"PALT") : if
XP=0 then return
650 XP=XP+4 : for I=0 to 15 : PAL(I)=deek(I*2+XP) : next I :
return
```

2.5 Fire control

2.5.1 Controlling the gun

Another vital element of your program, is the routine which is used to control the player's ship. I'll now present you with a general purpose control system which can perform this activity for you automatically. This routine can be freely used in your own games without any restrictions whatsoever.

Example 2.2 Universal Control System

```
10  rem Universal Control System
15  rem Don't bother to type in these REMs.
20  rem They are just for documementation purposes
25  rem Test routine. Load some sprites FIRST
30  mode 0 : rem Change for other resolutions
40  LX=10 : RX=300 : LY=150 : RY=180 : gosub 1000 : rem
Initialize UCS
45  rem Set movement increments and choose sprite image
50  IX=2 : IY=2 : SHIP=1
60  gosub 1100 : rem read joystick
70  if K=0 then 60 : rem Exit if FIRE or a mouse button is
pressed
80  stop
990 rem UCS
995 rem Initialization
996 rem Call this once at the start of your program
997 rem LX,LY = Top left corner of movement zone
998 rem RX,RY = Bottom right corner of zone
1000limit mouse LX,LY to RX,RY
```

```
1005SX=(RX+LX)/2 : SY=(RY+LY)/2
1010hide on : return
1060rem Universal control system
1070rem Ship = Image number of bat
1075rem sprite used is assumed to be number 1
1080rem inputs
1081rem SX,SY = coordinates of ship
1082rem IX,IY hold the increments which are added to the
current position
1083rem whenever the joystick is pulled. As the increment
increases
1084rem the sprite movements become faster but jerkier
1085rem Use increments of one or two for smooth movements
1086rem Use increments of three or four for maximum speed
1087rem LX,LY = Top left corner of movement zone
1088rem RX,RY = Bottom right corner of zone
1089rem You can restrict the movement directions using
LX,LY,RX,RY
1090rem If LX=RX then only vertical movements will be
detected
1091rem If LY=RY then only horizontal movements will be
performed
1092rem k=status of mouse key
1095rem outputs
1096rem SX,SY = coordinates of ship
1097rem k=status of mouse key
1098rem Note there are seperate routines to read the mouse
and joystick
1099rem Read mouse
1100SX=x mouse : SY=y mouse : K=mouse key : sprite
1,SX,SY,SHIP : return
1110rem Read joystick
1115rem Note the optimization
1120if jleft and SX>LX then SX=SX-IX : goto 1140
1130if jright and SX<RX then SX=SX+IX
1140if jup and SY>LY then SY=SY-IY : sprite 1,SX,SY,SHIP :
K=fire : return
1150if jdown and SY<RY then SY=SY+IY : sprite 1,SX,SY,SHIP :
K=fire : return
1160sprite 1,SX,SY,SHIP : K=fire : return
```

2.5.2 Firing a missile

This routine requires your to perform two separate activities. Firstly, you need to have some way of moving the missile across the screen. The MOVE Y instruction is ideal for this purpose, as it allows you to fire your missiles in just a couple of lines of STOS Basic.

```
move y S,"(1,-5,0)L":rem Fires missile S straight up
move on:rem Start the movement running
```

In addition, you can easily add a little animation to your missiles with the ANIM command. That's how the weird "wriggling" missiles found in Zoltar were produced.

Before you can fire your missile however, you will need to allocate it to one of the currently available sprites. This is important, because the number of missiles in motion will vary from moment to moment during the game.

After you've allocated the sprites for the rest of your objects, you will normally be left with a mere 2 to 4 sprites for your missiles. You therefore need to select one of the available sprites which is currently unused. This can be done by individually checking the current status of each missile using the MOVON function.

Example 2.3 Firing a missile

```
load "back.mbk":rem load sprites from STOS accessory disk
10 rem Fire a missile
20 s=12:n=4
30 rem s=first sprite used for a missile
40 rem n= number of sprites used for a missile
50 for I=s to s+n
60 if movon(i)=0 then sprite y,i*20,199,24: move y i,"(1,-
5,80)l'':move on
70 next i
80 goto 50
```

The effect of Example 2.2 is to repeatedly fire off a salvo of missiles from the bottom of the screen. The same idea can be seen from the equivalent routine on line 10480 of Zoltar.

2.6 Collision detection

Once you've animated your sprites, and fired off your missiles, you'll need to be able to detect the inevitable collisions. In most cases the objects to be checked are both sprites, so you will need to use the COLLIDE function from STOS Basic.

COLLIDE is hardly the most intuitive command, and unless you have a good grasp of binary notation, it's easy to get totally confused.

Instead of boring you with a lot of abstract programming theory, I'll present you with a couple of cook-book solutions which will allow you handle most types of collisions reasonably efficiently. These can be freely modified for use with your own programs.

2.6.1 Collisions between the player's ship and a missile

Load a variable with the binary number %1111111111111110 during initialisation. This number is known as the mask and contains the list of all of the sprites which are to be moved on the screen. Now set the bits representing your ship and its missile to zero with the BCLR command like so:

```
100 shipmask=%1111111111111110:bclr shipno,shipmask
110 bclr missno,shipmask
```

where:

shipno = the number of the sprite used for your ship
missno = the sprite used for your players missile

This situation corresponds to the simplest case, where all fifteen of the available sprites are being moved off the screen. If your program uses fewer sprites, you should also remove the unused sprites from consideration by clearing the appropriate bits in the mask.

You can now detect for a collision between the ship and any other sprite using the line:

```
1000 CS=collide(shipno,16,8) and shipmask:if CS<>0 then
gosub 2000:rem Where your explosion routine was at 2000
```

2.6.2 Collision between attacker and a missile

You can use a similar technique to check for the destruction of one of the attackers. This time you start off with a mask containing a string of binary zeros. Whenever you load up an attack wave, you should now set the binary digits representing the alien sprites to a one.

Supposing you had implemented your alien fleet using the sprites from 3 to 5. In this case, you would initialise the detection mask with the line:

```
3000 attmask=0:bset 3,attmask:bset 4,attmask:bset
5,attmask
```

You could now detect the collisions between your missile and the attacking fleet with:

```
3500 ca=collide(missno,16,8) and attmask: if ca<>0 then
4000:rem jump to routine to act on the collision.
```

Note that the above code only detects that a collision has occurred. If you want to determine which of the attackers has been hit, you will need to check the relevant bits for each ship in the formation. This could be accomplished using the BTST function, as follows:

```
4000 for i=3 to 5
4010 if btst(i,ca) then killed=i:gosub 5000
4020 next i
5000 rem kill off an attacker
5010 move off killed:bclr killed,attmask:rem Destroy ship
5020 rem Do explosion
```

See how line 5010 removes the killed ship from the detection list held in attmask. This ship will not be tested for a collision when the check is performed again at 3500.

2.7 Animating the background

Many arcade games such as Galaxians, require dozens of aliens to be moving across the screen at once. This is clearly impossible if you are forced to rely on the 15 sprites available from STOS Basic. The key to the solution of this problem is to realise that most of the ships are moving relatively slowly in a simple holding pattern. It's therefore possible to animate the main attack formation in the background, while your sprites are reserved for those ships which are actively attacking.

STOS Basic provides you with several possible methods of achieving this effect. The simplest of these, is to move the entire pattern around on the screen with SCREEN$.

If you decide to use this technique, you'll obviously need to be able to detect collisions between the ships making up the background screen, and the player's missiles. This can be implemented with the DETECT function, which returns the background colour of the pixel currently underneath one of your STOS Basic sprites.

Providing you keep the background colour different from the colours used for the animation, you can instantly detect collisions between a missile and the holding pattern. You can now use the position of the missile to determine precisely which ship has been affected. This can be subsequently removed using CLS, and you can add the normal explosion affect to make things realistic.

2.8 Inside Zoltar

I'll now examine some of the ideas behind the excellent Zoltar program supplied on the STOS Basic games disk. This was written in a matter of days by Francois Lionet, one of the original STOS Basic programmers. It embodies most of the principles I have been discussing in this chapter, and provides a superb example of what you can achieve with a little ingenuity and a lot of talent.

2.8.1 Initialisation

The program commences with an initialization section from lines 10 to 1000. This defines all the variables needed by the game and unpacks a number of important screens. The title screen is loaded from bank 5 at line 300 and placed into the string TTLE$ using SCREEN$.

The magedon is now unpacked from bank number 6. It is then copied into the string MAGEDON$(0) using the SCREEN$ function.

The magedon is then shifted sideways slightly and the process is repeated several times; the appropriate screen data is entered into the array elements MAGEDON$(1) to MAGEDON$(3). This allows the program to move the magedon smoothly across the screen without ever having to cross a 16 pixel boundary. During the initialisation process, the following four subroutines are called:

```
10050 Clears and resets screen
10100 Draws the game screen
10250 Set up an attack wave
10600 Initialise movement data
```

The menu bar is now created, and control passes to the Menu routine at line 11005.

2.8.2 Control loop

If the **play game** option is chosen, the program jumps to the main control loop at 1100. The action of this routine can be described using a little pseudo-code, as shown in Figure 2.5 below.

```
Initialise variables

while wave<maxwave
     load a phase from the disk
     repeat
          Play a single turn
          check status of player
     until lives<0 or aliens=0

wend
```

Figure 2.5 Pseudo-code for Zoltar's control loop

Line 1100 is of particular interest, because it defines the initial values of three important variables:

WAVE	Holds the number of the current wave
LIVES	Holds the number of lives left. This normally starts at three, but you can cheat by setting it to any number you like.
SCRE	Holds your current score

2.8.3 The play game routine

The play game routine, is split into two separate sections positioned at lines 10400 and 10800 respectively. The procedure at 10400 controls the action of a normal game, and the one at 10800 is used whenever the Magedon is selected. At first glance this routine appears rather impenetrable, but this is misleading. I'll now describe the action of this code in some detail.

The lines from 10400 to 10450 are concerned with initialisation. They create the display on the screen and prepare the attack wave data which has just been loaded from the disk. This data is contained in bank 11, and uses the following format:

Byte	*Meaning*
0-3	Identification code for a Zoltar wave
4-13	The ship numbers used for each of the nine aliens. These numbers range from 0 to 8
14	Release time in units of 4/50 seconds for ship 1
18	Release time for ship number 2
.	.
.	.
.	.
48	Release time for ship number 9
50	Fire rate
52	Magedon flag. $ff for magedon otherwise zero
54	Maximum number of hits needed to kill magedon
56	X coordinate of first position in movement table
57	Y coord of first position
58	X coord of second position
59	Y coord of second position
.	.
.	.
.	.
	movement table terminated by $ffff

The actual game begins with the loop at line 10455. In order to simplify things for you, I've produced the following pseudo-code expansion of this routine. Alongside each statement, I've added the number of the appropriate line in the program.

Action	*Lines*	*Comment*
`repeat`	10455	
`    move player`	10460	Using SPRITE 1
`    player fires a missile?`	10465	
`    animate background`	10470	See Note 1
`    move aliens`	10470	See Note 2
`    If Alien fires missile`	10475	
`        then`		
`            Choose alien`	10480	
`            move missile`	10485	
`    If missile destroys alien`	10490	
`        then`		
`            Which alien?`	10495	
`            Explode alien`	10500	
`            Increase score`	10505	
`    If missile destroys player`	10510	
`        then`		
`            Explode player`	10515	With ANIM command
`            End turn`	10520	
`    wait for next clock tick`	10525	See Note 3
`    screen swap`	10530	See Note 1
`    until (aliens dead`	10535	
`        or player is killed`		
`        or wave finished)`		

Figure 2.6 Breakdown of Zoltar's play game routine

Notes:

1 The actual background animation is performed by a routine at 10200. This procedure scrolls the background around the screen. In order to avoid an annoying flicker in the rotation, all the screen manipulation is performed on a separate logical screen which is not currently being displayed. The logical screen is then switched with the existing physical screen using the SCREEN SWAP instructions at line 10530.

See how the SYNCHRO command has been used to syncnronise the animation with the various sprite movements. This instruction is essential if you wish to produce really smooth background animation. If you require further information about the above technique, you will find a full explanation under the section in Chapter 10.

2 The procedure to move the aliens through their attack wave starts at line 10300. It works by repeatedly accessing a version of the movement table I showed your earlier. This is contained in memory bank 11, with the coordinate lists starting at byte number 56. If you examine this code, you'll come across several strange variables, as follows:

T(n) – This array holds a copy of the release time for ship number n, measured in units of 4/50 of a second. n can range from 0 to 8.

A(n) – Holds the address of the next entry in the movement table, for each of the nine sprites.

I(n) – Set to >0 is alien n has been released, otherwise zero.

Notice the unusual format of sprite instruction at line 10305. This is an undocumented feature which changes the position of a sprite which has previously been placed on the screen. The format of this instruction is:

```
SPRITE n,X,Y
```

As you can see, there's no image specified in the instruction at all. STOS Basic expects your program to have already selected this image with a normal SPRITE command. The advantage of this format, is that it enables you to move a sprite without interfering with the animation effects performed by the ANIM instruction.

3 The line at 10525 is used as a sort of clock. Every 4/50 of a second it produces one ''tick''. If the program has executed especially quickly, it halts the system until the next clock tick. This synchronises the sprite movements with the rate which was set up during the creation of the wave.

2.8.4 The Magedon!

The Magedon routine at 10800 is very similar to the one at 10400. The differences can be summarised by the following table:

Table 2.1 Magedon routine

Lines	*Description*	*Comment*
10820-10825	Move MAGEDON	This uses the same principles as the code at 1030 with the sprite commands being replaced by the appropriate SCREEN$ instructions.
10845	Magedon Hit	The collision detection routine simply uses the X SPRITE and Y SPRITE commands to determine whether a missile has intersected with the area enclosed by the magedon.
10900	Explode Magedon	This produces an impressive explosion when the magedon is destroyed. It comprises of a complex list of SPRITE commands which are animated with ANIM.

2.8.5 Possible enhancements

A good way to learn about games programming, is to try your hand at enhancing an existing game. Zoltar provides you with the perfect opportunity for this sort of experimentation. Here a few ideas:

1 Change the scoring system. At the moment each ship scores between 200 and 300 points. By modifying line 10505, you can introduce any alternative strategy you like.

2 Currently, a life is lost automatically if you fail to destroy an attack wave before it has been completed. It's possible to modify the movement routine at 10300 to repeat each wave until either your ship or the aliens are destroyed.

3 Add sampled sound to your game. This is very easy – full details are provided with the STOS Maestro package.

4 Give each type of alien its own attack wave. This would require you to modify the information used in the movement table loaded from the disk. You would also need to change the animation routine at 10300.

5 Add different screen types. Zoltar already includes two types of screen (normal and magedon). It would be relatively easy to incorporate a whole list of similar screens.

If you come up with something really special, be sure to send it to Mandarin for evaluation. Who knows, it might even be included with the latest version of STOS Basic!

3

Rebound games

3.1 Introduction

The first ever rebound game was a crude two-player version of table tennis called Pong. Each player was given control of a small bat, and a ping-pong ball was represented by a large blob which was flipped erratically from one side of the screen to another. Although pong looks absolutely horrendous by modern standards, it was a hailed as a real breakthrough at the time. It made its inventor, Nolan Bushnell a small fortune, and directly led to the founding of a small inconspicuous little company later known as "Atari".

It wasn't long before Pong was consigned to the rubbish bin of history. The fact was, the next generation of arcade games which quickly followed in its steps were so unimaginably superior that they wiped poor old Pong off the map. These games incorporated such new and innovative features as "colour" and "graphics". With that sort of competition, Pong didn't stand a chance!

Old computer games never die however, they just linger on and on until everyone has forgotten about them completely. Then just when we are certain they are dead and buried, some whiz-kid brings out a new version, and we all gasp in stupefied amazement at its originality.

Breakout was a typical example of this sort of development. The actual game-play was surprisingly similar to pong. But instead of playing against another player, we were now trying to destroy a set of coloured rectangular blocks. Whenever a ball hit one of these blocks, it would rebound away in an unusual direction, destroying the block in the process. The aim of the game was simply to clear the screen whilst achieving the maximum possible score.

For a while, Breakout was a phenomenal success, and was the inspiration for literally dozens of similar games. But by the early eighties, it had all started to look increasingly old-fashioned, and reviewers began making plaintive noises about the increasing number of boring Breakout clones which were starting to litter their desks.

Then, from out of nowhere, came an astonishing new game which breathed new life into the tired old format. Yet again! I am, of course, referring to the arcade classic Arkanoid. The most exciting improvement was in the game play. The player was now confronted with a vast range of obstacles which needed to be carefully avoided.

The precise effect of hitting a block varied depending on its type. Certain blocks released bonus pods which gave the player extra equipment, or added to the number of lives. Also, some blocks required several hits before they could be completely destroyed.

The result was a game which combined fast action with an intriguing strategic element which kept the player thinking. To this day, Arkanoid remains one of my favourite arcade games of all time, and in the unlikely event that this game is not already a valued part of your software collection, you are strongly recommended to rush out and buy a copy immediately. It really is *that* good.

Arkanoid may seem like a rather tough act to follow, but it's still possible to produce an acceptable alternative directly within STOS Basic. This can be seen from the excellent Orbiter program included on the STOS Basic games disk. Incredibly enough, Orbiter actually compares remarkably well to its famous predecessor. But remember that Orbiter was written entirely in STOS Basic, whilst Arkanoid required the extensive use of fast 68000 machine code.

In this Chapter, I will be giving you a guided tour of some of the programming techniques which were used to make this superb program possible.

3.2 Game plan of a rebound game

I'll begin with a generalised game plan of a rebound game, shown in Figure 3.1 on the next page.

As before, I'll take this game plan, and break it down into its component parts.

3.2.1 Critical routines for rebound

- ❑ Initialise main screen;
- ❑ Load a screen;
- ❑ Initialise level;
- ❑ Position bat;
- ❑ Control bat;
- ❑ Release ball;
- ❑ Move ball;
- ❑ Calculate rebound direction with wall;
- ❑ Calculate rebound direction with block;
- ❑ Rebound ball;
- ❑ Destroy block;
- ❑ Handle special block.

```
Initialise main screen

Repeat
     Load a level
     Initialise level
     Position bat
     Release ball
     Repeat
          Move ball
          If ball reaches bottom of screen
            then
               Lives=Lives-1
               If Lives>0
                    then
                         Position bat
                         Release ball
                    endif
               endif
          Control Bat
          If ball collides with bat
            then
               Calculate rebound direction with bat
               Rebound ball
            endif
          If ball collides with wall
            then
               Calculate rebound direction with wall
               Rebound ball
            endif
          If ball collides with block
            then
               Calculate rebound direction with block
               Rebound ball
               If normal block
                    then
                         Destroy block
                    else
                         handle special block
               endif
            endif

     Until Lives=0 or blocks=0

Until Lives=0
```

Figure 3.1 Game plan of a rebound game

I will now describe the internal workings of some of these activities in a little more detail.

3.3 The game screen

3.3.1 Designing the screen

You first need to design the basic screen format for your game. This will involve choosing the dimensions of the blocks and carefully setting out an invisible grid on the screen. Each slot in the grid will be just big enough to contain one individual block. Additionally, it will be illegal for a block to occupy more than a single slot.

In practice, you will quickly discover that it's essential divide up the screen into units of a single sprite. It's also important to leave a space between the end of the blocks and the edges of the screen. This will improve the quality of the action by allowing the ball to ricochet between the blocks and the walls.

The Orbiter game uses a grid of size 16x8. Each block is placed in one position in this grid, and there are gaps one unit wide between the grid and the walls. The grid occupies only about two-thirds of the total screen area, with the rest of the space being reserved for the scoreboard and the title screen.

The size and position of the playing area is totally up to you. There's certainly no reason why you can't use a much larger proportion of the screen for the game screen, and indeed this is the approach which was adopted by the original Arkanoid.

You can also experiment with larger grid sizes such as 16x16 or even 32x16.

3.3.2 Creating a screen

Once you've decided on the screen format, you will need to generate the various levels which will be included in your final game. There are two possible methods of producing these screens:

Firstly, you can use the map definer program found on the STOS Basic accessory disk. This is makes absolutely no assumptions as to the size or format of your screen. It's therefore ideal for creating screens which are slightly different from the usual format. Before you use this program, you should always remember to create a set of sprites for your blocks using the sprite definer. You can now load up the map utility, and produce your game screens with ease. These can then be saved to disk and incorporated directly into your rebound game.

The data produced by the map program starts off with a small header on line 50005.

```
50005 data DIST,screens
```

DIST is a record of the number of data statements which hold a single map, and screens is just the number of maps which have been generated by the definer. Each game screen starts with two pieces of data containing the width and height of the sprites making up the screen.

The data itself consists of a list of the sprite numbers which occupy the appropriate slots in your grid. The entire level can now be displayed automatically by the map definer, using a simple call to the output routine at 50000.

```
1000 ROOM=1:gosub 50000:rem draw level 1
```

All maps are drawn on the screen a column at a time. So the first line contains all the sprites in column number one, the second line contains the sprites in column two, etc. It's useful to load this data directly into an array, as this enables you to keep track of the block numbers which have been destroyed or changed during the course of your game.

```
99 read map data into an array
100 rem read data lines per screen and no of screens
110 read LS,NSCR
115 dim MAP(NSCR*20,50):rem reserve plenty of space
120 for s=0 to NSCR-1
130 rem get sizes of sprites
140 read W,H:cols=199/h:rows=319/w
150 d=200-cols*h:rem do the sprites divide evenly into
screen
160 for c=0 to cols-1
170 for r=0 to rows-1
180 read MAP(s*rows+r,c)
190 next r
```

You now have instant access to the status of the block which has been drawn at any position. This will be vital for the execution of your game.

One slight problem with the map definer is that it was not designed specifically for use with rebound games. This means that there are no facilities for setting the attributes of a block individually, because the definer records only the type of the block in a particular position, not the number of hits it can take, or the type of pods it can release. As the data in the map is the only information available to your program during the game, you are therefore limited to allocating the characteristics of an entire block type, rather than a particular slot on the grid.

Of course, all this can be surmounted by defining a set of blocks which look identical but are treated separately by your program. This is however, fairly cumbersome, so you might find it rewarding to use a slightly different approach.

This can be achieved by using Orbiter's own screen definer to generate your screens directly. Obviously this will restrict your game to a similar format to that of orbiter, but you will be able to set the number of hits which can be taken by each particular block before it can be destroyed.

The level data used by the game is held on the disk in the following format:

```
block type,no of hits
```

There's one entry in this list for every allowable block position on the screen. If the block is set to zero, then the appropriate slot is empty. A further explanation of this system can be found in section 3.8: *Inside Orbiter*.

3.3.3 Drawing the blocks on the screen

After you've produced your game screens, you'll obviously need to display them on the screen. If you've created the screens with the map definer this will not be a problem, as you can simply call up the DRAW MAP routine included as part of your map data.

It is however, well worth examining another technique which was exploited by Orbiter. This speeds things up significantly by loading the sprite data into a string with SCREEN$. The blocks can now be drawn on the screen using a successive set of screen$ assignments. The advantage of this approach is that it avoids the need for the WAIT VBL or UPDATE instructions. These tend to slow down the drawing process considerably. Here is a new version of the output routine from the map definer which utilises this technique. Replace lines 50000 from the data file produced by mapper with:

```
49995 rem New version of Map output program
49996 rem Rewritten using SCREEN$ for extra speed
50001 restore 50005 : read NL,NROOM : if ROOM>NROOM or
ROOM<=0 then return
50002 restore 50010+(ROOM-1)*NL : read GRIDW,GRIDH : cls
physic
50003 for I=0 to 319/GRIDW:for J=0 to 199/GRIDH:read S: if
S>0 then screen$(physic,I*GRIDW+1,J*GRIDH)=SEG$(S)
50004:next J : next I :return
```

Before calling this routine, you would first need to load the sprites into a SEG$ array which you have previously defined at the start of your program.

```
40000 rem Enter sprite images in SEG$ array
40010 cls physic : cls back
40020 for I=0 to 30
40030 cls physic,0,0,0 to 16,16
40040 sprite 1,0,0,I+1 : put sprite 1 : wait vbl
40050 SEG$(I+1)=screen$(physic,0,0 to 16,16) : next I
40060 sprite 1,-100,-100,1:return
```

Oddly enough, the original specification of the map definer was intended to use exactly the same system. But due to encroaching deadlines, there wasn't time to implement it in the final program.

3.4 The bat

3.4.1 Controlling the bat

When you're writing a game like Orbiter, it's tempting to leave the control of the mouse cursor entirely to STOS Basic. You can after all, assign any sprite image to the mouse cursor using a single call to the CHANGE MOUSE command. So why bother producing your own movement routine?

Unfortunately, in practice this approach is doomed to failure. The problem, is that the mouse cursor can be moved completely independently of the rest of your Basic program. This is incredibly dangerous as it's now impossible to know the exact position of the bat any given instant. All the program can do, is sample the mouse cursor as often as possible. Because of the sheer speed of the built-in mouse routine, this is never quite enough.

Imagine what would happen if the bat was moved from the ball just after a collision had been detected.

The ball would then be seen to rebound from the empty screen position previously occupied by the bat. You would also get situations where the collision tests missed the new location of the bat completely. This would allow the possibility of the ball falling through your waiting bat as if it didn't exist.

I'm afraid this type of problem is inevitable when you are trying to synchronise several sets of separate activities in a Basic program. The solution is simply to manipulate the bat directly from your program. This has the added advantage of allowing you to incorporate facilities for joystick control in the same routine.

Luckily, it's very easy to write such a routine in STOS Basic. Here's an example:

Example 3.1 Mouse driver

```
load "back.mbk":rem From accessory disk
10 hide mouse:rem Remove mouse pointer from view
20 sprite 1,x mouse,y mouse,1:rem Move sprite according to
mouse
30 locate 10,10:print "Do rest of program"
40 goto 20
```

In this case, the bat movement is only performed at the most convenient point in the program. This neatly avoids any possible synchronisation problems, whilst keeping the mouse control beautifully smooth. An example of this type of routine can be found in the Universal sprite controller described in Chapter 2.

3.4.2 Positioning the bat

After initialisation, the bat is generally placed at the centre of the playing area. If you are intending the use the joystick routine from Chapter 2 (Example 2.2), you can centre the bat by simply setting the variables SX and SY to the required coordinates. But how do you explicitly change the current position of the mouse pointer within a STOS Basic program?

Interestingly, there's an undocumented feature of STOS Basic which allows you to do just that. All you need to do is to assign the appropriate coordinates to the X MOUSE and Y MOUSE functions as if they were normal variables.e.g.

```
x mouse=10:y mouse=10:rem moves mouse to coordinates 10,10
```

3.5 The ball

3.5.1 Initial conditions (gluing the ball to the bat)

At the start of a rebound game, the ball is fixed on the bat waiting to be released in its final trajectory. The universal control system I showed you earlier, returns both the position of the bat, and the status of the mouse button (or fire key). You can use this information to effectively "glue" the ball to the ball using the SPRITE command in the following way:

```
2000 gosub 1000:rem Initialize universal control system
2000 gosub 1110:rem call universal control system
2005 rem Assume LBAT=width of bat and BALL is image no of ball
2010 if k=0 then sprite 2,bx+lbat/2,by-5,ball:goto 2000
2020 rem Release ball
```

If you wanted to control the bat with the joystick rather than the mouse, you would replace 2000 with:

```
2000 gosub 1100
```

3.5.2 Releasing the ball

As the mouse key (or fire button) is pressed, the ball is released, and flies headlong towards the bricks. The direction of flight can either be completely random, or can depend on the position of the ball relative to the bat. See section 3.8 on Orbiter for more details.

3.5.3 Moving the ball

Once the ball has been released, it will obviously need to be moved across the ST's screen. The STOS Basic MOVE commands provide you with the perfect mechanism for this operation. You do, however, need to calculate the required movement strings by careful experimentation. A full blown sprite experimenter program can be found in Chapter 1. This will allow you to play around with the possible movements before deciding on a particular set of strings.

If for instance, you wanted to move the ball diagonally,you could use a pair of instructions like:

```
move x 1,"(1,1,1)1":move y 1,"(1,1,1)1"
```

This sequence could then be activated using the MOVE ON statement like this:

```
move on 1
```

Although the movement commands themselves are trivial, you do need to decide carefully about the number and type of the directions you will assign to the ball. The minimum practical number of rebound directions is four, but if you want to produce a really believable effect, you will need to generate at least eight different movement paths. (See Figure 3.3 on the next page).

You will also need to provide each direction with several speeds. This allows you to

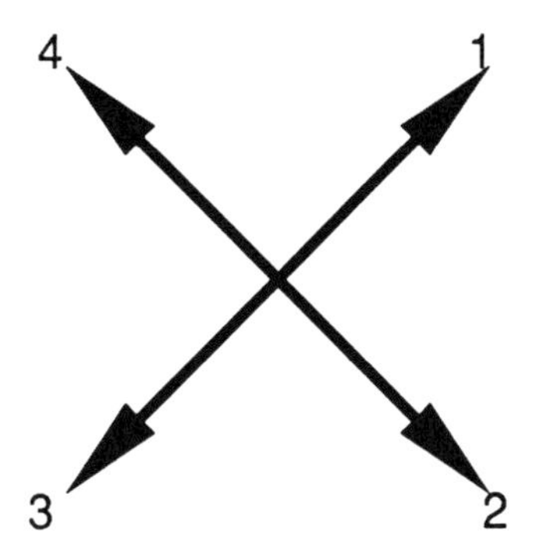

Figure 3.2 Movement directions (four)

increase the speed of the ball steadily during the course of a game, adding a whole new dimension to the game play.

The movement strings specifying each possible direction would be held in a set of arrays. These would be defined at the start of the program in the following way:

```
dim x$(no_of_directions,no_of_speeds)
dim y$(no_of_directions,no_of_speeds)
```

You would then load these strings with the appropriate values during the initialisation process. Let's assume that you wished to start the ball moving in direction number one with a speed of three. You could now use the following line in your program:

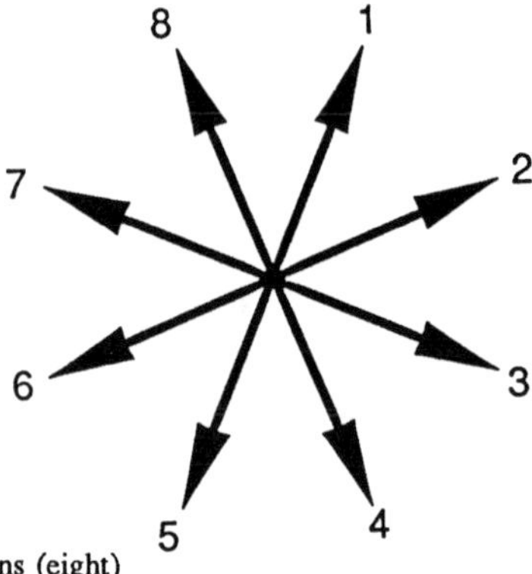

Figure 3.3 Movement directions (eight)

```
move x 2,x$(1,3):move y 2,y$(1,3):move on:rem sprite 2=ball
```

Orbiter uses a total of twelve possible movement paths, each of which has five different speeds. It's well worth having a look at these definitions, as they provide a perfect practical example of the technique in action. The movement strings can be found from lines 50000-50300. The first string in each line is used by the MOVE X instructions, and the second by the MOVE Y.

3.6 Collisions

3.6.1 Detecting a collision with the bat

The easiest collision to detect is that between the bat and the ball. This can be accomplished with a single call to the COLLIDE command. Supposing you had allocated sprite 1 for the bat and sprite 2 for the ball. You could now test for a collision using:

```
C=COLLIDE(1,W,H)
```

If a collision had been successfully detected then C would be loaded a binary number holding the sprite number used by the ball.

This could be tested with the BTST function like this:

```
if btst(SP,C) then 4000
```

where:

4000 is the location of your explosion routine
SP is the sprite number you've allotted to your ball, and
W and H specify the sensitivity of the test. The ideal values for these variables will depend on the size of the bat, but it's best to keep them both as small as possible.

Since all collision checks are performed in relation to the hot spot of the sprite, it's logical to set this to the centre of the bat. This will allow you to combine the maximum accuracy with the smallest detection zone.

3.6.2 Collisions between the ball and the block

In order to test for a collision between the ball and one of the blocks, you can make good use of the STOS Basic ZONE function. Each block is allocated one of the 128 possible screen zones during the initialization process. This can be demonstrated by the following program fragment:

```
500 for i=0 to BLOCKS
510 reset zone i:rem Free zone for block no i
520 set zone I, BLOCKX(I)-1,BLOCKY(I)-1, BLOCKY(I)-4 to
BLOCKX(I)+13,BLOCKY(I)+9
530 next I
```

BLOCKX and BLOCKY are assumed to be previously defined arrays which have been loaded with the X and Y coordinates of each block.

You can now instantly determine the number of any block which has just been hit by the ball:

```
BLOC=zone(2):rem ball is sprite number two
```

If BLOC contains the number of one of the existing blocks, then the collision has taken place. Otherwise, your program can continue unaffected.

You obviously need to make provision in your program to remove the blocks from consideration after they have been destroyed. This can be done with a single call to the RESET ZONE command.e.g.

```
reset zone BLOC:rem Destroys block number BLOC
```

3.6.3 Collisions between a ball and the walls

There are literally dozens of ways you can check collisions between the ball and the edges of the playing area. The most obvious method involves the use of the X SPRITE and Y SPRITE functions. If you wanted to detect a collision between the ball and the left hand wall, you could use something like:

```
if x sprite<=TX then gosub 2000:rem do collision with Left
wall
```

The variables TX,TY are assumed to contain the coordinates of the top of the playing area, and DX,DY the position of the point diagonally opposite.

You can also exploit exactly the same idea to test for a collision between the ball and one of the other walls. e.g

```
if x sprite>=DX then gosub 2100:rem do collision with right
if y sprite<=TY then gosub 2200:rem do collision with top
if y sprite>DY then 2300:rem lose a life
```

Note that the routines at 2000,2100,2200 and 2300 have not yet been defined. They are assumed to refer to subroutines which you have written earlier in your program to handle to various types of collision.

Alternatively, you can enclose the edges of the playing area with a set of screen zones. This enables you to use a single call to the ZONE function to detect collisions between both the edges of screen and the blocks. Each of the three edges is now assigned a particular screen zone using SET ZONE.

Here is a fragment of code which demonstrates this process:

```
100 rem Set up zones
110 set zone 100,tx,0 to dx,ty:rem Top
120 set zone 101,0,ty to tx,dy:rem Left
130 set zone 102,dx,ty to 319,dy:rem Right
200 rem read zone
210 z=zone(2):if z=0 then 210
220 if z<100 then gosub 3000:rem Collision with brick
220 rem collisions with wall
        :       :
```

One minor flaw with this technique, is that it ignores the possibility of the ball hitting one of the corner points. This will lead to slightly unpredictable behaviour when the corners are hit, as the rebound effect will vary depending on which zone was entered first. The solution is simply to define a couple of extra zones to specifically cover the corner points.e.g.

```
140 set zone 103,tx,ty to tx+10,ty+10:rem Top left corner
150 set zone 104,bx-10,ty to bx,ty+10:rem Top right corner
```

In the vast majority of rebound games, the bottom corners of the playing area can be safely ignored by this routine, because they do not produce rebounds.

3.6.4 Collisions with the ball and an irregular object

Normally, all the objects in a rebound game are rectangular. But if you're attempting to write something refreshingly original, you might wish to introduce circular or even triangular obstacles to your game. Supposing you wanted to create a version of pin-ball.

Collisions between the ball and your blocks could now be discovered using DETECT. This returns the number of the colour underneath the hot spot of the ball. Providing you kept the background colours of your screen separate from those used in the objects, you would be able to quickly distinguish between your blocks and the background, and thus detect any collisions.

Unfortunately, you would still have no idea about which particular object the ball had actually hit. Luckily, there's a delightfully sneaky way of solving this problem with very little effort. All you need to do, is enclose your object in a rectangular screen zone. If you've detected a collision, the ball has to lie within one of the rectanglar zones. So then it's just a matter of finding the zone using using the ZONE function to get the precise identity of the object in question.

3.7 Rebounds

Whenever the ball hits an object, it will rebound in a distinctive direction. If your game is to appear realistic, it is essential that you choose the correct rebound effect for every possible eventuality.

During the game, the ball can rebound off the walls, the blocks, or the bat. The principles of these rebounds are similar for all three situations.

3.7.1 Rebound tables

The standard way of handling these rebounds is to calculate all the possible rebound directions in advance. These can then be placed in a look-up table and the required movement string can be accessed immediately by the appropriate collision handler in your program. Every distinct type of object in your game will have its own specific set of rebound directions. Since the rebound of the ball varies according to the point it hits a block, each face will need to be treated separately.

3.7.2 Rebounds with a wall

The playing area of a rebound game is usually surrounded by three walls. You could therefore hold the entire rebound table for these walls in an array.e.g.

```
dim WALL(3,REBOUNDS)
```

REBOUNDS is just a simple variable holding the number of rebound directions you have chosen.

This array would then need to be loaded with the appropriate rebound information. You could now get the direction of rebound of the ball from wall number one, using a line like:

```
d=WALL(1,d)
```

D is assumed to hold the number representing the direction of the ball before the collision took place.

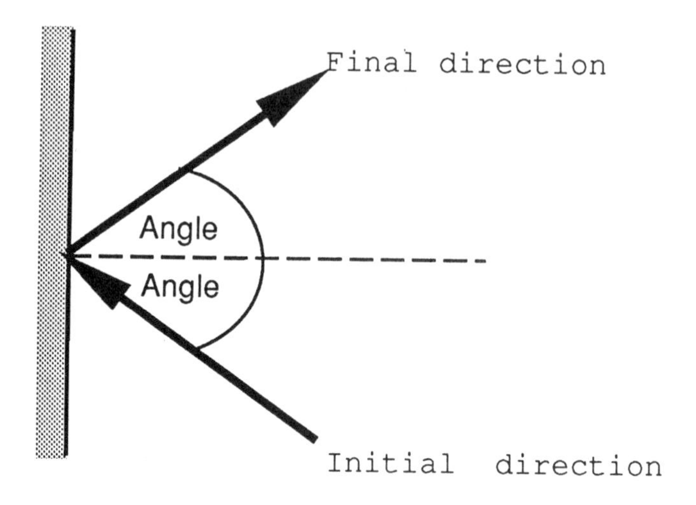

Figure 3.4 Collision between the ball and a wall

Supposing the ball was to hit wall number one from direction number four (see Figure 3.2). The rebound table would now be accessed to work out the correct rebound direction for the ball.

```
D = WALL(1,2)
```

In the case of the situation in Figure 3.4, the required rebound would occur in direction one. Once you have found the rebound direction, you can simply reset the motion of the ball using the movement strings you defined earlier for MOVE X and MOVE Y.

If you had decided on eight possible movement directions, these arrays dimensioned like this:

```
dim X$(8),Y$(8)
```

X$ contains the strings needed for the horizontal part of the motion, and Y$ the vertical component. So the entire rebound effect could be generated using:

```
-D=WALL(1,D)
move x 2,X$(D)
move y 2,Y$(D)
move on
```

The really nice thing about this technique is that it's extendible. This allows you to start off with a minimum of four directions, and steadily expand these during the development of your game.

I'll now demonstrate the use of rebound tables with a practical example.

Example 3.2 Rebound tables

```
10  rem Example 3.2
20  rem Rebound
30  TX=0 : rem TX=X coordinate of left wall
40  BX=319 : rem BX=X coordinate of right wall
50  TY=0 : rem TY=Y coordinate of top wall
60  BY=199 : rem BY=Y coordinate of bottom wall
70  rem set up screen
80  mode 0 : cls physic : cls back : locate 10,2 : centre
"Rebounds" : curs off : box TX,TY to BX,BY : hide
90  rem Initialization
100 dim WALL(4,4) : rem four walls and four directions
110 rem load rebound table
120 for W=1 to 4 : for D=1 to 4 : read WALL(W,D) : next D : next
W
130 dim H$(4),V$(4) : rem define movement strings
140 rem load movement strings
150 for M=1 to 4 : read H$(M),V$(M) : next M
160 sprite 1,160,100,25 : rem Draw sprite at centre
170 REBOUND=1 : rem initial direction of motion
180 rem for R=1 to 4 : sprite 1,160,100,1 : move x 1,H$(R) :
move y 1,V$(R) : move on : print R : wait key : next R
190 move x 1,H$(REBOUND) : move y 1,V$(REBOUND) : move on
200 rem left wall (surface 1)
210 if x sprite(1)<=TX then REBOUND=WALL(1,REBOUND) : move x
1,H$(REBOUND) : move y 1,V$(REBOUND) : move on : shoot
220 rem right wall (surface 2)
230 if x sprite(1)>=BX then REBOUND=WALL(2,REBOUND) : move x
1,H$(REBOUND) : move y 1,V$(REBOUND) : move on : shoot
240 rem Top wall (surface=3)
250 if y sprite(1)<=TY then REBOUND=WALL(3,REBOUND) : move x
1,H$(REBOUND) : move y 1,V$(REBOUND) : move on : shoot
260 rem Bottom wall (surface 4)
270 if y sprite(1)>=BY then REBOUND=WALL(4,REBOUND) : move x
1,H$(REBOUND) : move y 1,V$(REBOUND) : move on : shoot
280 goto 210
290 rem rebound table
300 data 1,2,2,1
310 data 4,3,3,1
```

```
320 data 2,2,3,3
330 data 1,1,4,4
340 rem movement strings
350 data "(1,6,4)1","(1,-6,4)1"
360 data "(1,6,4)1","(1,6,4)1"
370 data "(1,-6,4)1","(1,6,4)1"
380 data "(1,-6,4)1","(1,-6,4)1"
```

3.7.3 Rebounds with the bat

The bat is the only part of the program which is directly controlled by the player. It's therefore essential to get the rebounds from the bat as accurate as possible. Since the bat only has a single surface, the rebounds are delightfully straightforward. You could, for instance, treat the bat as just a moving wall, and implement the rebounds directly using a simple rebound table.

If you tried to implement this idea in practice, the path of the ball would quickly degenerate into a predictable pattern which would quickly become boring. This robs the game of much of its appeal in one foul stroke. The solution is to introduce some variety into the rebound process. The rebound mechanism between the ball and the bat provides you with a perfect opportunity to implement this type of system. Here are a few ideas:

1. The rebound direction depends on the point the ball hits the bat. If you've placed the hot point of the bat at the centre, the position can be calculated from the following formula:

   position = (width of bat)/2 +x sprite(ball) - x sprite(bat)

   This value can now be looked up in a rebound table containing the appropriate rebound directions for each point on the bat. In the case of Orbiter, each bat has a rebound table containing 48 distinct elements.

2. Let the rebound table vary depending on the size of the bat. This is extremely useful in games like Orbiter which include several different bats. The smaller the bat, the tighter the rebound angle. This can be reflected in the appropriate rebound table.

3. Test for the speed of the mouse movement. If the player slices the ball, the angle of rebound will be higher and the ball will be faster. The speed of the movement can be calculated by keeping a record of the last bat position. So speed = ABS(last X coordinate - current X coord). (The ABS just removes the sign from the speed indicator).

4. Change the rebound direction depending on the speed of the ball. Normally the speed will already be known. So it's just a matter of creating a rebound table holding the directions for each speed. Fast speeds should have tight rebound angles and slow speeds should have shallow ones.

3.7.4 Rebounds with the block

The final type of rebound effect is generated by a collision between the ball and one of the blocks. It should be obvious that the direction of the rebounding ball will depend on the side of the block at which the impact occurs. This is shown in the diagram in Figure 3.5.

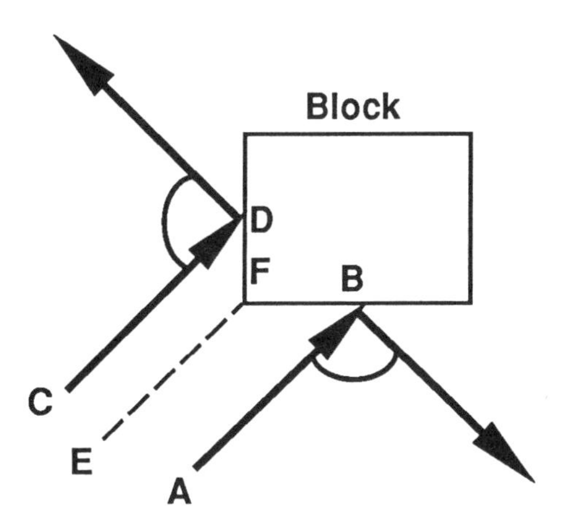

Figure 3.5 Rebound directions

As you can see, the rebound direction is completely different when the ball hits at B from when it impacts at D. Assuming the two paths are parallel, the eventual rebound direction will be determined entirely by the initial position of the ball. If the ball starts at the left of the line E F, the ball will be reflected off the left face, but if the ball starts to the right, it will collide with the bottom edge of the block.

A small distance between the two starting points can have a profound effect on the final result. This presents the programmer with an extremely difficult problem, which is further complicated by the ball's speed across the screen.

There are several possible solutions to this situation. The best I've seen so far was devised by Francois Lionet in his excellent Orbiter program. This divides up the area around the block into the eight sections shown in Figure 3.6, on the next page.

Whenever the ball is in flight, a record is kept of its current coordinates. This record is invaluable when the ball hits one of the blocks, as it gives a good indication of the original path of the ball. You can now use this information to calculate which side of the block has been hit.

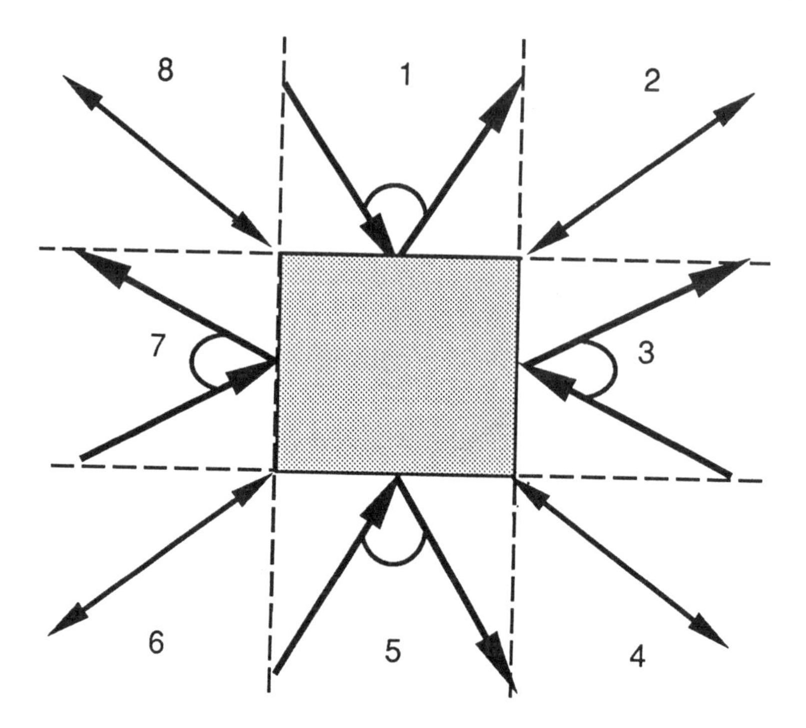

Figure 3.6 Rebound Zones

If, for instance, the old coordinates of the ball lie in region one, then the ball has almost certainly collided with the uppermost face of the block. Likewise, regions three, five and seven indicate a collision between the right, bottom and left sides respectively.

From these facts, it's easy to get the rebound direction straight from a rebound table you have defined previously. But what happens if the ball has moved from regions two, four, six or eight? In this case, the situation is far less clear. Take a look at the diagram in Figure 3.7 on the next page.

You can get a good approximation of the path of the ball, by checking whether the ball originated from above, on, or below the diagonal line A B which divides the zone neatly in two.

If the ball lies above the region then it is likely that the impact point is somewhere along the left face.

Similarly, if the ball started from below the region then it probably collided with the top of the block. By checking the relative distances between the old position and corner points, you can work out which zone the ball has moved from.

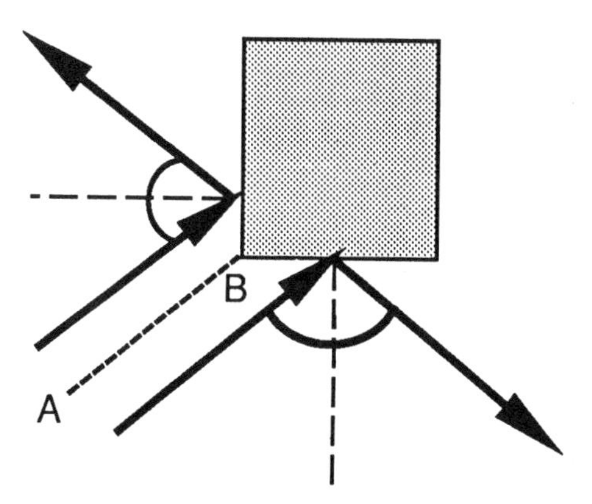

Figure 3.7 Diagonal hits

This can be used to estimate the final impact point, which can be passed on to the rebound table in the usual way. If, incidentally, the ball enters along the diagonal line, then the ball will have hit one of the corners. This situation will require its own entry in the rebound table.

Unfortunately, it's quite possible to fool the system completely because it assumes that the motion of the ball is parallel to the line A-B. If you're using more than four movement directions in your game, this condition is not always satisfied.

There's no way you can surmount this entirely, but you can add an extra test to reduce its likelihood. Before your program guesses the collision, it should first check the condition of some of the adjacent blocks. If you find that a block along the predicted pathway is still in existence, you can be pretty sure that the collision point which you have calculated will be wrong.

So far, I've limited my discussion to theory. Here, in Figure 3.8 on the next page, is a pseudo-code description which might make things a little less opaque.

I appreciate that the above pseudo-code looks rather complicated, but this is simply a reflection of the difficulty of the problem. The best way to get an understanding of this procedure, is to laboriously go through the description by hand. It helps to make a sketch of each zone on a piece of graph paper. You can then trace through the method, and see how every conceivable path is handled by the system.

Surprisingly enough, the final STOS Basic routine is remarkably small. In the Orbiter game, Francois Lionet cleverly managed to compact the whole thing down to just six lines of instructions!

```
(Note that last X, last Y are the last known coordinates of the
ball. Block X and Block Y are the coordinates of the top left
hand corner of the block which has been hit. Length and Height
are the dimensions of the block)

Detect collisions
If collision
    then
        face=unset
    If last X>blockX and last X<block X+Length
    and last Y<block Y
        then
            zone=1
            face = top
            rebound ball
        endif
    If last X>blockX and last X<blockX+Length
    and last Y>block Y
        then
            zone=5
            face = bottom
            rebound ball
        endif
    If last Y>blockY and last Y<blockY+Height
    and last X>block X
        then
            zone=3
            face = right
            rebound ball
        endif
    If last Y>blockY and last Y<blockY+Height
    and last X<block X
        then
            zone=5
            face=left
            rebound ball
        endif
    If face=unset
    then
        handle diagonal
    else
Store last X
Store last Y
Endif
```

Figure 3.8 Rebound system for blocks

3.8 Inside Orbiter

Of the three games which are included in the STOS Basic package, Orbiter has to be my personal favourite. Not only is the action both fast and furious, but the overall quality of the game approaches that of the original Arkanoid program.

I'll now provide you with a detailed look at the inner workings of this fascinating program.

The intention is to give you enough information to allow you to modify the game to your own needs. This would be particularly useful for those of you who are restricted to a monochrome monitor, as it would enable you to convert the game into high resolution. I'll also be demonstrating some of the spectacular tricks used to squeeze the maximum possible speed out of the STOS Basic system.

3.8.1 Initialisation

The program lines from 10-500 perform a variety of useful initialisation steps. The first action is to fade out the screen and enter low resolution graphics mode. Line 15 now defines a number of important constants.

NXBLOCS = The maximum number of blocks per row (11)

NYBLOCS = The maximum number of rows per screen (10)

MBLOCS = The maximum number of blocks on the screen (110)

SPEEDMAX = The number of possible speeds for the ball (6)

The numerous arrays required by the game are now defined at line 20.

The rectangular blocks are displayed on a grid with elements numbered from 1 to 110. This grid is stored in the arrays WAVE and BLOC. If an element contains a zero, then there is no block at the current position. Any other value represents the type of the block which is present on the screen.

The numbering system starts from the top left corner of the screen and progresses from left to right. So the number of the slot at row R and Column C is given by the following formula:

Slot number = (R-1)*MXBLOCS+C

If MXBLOCS=11, then the slot at row five, column two has an identification number of:

(5-1)*10+2=42

The other arrays defined at line 20 are:

WAVE: This holds a permanent copy of the current game screen. It is only changed when a new wave is loaded from the disk.

BLOC: holds a temporary copy of the screen which will be altered as blocks are destroyed during the game.

WAVEHITS: This is an array containing the number of hits which can be taken by each block before it will be destroyed. Like WAVE, the information in this array is permanent.

HITS is a temporary version of the WAVEHITS array, which is changed after every successful hit.

XBLOC: holds the X coordinate of the top left hand corner of each slot in the game grid. There's an entry in this table for every possible position, even if it does not contain an actual block.

YBLOCK: holds the Y coordinate of the top corner of the slots.

B$: is an array of thirty strings which will be subsequently loaded with the images of the block graphics using the SCREEN$ command.

MX$: is a string array containing the movement strings describing the balls horizontal motion for use with the MOVE X instruction. The ball can move at six speeds and in twelve directions. There is one movement string for each of these possibilities.

MY$: is an array of strings containing the vertical component of the balls movements for use with the MOVE Y command.

REBAT holds the rebound table for the bat. The data for this can be found at line 60000 in Orbiter.

REWALL: contains the rebound table for all three walls, along with the two top corners. Each possibility is managed by its own set of twelve rebound directions. This data is at line 60100.

REBLOC: This is the rebound table for the blocks. The rebound direction depends on the face of the block which has been hit, and the initial direction of travel. The information needed for this table is stored from line 60200.

The **EFFECT** array holds the location of the subroutines used to handle special effects such as the bombs and the hyperspace feature. The starting lines of each routine are loaded in the array using the data at 61000. The appropriate routine can then be executed like this:

```
gosub EFFECT(n)
```

Where n is the number of the effect which is to be executed.

TURN$: contains a set of twelve animation strings which add a spinning effect to the ball. Six strings are allocated to turns in a clockwise direction, and six for an anticlockwise rotation. There is a different string in each direction and for the twelve possible speeds. This data is generated during the game at line 145.

DX = X coordinate of top corner of movement zone for bat.

DY = Y coordinate of top corner of movement zone.

FX = X coordinate of bottom right corner of movement zone

FY = Y coordinate of bottom corner of zone.

The sizes of the movement zones will vary according to the bat which has been selected. There are therefore three sets of each of these coordinates.

The LB array contains the lengths of each bat. There are three possible bat sizes, 16,32 and 48 units long.

The graphics for the blocks are initially held in the form of sprites. In order to speed up the block drawing routine, Orbiter loads each sprite into one of the strings in the B$ array. This is achieved by the routine starting at line 200.

NBBLOC is loaded with the number of different block types.

SPBLOC contains the starting position of the first sprite image used to contain a block.

The lines from 300 to 1000 now generate the title screen and allow the player to begin playing the game.

3.8.2 The control loop

The main control loop for the Orbiter game commences at 1000.

The first action is to set up the initial conditions:

WAVE = The number of the wave
NBATS = The number of bats
SCRE = The initial score
WIN = The status of the player.

During the game WIN can take one of the following three values:

WIN = 0 (Player has started a wave)
= 1 (Player has destroyed a wave)
=-1 (Player has been destroyed)

The activities of the main control loop can be summarized with a little pseudo-code:

The main control loop from Orbiter

```
Draw screen           (Calls routine at 10000 and clears space
                      needed for blocks)

Repeat
     Load wave
     Copy wave data into temporary storage
     Repeat
          Play one game (Calls play game routine at 1200)
     Until Lives<0 or wave defeated

Until Lives<0 or no more levels
```

All the waves are stored on the disk in the form of 110 pairs of numbers with one pair for each element in the grid. The first number contains the type of the block at this position. A value of zero indicates that the current position is empty. The second number holds a record of the amount of damage which can be suffered by a block before it is destroyed.

3.8.3 Playing a game

The "play game" routine itself can be found from line 1200. I'll demonstrate how it works with a line by line breakdown of the various activities in Table 3.1, below.

Table 3.1 "Play Game" routine

Action	*Lines*	*Comment*
Initialise game	1200	See Note 1
Redraw blocks	1210	Calls routine at 10200. Uses temporary data
If new bat slides out "cage"	1215	Calls routine at 10100
Set WIN to zero	1225	
Centre ball on bat	1225	DXBALL=position
Release ball	1225	Calls routine at 2000
Repeat	1300	Start of main loop
Control Bat	1300	Call control routine at 2045

Table 3.1 "Play Game" routine (continued)

If bat and ball collide	1305	Call rebound routine at 2025 or release bat routine if bat "sticky"
Has ball entered a new zone?	1310	OLDZ=Old zone number. If it hasn't, jump to end of loop at 1385
Increase speed of ball?	1315	When SPEEDCPT=0
Has ball hit a wall?	1320	Handle and jump to 1385 See Note 2
Ball hits block	1325	
Is block destroyed?	1325	If DESTROY Flag set. Check NHITS and exit to end of loop; see Note 3
Stop ball moving	1330	
Get row of current block	1330	Store in Y
Get column of current block	1330	Store in X
Set horizontal distance to dummy	1330	Loads DX with 100. See Note 4
Set vertical distance to dummy	1330	Loads DY with 100. See Note 4
Did ball approach from left?	1335	Ball hit top, bottom or left; see Note 5
Did ball approach from right?	1340	Ball hit at top, bottom or right; see Note 5
Did ball approach from top?	1345	Ball hit at top, left or right; see Note 5
Did ball approach from below?	1350	Ball hit at bottom, left or right; see Note 5
Did ball impact at corner?	1355	See Note 4
Set face of impact	1360	See Note 5
Choose rebound direction	1365	Using REBLOC table
If diagonal hit choose random direction	1365	Adds a little unpredictability

Table 3.1 "Play Game" routine (continued)

Start ball moving in new rebound direction	1370	Uses MOVE X and MOVE Y with strings in MX$ and MY$
Control mouse	1370	Call routine at 2045 again
Destroy block?	1375	Check number of hits
Special effect?	1375	IF number of hits<>0 gosub EFFECT(type); see Note 6
if normal block	1375	Destroy block
Get old zone number	1385	OLDZ=Z
Get last X and last y	1385	Load in OLDX and OLDY
Check for collision with bomb	1390	Bomb=sprite 5
Check for Escape key	1391	
Until no more blocks or ball reached bottom of screen	1395	

Notes:

1 This section sets up the following variables:

SPEEDCPT=3	Speed of ball
REVERSE=0	Set to one if the mouse action is reversed. See line 2800 of Orbiter.
DESTROY=0	Set to one for Superball (See line 2700 of Orbiter)
GLUE=0	Sticky bat. This is loaded with one at 3700.
BOMB=0	No bombs on screen. Bomb launched by routine at 2600.
YMOVE=0	Set one if UP/DOWN movements are allowed.
BON$=""	String containing B O N U S sequence
QUIT=0	Set to one if user presses escape

2 If the ball is in a zone with a number greater than that used by a block, then it must have hit one of the walls. This line uses a rebound table stored in REWALL to determine the rebound direction.

3 This line is only applicable if the superball option has been set. The ball then destroys the block and continues regardless, with no rebound.

4 DX holds the difference between the last recorded X coordinate of the ball and the corner of the block.

DY holds the equivalent distance between the Y coordinates.

At the start of the routine, DX and DY are loaded with dummy values of a 100. These values are changed by the tests at lines 1335-1350. If only one test proves true, then the ball has approached from the directions 1, 3, 5, or 7 and the impact point is obvious. Since 100 is much larger than a real distance, the line at 1360 automatically selects the impact point chosen by whichever test was successful.

If however, both values are set, then the impact point will depend on the relative sizes of DX and DY. This can be clearly seen from Figure 3.9, which illustrates the three main possibilities.

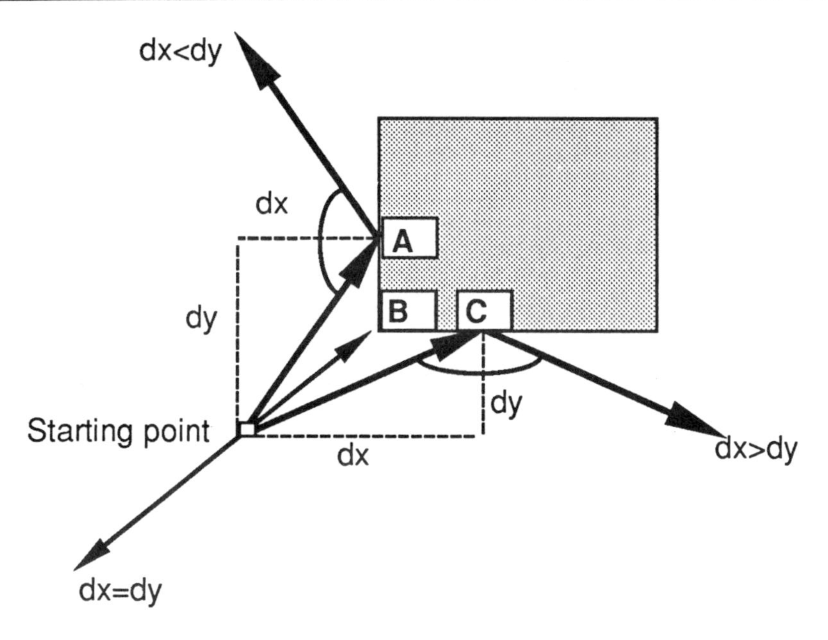

Figure 3.9 DX and DY

If both values are equal, the ball will have hit at the point B. Otherwise it will impact at either A or C, depending on the values of DX and DY.

5 Notice the checks for the contents of the adjacent blocks.

If none of these blocks are free, the ball must have hit the block at one of its corners. In this case the variables DX and DY will remain at their initial values and this will be spotted at line 1355.

Ideas for improvements

1 Add your own types of block with their own effects. This is quite easy and could be accomplished by placing your own routines at the end of the program. You could then add this to the EFFECT array stored at line 61000. Don't forget to change the number of effects at 140.

2 Add moving aliens as in Arkanoid. This wouldn't be too hard, as you could use the movement system I described in Chapter 2. But you might find that the ball movements slowed down a little. After all, even STOS has its limits.

3 Incorporate another feature of Arkanoid, like the pods.

4 Increase the size of the playing area.

5 Add animation effects to the blocks when they are hit. The blocks could rotate into oblivion instead of just disappearing.

6 Include some really effective sound effects during the game play.

Hopefully, this section has convinced you that Rebound games are well worth your serious attention. After many years of deserved success, Arkanoid is now starting to approach the end of its useful life. Maybe you can create its successor!

4

Simulations

4.1 What is simulation

One of the most important applications of computers in the modern world is in the field of simulation. The art of computer simulation is to break down a complex real-world situation and capture its essence inside a computer program. These systems can then be used to make uncannily accurate predictions as to the outcome of any specific event, without the risk of disastrous and expensive mistakes. This allows us to test our theories so we can get things completely right first time.

When the scientists at NASA wanted to calculate the best orbit for the Voyager space probe, they didn't shoot off a couple of dozen ships in the hope that one would succeed. That would have been sheer lunacy. Instead they simulated the orbit with a computer, and simply checked through all the possible combinations until they found one they particularly liked. This allowed them to make full use of Jupiter's gravity field, to flick the probe from Jupiter to Saturn with just a minimum expenditure of fuel. Frankly, without the ability to simulate the mission, it's unlikely that the amazingly successful Jupiter flyby would ever have been attempted. Considering the eventual pictures, that would have been real loss to both scientists and space enthusiasts alike.

Of course, simulations are not always so effective. The met office regularly runs some of the largest simulations in the world, using computers of unimaginable complexity. But the reliability of the weather forecasts these systems produce is still a matter of heated debate!

Because simulations are essentially just lists of mathematical rules, they have always lent themselves especially well to computer games. These games have long been popular with computer science students, as many of the basic principles of simulation programs are naturally acquired as part of their studies. The earliest examples of the genre were games like Golf, Lunar lander, and Kingdom. Originally these programs were unbelievably crude, and their graphics were often almost non-existent. Despite this, the games were surprisingly enjoyable, and I still remember them with a great deal of fond nostalgia from my own days as a student.

Over recent years, the simulation game has evolved out of all recognition. Golf has been transformed from a grotty text oriented game using the keyboard, to the amazing World class Leaderboard with its superb graphics and accurate game play. Lunar lander has progressed from a crude simulation of a real spaceship to the fantastic imaginary world of Elite. Even Kingdom has been reborn in a new guise, with the advent of chilling political simulations such as Chris Crawford's excellent ''Balance of power''.

4.2 Simulation games

4.2.1 The game world

All the action in a simulation game takes place in an imaginary **game world**, whose events are controlled through a complex set of mathematical relationships. In a commercial simulation, there will hopefully be a some direct correspondence between the events in the real world and those in the simulation. But in a computer game, this link is purely arbitrary, and it's quite possible to simulate situations which would appear totally ridiculous in reality.

Take the Hyperspace sequences found in games like Elite. Ask a respectable physicist about the possibility of hyperdrive, and you will be greeted with hoots of derision. According to the best modern theories, it's totally impossible to travel faster than the speed of light. If however, you were to restrict the spaceships in a space simulation to sensible speeds, the vast distances separating even the closest stars would seriously disrupt the mechanics of the game.

But who cares about the accuracy of a computer game? You don't after all, need to believe that your planet is being invaded to enjoy a game of Galaxians. So why bother with the authenticity of your simulation game. Show the same respectable physicist the latest version Elite, and I'm sure he'll enjoy himself no end.

Conversely, if your game is a perfect simulation but is boring and difficult to play, then it is highly unlikely to be a conspicuous success.

You should therefore always feel at liberty to simplify the game world for your own convenience. This applies especially to the speeds and distances used in your calculations. The only possible exception to this rule would be if you were attempting to recreate the illusion of flying a particular aircraft. But even in the best such simulations, the programmers are usually forced to take some liberties with the system. Otherwise, what would be the use of those million pound flight simulators used by the RAF?

In practice, few people will care about the exact figures you have used in your program. So given the choice between authenticity and entertainment value, the sensible programmer always errs on the side of playability.

While you're designing your game, it's important to think very carefully about precisely which aspects of the situation you are actually attempting to simulate. Normally, the game world will be vastly simpler than the real world around you. This will allow you to concentrate on the interesting parts the game, ignoring any boring details. How many golfing simulations include the movements of the caddy? And although Elite has you rushing across the galaxy for "months" at a time, there's no simulation of your character eating lunch or going to the bathroom.

Of course, nobody would really go to those extremes. Once you've started working on your simulation however, it's all too easy to get carried away, and continue to add more and more detail, forgetting about the eventual consequences to the gameplay.

4.2.2 Game time

Since the game world only exists inside the computer, the time which passes in the simulation is completely separate to that experienced by the player. For the purposes of my discussion, I'll assume **game-time** to be the time that is apparently spent in the game world, and **real-time** as the actual time which takes place for the player.

In games like golf, the two time-scales will be pretty near identical, but if you are trying to simulate the economics of an entire country over a period of years, you might need to compress years of game-time into just minutes of real-time activity. By choosing the ratio of game-time to real-time carefully, you can play complicated scenarios which would require an enormous amount of time to complete in the real world, whilst still keeping the gameplay fast and furious.

The time in your game doesn't even need to be continuous. Most economic simulations only update the time after the player has entered a turn. A good example of this approach can be found in "Balance of power", which takes each turn to be a single year. So the length of one of these games depends entirely on the amount of time the player is prepared to spend pondering each move.

4.3 Simulating movement in space

The simulation process requires you to produce a detailed mathematical model of a real-life situation. This forces you to break down a complex physical process into a set of mathematical equations. At first glance this procedure would appear to be incredibly daunting, but fortunately most of these types of simulations only require you to understand a relatively few basic physical laws.

4.3.1 The equations of motion

The first reliable description of the laws which govern the motion of an object were discovered by Sir Isaac Newton. These allow you to calculate the position and speed of any object moving in three dimensional space. The beauty of the Newtonian laws, is that they apply equally well to a golf ball as a space ship. Suffice it say, Newton's equations have been successfully employed in many different types of simulations, up to and including the Voyager simulator I mentioned earlier.

I'll start off with a brief description of the laws of motion in a simple straight line. If you've done a little physics, you will already be fairly familiar with these equations. They can be summarised as follows:

Distance = ((Initial velocity+final velocity)/2) * time (1)

Final velocity = Initial velocity + acceleration * time (2)

Distance = Initial velocity*time+(acceleration*time^2)/2 (3)

Final velocity^2=Initial velocity^2+acceleration*distance*2 (4)

Velocity is measured as the distance per unit of time in a specific direction; e.g. 10 metres per second north.

It's important to realise that the velocity of an object is not the same as its speed. A velocity is the increase in distance in a specific direction. So 30 miles/hour is a speed, but 30 miles/hour due north is a velocity.

Also note that the units used to measure the distances and speeds purely arbitrary. The above equations work equally well for both British and Metric systems, and if you feel more comfortable with yards rather than metres, you can substitute them directly into my calculations. Treat a metre as approximately 39 inches or 3 1/4 feet. If you're really lazy, you can forget about the fraction completely and just assume that metres and yards are identical. This does however, reduce the accuracy of your calculations by around eight percent. So a really smart player might actually notice the difference!

Acceleration = Increase in velocity per unit of time

Acceleration is defined in terms of the increase in velocity which takes place over a given unit in time. If, for instance, an object accelerated from rest with an acceleration of 10 metres per second per second, the velocity would increase according to the pattern shown in Table 4.1.

Table 4.1 Acceleration at 10 ms^{-1}

Time	*Velocity*
0	0
1	10
2	20
3	30
.	.
.	.
.	.

Normally the "per second per second" part abbreviated to just "per second^2"

You might be asking yourself at this point what all this boring physics has to do with a simulation game. Surprisingly enough, however, you can apply these rules directly to create a simple moon lander program.

Example 4.1 Simple moon lander

Before entering this program, you will need to generate a sprite for the spaceship. It's quicker to borrow one of the sprites from Zoltar with:

```
load "zoltar.bas":rem From the STOS games disk
```

Place a fresh disk into your current drive and type:

```
save "sprites.mbk",1
new
load "sprites.mbk"
10  rem Lunar lander version 1
20  SHIP=45 : rem set ship to the image number of your
spaceship
30  cls : input "Enter difficulty level";D
40  rem Clear screen
50  mode 0 : curs off : hide on : cls physic : cls back
60  locate 0,0 : centre "Lunar Lander"
70  FUEL=100*(10-D) : HEIGHT=1000 : SPEED=0 : THRUST=0 :
G=2
75  VSPEED=0 : ACC=0
80  rem Set up initial conditions
90  sprite 1,150,0,SHIP : rem draw sprite
100 rem play game
110 while (HEIGHT>0)
130 if FUEL<=abs(THRUST) then X$="" : THRUST=0 : goto 160
140 if jup then inc THRUST : rem Increase thrust
150 if jdown then dec THRUST : rem Reduce thrust
160 FUEL=FUEL-abs(THRUST) : rem Fuel consumption
170 locate 0,16 : print "Thrust ";THRUST;" ";
180 locate 0,17 : print "Fuel ";FUEL;" ";
190 rem perform calculations
200 ACC=G-THRUST
210 FSPEED=SPEED+ACC : rem from (2) with t=1
220 D=(FSPEED+SPEED)/2 : rem from (1)
230 HEIGHT=HEIGHT-D : rem Calculate new height
240 SPEED=FSPEED
250 locate 0,18 : print "Height ";HEIGHT;" ";
260 locate 0,19 : print "Speed ";SPEED;" ";
270 if HEIGHT>0 then sprite 1,150,200-(HEIGHT)/5,SHIP
280 wend
290 if SPEED>5 then cls physic : cls back : boom : locate
0,0 : centre "You crashed" : wait 50 : wait key : goto 10
```

```
300 if SPEED<0 then locate 0,0 : centre "Boing!" : goto 110
310 if SPEED=0 then cls physic : cls back : locate 0,0 :
centre "Perfect landing" else cls back : cls physic :
locate 0,0 : centre "Landed safely"
320 wait 50 : wait key : goto 30
```

It's worth examining Example 4.1 in some detail, as it illustrates a number of interesting techniques. The ship starts off at a height of 1000 metres with a velocity of zero. The program then enters a loop at 110 which continues until the ship has reached the ground. The sprite command at line 270 converts the height of the space ship into a physical screen coordinate. If your game uses wire frame graphics, this translation process will be considerably more complex. See Chapter 7 for more details.

Note the definitions I've used for the thrust and the fuel. Thrust is a measure of the acceleration of the ship. A positive thrust represents an acceleration towards the ground, and a negative one denotes an acceleration upwards. The choice of direction is fairly arbitrary, and was determined by the assuming that the direction of the motion was positive. Since the force of gravity is in the same direction as the motion, this will be represented by a positive acceleration. But as your spaceships engine is thrusting against the downward motion, it will be assigned a negative acceleration.

The equation at line 200 adds the negative thrust to the positive gravity, and works out the total acceleration towards the moon. This is translated into the final velocity at line 210 using equation 2: (Final velocity = Initial velocity + acceleration * time)

The change in height is now calculated using the equation 1 at line 220, i.e

Distance = ((Initial velocity+final velocity)/2) * time

The new height is then updated accordingly, and the appropriate graphics are displayed on the screen. Incidentally, the fuel is defined in terms of acceleration. One unit of fuel is assumed to impart an acceleration of one metre per second per second. This is a classic example of the type of harmless simplification you can make to reduce the difficulty of your calculations.

Unfortunately, in real life, things are rather more complicated, and the acceleration per unit of fuel will decrease as the fuel is expended and the ship gets lighter.

That's why most modern spaceships are constructed in stages. As each stage runs out of fuel, it is immediately jettisoned. This vastly increases the effectiveness of the fuel stored in the remaining stages of the spaceship.

The relationship between mass and acceleration can be seen directly from yet another of Newton's famous formulae:

Force = mass * acceleration (5)

Mass is measured using the standard units of weight. On Earth, the mass and weight of an object are identical. But although weight can change according to the strength of gravity, the mass of an object depends on the quantity of matter it contains and is therefore a constant. Supposing you had a brick weighing five kilograms. If you were to take this brick to the moon, the weight of the object would be reduced to a single kilo, since the moons gravity is about a fifth of that of the Earth. The mass of the brick would however remain unchanged at five kilograms.

This difference between mass and **weight** may seem arbitrary, but it is a matter of life and death to astronauts. Although it's possible to move extremely large objects in zero gravity, the force required to start and stop the object's motion is the same as than on Earth. Forgetting the consequences of this fact could well lead to the astronauts being accidentally crushed by the mass of an object they were trying to position.

Force is measured in units called Newtons. One newton is strictly equal to the force required to produce an acceleration of 9.81 metres per second^2 to a mass of one kilogramme. In practice, you will can round this number up to just ten, with very little loss of accuracy. (Around two percent).

You can incorporate equation (5) into Example 4.1 by changing the thrust to a force rather than an acceleration. You can then calculate the acceleration produced by this force using (5): Thrust = Mass * Acceleration

So Acceleration = Thrust/mass

Try adding the following lines to Example 4.1.

```
76  REST=500:rem Mass of ship without fuel
130 if FUEL<=abs(THRUST/1000) then X$="" : THRUST=0 :
goto 170
140 if jup then THRUST=THRUST+1000 : rem Increase thrust
150 if jdown then THRUST=THRUST-1000 : rem Reduce thrust
160 FUEL=FUEL-abs(THRUST)/1000 : rem Fuel consumption
195 MSS=REST+FUEL
200 ACC=G-THRUST/MSS
```

See how I've had to modify some of the original equations in order to get things to work correctly. The thrust is now measured directly in newtons. Since the original mass of the ship at level five is 1000 (including fuel), it takes 1000 newtons of force to add an acceleration of 1 metre per second squared. e.g.

$$\begin{aligned} \text{Acceleration} &= \text{force/mass} \\ &= 1000/1000 \\ &= 1 \end{aligned}$$

Also note that each unit of fuel is assumed to weigh one kilogramme.

4.3.2 Motion in two dimensions

The problem with the equations I've so far discussed, is that they only apply for motion in a simple straight line. If you want to predict the path of a projectile, such as a golf-ball, you will need to be able to simulate far more complex motions.

All projectiles move in a curved path known as a **parabola.** An example of one of these parabolas can be seen from Figure 4.1

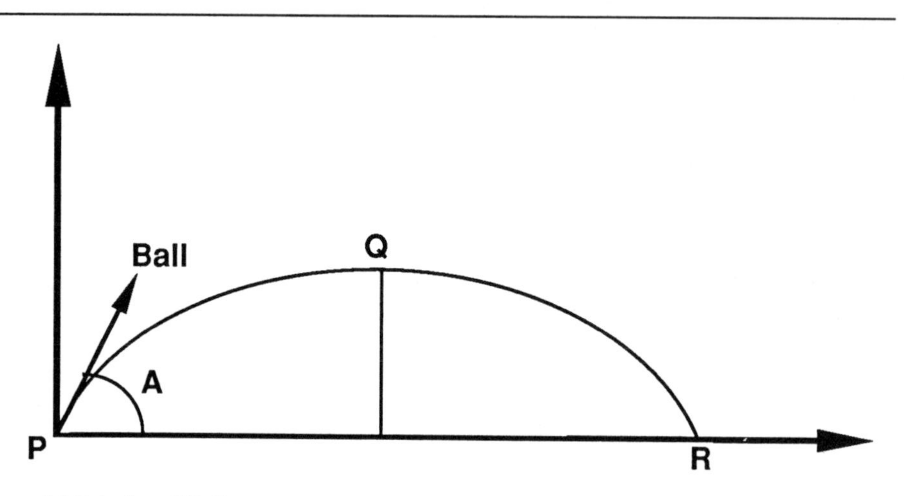

Figure 4.1 Path of a golf-ball

The golf-ball is struck at an angle A to the ground, and follows the path from P to R. The highest point in the motion occurs at position Q. Since the equations of motion will not work directly for a curve, they are apparently useless in the solution to this problem.

Fortunately, there's a trick which allows us to adapt the original equations for this new situation. Instead of trying to perform the calculation in one go, we can sneakily split the velocity into two separate components. One component represents the velocity of the ball vertically, and the other determines the velocity of the ball as it moves horizontally across the ground.

The sizes of each component can be calculated from the original velocity (V) using a little trigonometry.

Initial horizontal velocity = V * COS(A) (6)

Initial vertical velocity = V * SIN(A) (7)

Where A is the angle between the golf ball and the ground.

It's very similar to the section in Chapter 2 where I showed you how you could combine the MOVE X and MOVE Y instructions to move a sprite in two dimensions.

If the object is accelerating, the velocity components will continually be changing. So we will also need to divide the acceleration into two components. We can then work out the separate velocities using equations (1) through (3).

Horizontal acceleration = Total acceleration * COS(T) (8)

Vertical acceleration = Total acceleration * SIN(T) (9)

T is the angle of thrust. If the acceleration occurs in the direction of motion then T and A will obviously be identical. (See Chapter 7 for an explanation of the SIN and COS functions)

Once you've worked out the velocities and acceleration, using the formulae shown above (6-9), you can then treat each component completely independently, using the equations of motion.

Remember, these equations were given by:

Distance = ((Initial velocity+final velocity)/2) * time (1)

Final velocity = Initial velocity + acceleration * time (2)

Distance = Initial velocity*time+(acceleration*time^2)/2 (3)

Final velocity^2=Initial velocity^2+acceleration*distance*2 (4)

You can use these equations to find both the maximum range and the height of the ball respectively. You can also work out the total velocity of the ball at any time using Pythagoras' theorem.

Final velocity^2=(Horizontal velocity)^2+(Vertical velocity)^2 (10)

Here's a simple example to demonstrate these equations in practice. Let's assume that your golf-ball left the ground with a velocity of 20 metres per second at an angle of 45 degrees. The height of the ball after the first second of flight can be calculated from equations (1) and (4)

Initial_velocity (Vertical) = V*SIN(A)
= 20*SIN(45)
= 20*0.707
= 14.14 metres per second.

Final_velocity = Initial_velocity+acceleration*time (1)
= 14.14-10*1 (Acceleration is negative!)
= 4.14 metres per second

Height = ((Initial_velocity+Final_velocity)/2)*time
= (20+4.14)/2*1
= 12.07 metres

Since gravity only acts downwards, there is no acceleration affecting the balls horizontal motion. So the final velocity will be the same as the initial velocity and you can calculate the distance directly from (1).

Initial_velocity (horizontal) =Total_velocity*COS(angle)
= 20*COS(45)

Final_velocity =Initial velocity
=20*COS(45)

From (1)

Distance = ((Initial velocity+final velocity)/2) * time (1)

Distance = (20 * COS(45) + 20 * COS(45)) /2) * time
= (20*COS(45))
= 14.14 metres

Note that I've intentionally ignored the force of friction from my calculations. Generally the effect of this is fairly negligible anyway.

With a little mathematical wizardry you can substitute these equations into the Newtonian formulae to obtain the following rules:

Maximum height of ball = $V^2SIN(A)^2/2*G$ (11)

Time of flight = V*SIN(A)/G (12)

G = The acceleration of gravity (normally 10 M/S^2)

I appreciate that these formulae look pretty horrendous when you first see them. In fairness, the mathematics shouldn't tax anyone whose been educated up to O-Level physics. Thankfully you don't really need to understand any of these equations in order to use them in your programs.

I'll demonstrate this by incorporating the new equations into the moon-lander program in Example 4.1.

Example 4.2 A moon lander in 2D

```
10  rem Lunar lander version 2
20  SHIP=45 : rem set ship to the image number of your
spaceship
30  rem Clear screen
40  mode 0 : curs off : hide on : cls physic : cls back
50  rem Set up initial conditions
60  FUEL=1000 : HEIGHT=1000 : DISTANCE=1000 : VSPEED#=0
65  HSPEED#=50 : SPEED#=0 : THRUST#=0 : G=2 : ANGLE#=90
70  rem play game
80  while (HEIGHT>0)
90  if FUEL<=abs(THRUST#) then THRUST#=0 : goto 140
100 if jup then THRUST#=THRUST#+1 : rem Increase thrust
110 if jdown then THRUST#=THRUST#-1 : rem Reduce thrust
115 rem Turn thrust nozzle clockwise
120 if jleft then ANGLE#=ANGLE#-5
```

```
125 rem Turn thrust nozzle anticlockwise
130 if jright then ANGLE#=ANGLE#+5
140 FUEL=FUEL-abs(THRUST#) : rem Fuel consumption
150 locate 0,13 : print "Thrust ";THRUST#;" "
160 locate 0,14 : print "Angle ";ANGLE#;" "
165 locate 0,15 : print "Fuel ";FUEL;" ";
170 rem perform calculations
180 A#=rad(ANGLE#) : rem convert angle into radians
190 rem Get horizontal component of thrust
200 HTHRUST#=THRUST#*cos(A#) : rem from (8)
210 VTHRUST#=THRUST#*sin(A#) : rem vertical component
(9)
220 rem Calculate new horizontal velocity using (2)
225 rem thrust is against motion Time=1 (2)
230 FHSPEED#=HSPEED#-HTHRUST#
240 rem Calculate distance travelled across screen
250 DISTANCE=DISTANCE+(FHSPEED#+HSPEED#)/2 : rem From
(1)
260 HSPEED#=FHSPEED#
270 ACC=G-VTHRUST#
280 rem Work out new vertical speed
290 FVSPEED#=VSPEED#+ACC : rem from (2) with t=1
300 rem Calculate new height
310 HEIGHT=HEIGHT-(FVSPEED#+VSPEED#)/2 : rem from (1)
320 VSPEED#=FVSPEED#
330 rem Calculate total speed
340 SPEED=sqr(HSPEED#^2+VSPEED#^2) : rem from (10)
350 locate 0,16 : print "Height ";HEIGHT;" ";
360 locate 0,17 : print "Speed ";SPEED;" "
370 locate 0,18 : print "Hspeed ";int(HSPEED#);" "
380 locate 0,19 : print "Vspeed ";int(VSPEED#);" "
390 sprite 1,320-DISTANCE/4,200-HEIGHT/5,SHIP
395 rem Sweep ship across screen
400 if DISTANCE<-10 then DISTANCE=1000
410 if DISTANCE>1000 then DISTANCE=0
420 wait 10
430 wend
440 if SPEED>5 then locate 0,0 : centre "You crashed" :
goto 470
450 if SPEED<0 then locate 0,0 : centre "Boing!" : goto 70
460 if SPEED=0 then locate 0,0 : centre "Perfect landing"
else centre "Landed safely"
470 wait 50 : clear key : wait key : goto 20
```

As you can see, Example 4.2 is much more complicated than the original moon-lander. The core of the program lies between lines 130 to 340. These sequentially calculate the horizontal and vertical position of the spaceship during the flight as follows:

hthrust# and vthrust# are loaded with the vertical and horizontal components of the acceleration using equations (8) and (9).

Horizontal acceleration = Total acceleration * COS(T) (8)

Vertical acceleration = Total acceleration * SIN(T) (9)

These are used in conjunction which equations (1) and (2) to calculate the final speed and distance travelled in each direction.

Distance = ((Initial velocity+final velocity)/2) * time (1)

Final velocity = Initial velocity + acceleration * time (2)

The line at 340 combines the two components into the final velocity using Pythagoras' theorem.

$\text{Final velocity}^2 = (\text{Horizontal velocity})^2 + (\text{Vertical velocity})^2$ (10)

The movements of the rocket are measured relative to an arbitrary reference point at the bottom left-hand corner of the screen. These distances are translated into the actual position of the sprite on the screen using the statements at lines 390. As lunar landers go, Example 4.2 is rather crude; the graphics in particular are very limited.

Here are a couple of suggestions for possible improvements:

1 Add a fancy looking control panel for the controls. This can be generated with the Universal Control panel I shall be showing you later in this chapter.

2 Implement a smooth scrolling background moving with the ship. This would improve the game play no end, and could be easily be implemented using some of the techniques in Chapter 10.

3 Place a specific landing site somewhere on the moon, and give the player the task of landing on it.

4.3.3 3D Movements

In order to cope with the three dimensions you need to simulate a movement in the real world, you need to split up the motion into components along three different directions. Obviously there has to be some standard way of referring to a particular heading. For the sake of simplicity, I'll label my directions using the letters X,Y, and Z. A full explanation of this notation can be found in Chapter 7.

The best way of thinking about these labels is in terms of the points on a compass, as follows:

Label	*Directions*
X	East/West
Y	Up/Down
Z	North/South

Since the mathematical reasoning behind this procedure is pretty complex, I'll limit myself to presenting the results. I shall start by defining a couple of angles. These can be seen from the diagram in Figure 4.2.

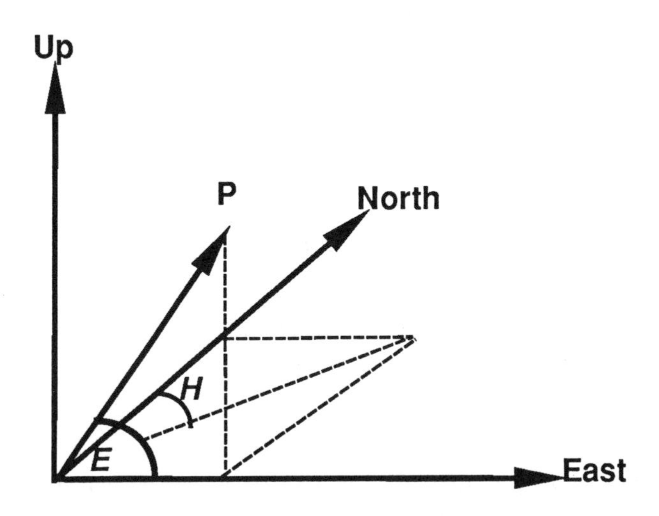

Figure 4.2 Motion in three dimentions

E This is the angle of Elevation between the velocity and the ground. An elevation of ninety degrees points straight up, and an angle of zero represents a purely horizontal velocity.

H H is for heading. This indicates the angle between the motion and due north. e.g

H=0	(North)
H=90	(East)
H=180	(South)
H=270	(West)

Now for the equations themselves:

Initial velocity in the Y direction (Up)

VY = V*SIN(E) (13)

Initial velocity in the X direction (East)

VX = V*COS(E)*SIN(H) (14)

Initial velocity in the Z direction (North)

VZ = V*COS(E)*COS(H) (15)

Total $\text{velocity}^2 = VX^2 + VY^2 + VZ^2$ (From Pythagoras)

If your object under is acceleration, each component will have its own acceleration. The size of this component will depend on the angles of thrust.

Acceleration in Y direction (Up) = Total acceleration * SIN(TE) (16)

Acceleration in X direction (East) =

Total acceleration * COS(TE) * SIN(TH) (17)

Acceleration in Z direction (North) =

Total acceleration * COS(TE)*COS(TH) (18)

Where:

TE is the angle between the thrust and the ground (XZ), and

TH is the angle between the direction of thrust and north.

These equations could be now applied to the moon-lander in Example 4.2 to produce a full blown space simulation. The only difficulty you would encounter would be to generate the illusion of the spaceship's motion in 3D space. This could be accomplished using some of the techniques in Chapter 10.

Another possible idea would be to create a realistic golfing simulation. Each club could impart a set velocity to the ball when it was hit by the player. This could be modified by the strength of the shot and the degree of slice. You could then work out the motion of the ball using the equations of motion. This would allow you to calculate the precise position where the ball would land on the green.

Note that the maximum height of the ball and the time of flight depend only on the vertical component of the motion. This has exactly the same size as the equivalent component in two dimensions. You could use equations (11) and (12) to predict the range of your golf-ball with impunity.

Maximum height of ball = $V^2SIN(A)^2/2*G$ (11)

time of flight = V*SIN(M)/G (12)

4.4 Flight simulators

A flight simulator places the player in control of an aeroplane which is moving through a three dimensional landscape. Normally this landscape is generated using some type of wire-frame graphics. (See Chapter 7).

The aim of the game is to master the aircraft controls and fly from your starting point successfully to some specific destination. Along the way, you will see the appropriate scenery in front of you on the screen.

Many games improve on this idea by adding a strategic element of some sort. The player is assigned a dangerous mission, which often involves the destruction of selected ground installations. These installations are hotly defended by a squadron of enemy ships. In order to survive the mission and complete the game, these ships will need to be destroyed. Other games such as Elite also include a trading option, which allows the player to earn money during the course of the game. This is normally used to add extra features to the basic space ship.

4.4.1 Game plan of a flight simulator

```
Initialise game world
Set up the screen
While game is played

   Handle takeoff
   While (Airborne)

           Read the controls
           Calculate accelerations in all three dimensions
           Calculate new velocities in each direction
           Work out new position of the ship
           Update screen display
           If landing sequence then
                       Do landing
                 endif
           If combat sequence then
                 Handle combat
                 endif
   wend
   If plane crashed then
                 Destroy ship
           endif
Wend
```

Obviously, this code only gives an general overview of the design of one of these games. In practice it would need to be expanded a great deal before you could use as part of a real game plan.

4.4.2 Reading the controls

STOS Basic provides you with many mechanisms for entering the player's commands.

The angle of thrust can be controlled directly using the joystick. When the player pulls the joystick down the vertical thrust angle will be increased and the plane will climb. A forward motion on the joystick will cause the angle to decrease, forcing the plane to descend. Similarly, moving the joystick left or right will produce a turning effect.

Example 4.3 Joystick handler for a flight simulator

```
10  rem Simple joystick controller for a flight simulator
20  rem Climb=angle of ascent (horizontal=0 degrees)
30  rem turn=angle of turn (Straight north = 0)
40  if JLEFT then inc turn
50  if JRIGHT then dec turn
60  if JDOWN then inc climb
70  if JUP then dec climb
80  if FIRE then attack=1
90  return
```

See how carefully I've chosen the directions of the angles to be as simple as possible.

4.4.3 Control panels

All modern aircraft have complex and exciting looking control panels. You can simulate these systems using the STOS Basic ZONE command. Here is a general purpose control panel program for use with your own games:

Example 4.5 Universal control panel

The program is split into three separate parts. The first section initialises the screen zones and defines the arrays SWITCH and STATUS. SWITCH holds the coordinates of the top left and bottom right of the switch. The STATUS array contains a number indicating the current status of the switch (0 for OFF, -1 for ON)

```
1000rem initialise control panel
1010read NZ : reset zone
1020if NZ<0 or NZ>127 then stop
1030dim SWITCH(NZ,4),STATUS(NZ)
1040for I=1 to NZ
1050for J=0 to 3
1060read SWITCH(I,J)
1070next J
1080set zone I,SWITCH(I,0),SWITCH(I,1) to SWITCH(I,2),
SWITCH(I,3)
1090if DEBUG then box SWITCH(I,0),SWITCH(I,1) to
SWITCH(I,2),SWITCH(I,3)
1100next I : return
```

DEBUG is a variable which allows you to actually see the position of the switch which is being implemented. The graphics of a control panel are usually created using a drawing package such as Neochrome or DEGAS. While you are drawing this picture, it's easy to make a note of the coordinates of the various buttons. But these measurements are very approximate, and mistakes are inevitable. The debug option therefore allows you to synchronise your graphics precisely with the zones of the control panel.

The second part of your routine tests whether the user has selected one of the buttons with the mouse, and sets an appropriate variable:

```
1200 rem check zone
1210 Z=zone(0) : if Z=0 or mouse key=0 then return
1220STATUS(Z)=not(STATUS(Z))
1230 if debug then locate 0,10 : print STATUS(Z),Z;
1240 return
```

Finally, there is a small routine which can be used to highlight the switch which has just been pressed. This works by drawing over it using writing mode three (XOR). You may need to choose your background colours carefully in order to achieve a reasonable effect.

```
1300 rem Invert a box
1310 wait 5 : gr writing 3 : ink 1
1320 bar SWITCH(Z,0),SWITCH(Z,1) to
SWITCH(Z,2),SWITCH(Z,3)
1330 gr writing 1 : return
```

Now for a small program which tests these routines.

```
5   cls physic : cls back : DEBUG=1
10  restore 1400 : gosub 1000
20  gosub 1200 : goto 20
100 stop
200 data 3
210 data 100,100,150,150
220 data 10,10,30,50
230 data 250,10,300,60
```

A further example of this routine can be found in the combat system (Example 5.5) in Chapter 5.

4.5 Space simulations

If you're writing a space simulation like Elite, you can reduce the complexity of the equations of motion by ignoring the acceleration completely.

Instead of simulating an object accelerating smoothly through space, you can increase the velocity in fixed steps, assuming that the ship accelerates to the new speed practically instantaneously. This reduces equation (1) to:

v=speed(n)

Speed is just an array containing the new velocity for each speed setting. The distance travelled in all three directions can then be calculated directly from equations (13) to (15) without having to bother with any of the usual thrust computations.

4.6 Other simulations

Up until now, I've concentrated almost completely on simulations involving some sort of movement through space. In practice however, it's quite possible to simulate almost anything from the managing of a football team to the running of a nuclear power station. Many of these simulations can be developed into excellent games.

4.6.1 Creating a simulation

The main problem with this type of simulation, is that you are generally left on your own. There are no simple textbooks full of useful formulae for you to cheat with. All the mathematics will need to be generated by yourself. This involves listing the range of possible outcomes for the simulation, and then trying to isolate a set of factors which will determine each of these events.

You can then attempt to develop a crude set of mathematical equations which will allow you to predict the likely outcome of any action by the user. This can be derived from the factors you have discovered. Some factors will be used internally by your program, whilst others will be changed by the player as the game progresses.

Although this technique may seem a pretty tall order, it can often prove surprisingly simple. After all, providing your game world is believable, it doesn't have to be particularly accurate.

4.6.2 Economic simulation

The classic simulation game Kingdom, simulates the problems faced by the ruler of a small primitive culture. The player is given limited control over the economic resources of the country, and the outcome in terms of population growth and total income are calculated by the program. The population growth depends on the available food supply. This in turn depends on the number of crops which have been planted in the previous year. The aim of the game is simply to survive your term of office without getting lynched by your disgruntled subjects.

A simple version of the game might ask the player just four questions in each turn.

Question 1 How many bushels of wheat do you wish to buy?

Question 2 How many bushels of wheat do you wish to sell?

Question 3 How many bushels of wheat do you wish to plant?

Question 4 How many bushels of wheat to you wish to give to your people?

The crucial factors in this simulation are as follows:

grain = the quantity of grain in the storehouse

money = the amount of money in the treasury

price = the price of grain on the market

sell = the number of bushels sold

buy = the number of bushels bought

crop = the number of bushels which have been harvested

planted = the amount of grain which has been planted previously

lost = Grain lost because of pests

total food = total food allocated to subjects

food = the amount of food for each subject

subsistence= the minimum amount of food for a person to live one year.

people = the total number of people

growth = the number of people born/starved

If you look at these factors very carefully, you should be able to deduce a number of general rules which will govern the simulation.

money = money + sell*price - buy*price

crop = planted*yield

food = (total food)/people

newpeople = (total food)/subsistence

growth = (new people)-people

satisfaction= food/subsistence

I derived these equations directly from the factors I originally isolated, using a combination of guesswork and experimentation. Although they omit dozens of features found in the real world, they still provide a useful basis for a version of kingdom.

Example 4.6 Kingdom

```
10  rem Example 4.6
20  rem The simulation model here may be crude
30  rem But you can have great fun playing around with it
40  rem Kingdom!
50  mode 0
60  rem set up menus
70  menu$ (1)="Game "
80  menu$ (1,1)="Next turn"
90  menu$ (1,2)="---------" : menu$ (1,2) off
100 menu$ (1,3)="New game"
110 menu$ (1,4)="---------" : menu$ (1,4) off
```

```
120 menu$ (1,5)="Quit"
130 menu$ (2)="Economy "
140 menu$ (2,1)="Buy food"
150 menu$ (2,2)="Sell food"
160 menu$ (2,3)="Check coffers"
170 menu$ (3)="Policy"
180 menu$ (3,1)="Plant seed"
190 menu$ (3,2)="Distribute food"
200 menu on
210 windopen 2,0,14,40,10
220 windopen 1,0,1,40,23
230 curs off
240 on menu goto 280,860,1170
250 on menu on
260 goto 260
270 rem Game menu
280 bell : CHOICE=mnselect
290 if CHOICE=3 then gosub 340 : rem new game
300 if CHOICE=1 and GAMEOVER=1 then gosub 460 : rem next
turn
310 if CHOICE=5 then menu off : stop
320 goto 240
330 rem New game
340 curs on : locate 0,10 : input "What's your
name?";NAME$ : print "Welcome to Mundania King ";NAME$ :
wait 40 : clw : curs off
350 PEOPLE=1000+rnd(200) : MONEY=PEOPLE*24
360 GRAIN#=rnd(1000)+3000 : NGRAIN#=GRAIN# : CROP=0 :
SATISFACTION#=1 : PLANTED=0 : LOST=0 : FOOD=0 : SCRE#=0
370 YEAR=1 : GAMEOVER=1
380 SUBSISTANCE=3 : BUY_PRICE=8+rnd(3) :
SELL_PRICE=BUY_PRICE-2
390 rem assuming 1 bushel=100kg of grain, and 2kg of grain
= 1kg of cornflakes
400 rem Thats around one large packet of cornflakes a day
410 rem What an unpleasant prospect. You probably
wouldn't starve however
420 rem Ok, so the derivation may be a LITTLE unorthodox
430 rem But who worries about acurracy when they're having
fun
440 LOST=0 : PEOPLE_NEW=0 : FOOD_RATION=0 : return
450 rem next turn
460 rem Set yield per bushel. Tweek as desired
470 YIELD#=2+(rnd(3)/10.0)
480 rem Reap Crop. I've assumed wastage is always at least
10 percent
```

```
490 CROP=PLANTED*YIELD# : LOST=rnd(CROP/10+1)+CROP/10
500 rem In order keep the game challenging I've assumed
that
510 rem wastage increases for larger crops
520 rem This can be justified if large crops attract
swarms of locusts
530 rem That's my excuse anyway.
540 if CROP>10000 then CROP=CROP-rnd(5000)
550 ROTTED=rnd(NGRAIN#/3+1)
560 GRAIN#=NGRAIN#+CROP-LOST
570 FOOD_RATION#=FOOD/PEOPLE : rem calculate ration for
each person
580 rem Assume no of people rises along with increasing
prosperity
590 PEOPLE_NEW=FOOD/SUBSISTANCE : rem calculate people
at end of year
600 GROWTH=PEOPLE_NEW-PEOPLE
610 PEOPLE=PEOPLE_NEW
620 BUY_PRICE=7+rnd(4) : SELL_PRICE=BUY_PRICE-2
630 if GROWTH<0 then STARVED=abs(GROWTH) : INFLUX=0 else
STARVED=0 : INFLUX=GROWTH
640 under on : locate 0,1 : print "In the year ";YEAR;" of
king ";NAME$ : under off
650 SATISFACTION#=FOOD_RATION#/SUBSISTANCE
660 locate 0,4 : print INFLUX; : locate 7,4 : print "
people entered the city"
670 locate 0,5 : print STARVED; : locate 7,5 : print "
people starved"
680 locate 0,7 : print " Thy people harvested ";CROP;"
bushels"
690 locate 0,8 : print LOST;" bushels were eaten by
locusts"
700 locate 0,9 : print ROTTED;" bushels rotted in the
warehouse"
710 locate 0,11 : print " Thy treasury containeth ";MONEY;
720 locate 0,12 : print " Thy warehouse holds ";GRAIN#;"
bushels"
730 locate 0,13 : print " Thy subjects number ";PEOPLE;"
citizens"
740 inc YEAR : NGRAIN#=GRAIN# : PLANTED=0 : FOOD=0
750 locate 0,17 : clear key
760 SCRE#=SCRE#+SATISFACTION#
770 if SATISFACTION#>=1 then print "Prosperity reigns in
Mundania" : print "All hail the name king ";NAME$
780 if SATISFACTION#<1 then print " Famine rages through
the land"
```

```
790 if SATISFACTION#<0.5 then print " Thy people are in
revolt!" : print " Thy reign of terror ends at year ";YEAR
: print " King ";NAME$;" is DEAD!" : print " Long live the
king!" : GAMEOVER=0 : goto 1420
800 if YEAR>10 and SCRE#>7 then print "After ten happy
years" : print "Your term of office has expired." :
GAMEOVER=0 : goto 1420
810 if YEAR>10 and SCRE#>=5 then print " Your term of
office has expired." : print "Hurray!" : GAMEOVER=0 : goto
1420
820 if YEAR>10 and SCRE#<5 then print " Your term of office
finally terminated" : print " The surviving people are
dancing in the streets" : GAMEOVER=0 : goto 1420
830 locate 0,20 : centre "press any key to continue" : wait
key : clw
840 return
850 rem economy
860 CHOICE=mnselect
870 if CHOICE=1 and GAMEOVER=1 then gosub 920
880 if CHOICE=2 and GAMEOVER=1 then gosub 1020
890 if CHOICE=3 and GAMEOVER=1 then gosub 1110
900 goto 240
910 rem buy grain
920 PRICE=BUY_PRICE
930 if PRICE<2 then PRICE=2
940 window 2 : clw : locate 0,0 : centre "Buy Grain"
950 locate 0,2 : print "Grain costs ";PRICE;" per bushel"
960 locate 0,3 : print "You have ";MONEY;" pieces of gold"
970 locate 0,4 : print space$(40); : locate 0,4 : input
"How many bushels wilt thou buy";BUY
980 if BUY=0 then print "You leave the trading hall" : wait
40 : window 1 : return
990 if BUY*PRICE>MONEY then print "You don't have enough
money" : wait 40 : locate 0,5 : print space$(40) : goto 950
1000MONEY=MONEY-BUY*PRICE : GRAIN#=NGRAIN#+BUY :
NGRAIN#=GRAIN# : window 1 : return
1010rem sell grain
1020PRICE=SELL_PRICE
1030window 2 : clw : locate 0,0 : centre "Sell Grain"
1040locate 0,2 : print "Grain costs ";PRICE;" per bushel"
1050locate 0,3 : print "You have ";NGRAIN#;" bushels in
the store"
1060locate 0,4 : print space$(40); : locate 0,4 : input
"How many bushels wilt thou sell";SELL
1070if SELL=0 then print "You leave the trading hall" :
wait 40 : window 1 : return
```

```
1080if SELL>NGRAIN# then locate 0,5 : print "You don't
have enough grain" : wait 40 : locate 0,5 : print
space$(40) : goto 1060
1090MONEY=MONEY+SELL*PRICE : GRAIN#=NGRAIN#-SELL :
window 1 : NGRAIN#=GRAIN# : return
1100rem check status
1110window 2 : clw : locate 0,0 : print "Status report for
Mundania (Year";YEAR;")"
1120locate 0,2 : print " Thy treasury containeth ";MONEY;
1130locate 0,3 : print " Thy warehouse holds ";NGRAIN#;"
bushels"
1140locate 0,4 : print " Thy subjects number ";PEOPLE;"
people"
1150locate 0,6 : print "Press any key to continue" : wait
key : window 1 : return
1160rem Policy menu
1170CHOICE=mnselect
1180if CHOICE=1 and GAMEOVER=1 then gosub 1220
1190if CHOICE=2 and GAMEOVER=1 then gosub 1320
1200goto 240
1210rem Plant seed
1220window 2 : clw : locate 0,0 : centre "Plant crops"
1230OLD_PLANTED=PLANTED
1240locate 0,3 : print "Thou hast ";NGRAIN#;" bushels in
the store"
1250input "How many bushels wilt thou plant";PLANTED
1260if PLANTED=0 then input "Are you sure?";AN$ : if
AN$="y" or AN$="Y" then window 1 :
NGRAIN#=NGRAIN#+OLD_PLANTED : return else goto 1250
1270if PLANTED>NGRAIN# then print "You don't have enough
grain" : wait 40 : PLANTED=0 : goto 1250
1280if PLANTED<OLD_PLANTED then
NGRAIN#=NGRAIN#+OLD_PLANTED-PLANTED : goto 1300
1290NGRAIN#=NGRAIN#-PLANTED
1300window 1 : return
1310rem Feed people
1320OLD_FOOD=FOOD
1330window 2 : clw : locate 0,0 : centre "Distribute food
ration"
1340locate 0,3 : print "Thou hast ";NGRAIN#;" bushels in
the store"
1350input "How many bushels wilt thou distribute";FOOD
1360if FOOD=0 then input "Are you sure?";AN$ : if AN$="y"
or AN$="Y" then window 1 : NGRAIN#=NGRAIN#+OLD_FOOD :
return else goto 1350
```

```
1370if FOOD>NGRAIN# then print "There isn't enough grain"
: FOOD=0 : goto 1350
1380if FOOD<OLD_FOOD then NGRAIN#=NGRAIN#+OLD_FOOD-FOOD
: goto 1300
1390NGRAIN#=NGRAIN#-FOOD
1400window 1 : return
1410rem another game?
1420wait 50 : gosub 1110 : rem check status
1430print "Another game" : input A$ : if A$<>"Y" and
A$<>"y" then menu off : stop else clw : gosub 330 : goto 230
```

If you're really interested in this sort of simulation, it's worth getting a copy of Chris Crawford's book *Balance of power* which explains how an excellent political simulation was developed. Fascinating reading!

4.7 Conclusions

Simulations are one of the most challenging areas of computer gaming. They are also one of the most engrossing. The range and depth of the subject is immense, and it's impossible to encompass the entire subject in a single chapter. But don't be put off by its apparent complexity. If these games are within the reach of computer students using crude mainframe versions of basic, they should be well within the reach of any experienced STOS Basic programmer. The fact is, simulation can be fun. So go out and simulate something today!

5

Role-playing games

5.1 History

Role-playing games first appeared with the emergence of the Dungeons and Dragons game in the early seventies. D&D took a small group of people on an exploration of a vast imaginary world where magic and adventure were really possible. The intention was to try to simulate the action and excitement of a fantasy novel from the viewpoint of the people actually experiencing it.

One player, known as the referee, played the part of the story teller, and the other participants assumed the roles of the various characters. These characters were able to roam through the game world at will, solving puzzles, rescuing princesses, and killing the occasional monster. Whenever something interesting happened, such as a monster appearing, dice would be rolled and tables consulted to determine the eventual result.

Surprisingly enough, the market for these games turned out to be immense. So it wasn't long before a whole range of competitors sprung into existence. Some of these were based around a similar world of swords and sorcery as the original D&D.

Other games however, branched out into different areas of fiction, such as SF and Crime. Typical examples of these games include TRAVELLER™, SUPER-HEROES™, and STAR TREK™.

Over the course of time, D&D has been steadily evolving and improving. The latest "Advanced version" is now known under the name of AD&D, and even this is currently undergoing a major revamp to prepare it for the nineteen nineties.

The biggest attraction of these role-playing games, (or RPGs for short) is that they are open-ended. Games can last from a couple of hours, to months or even years. Also, RPGs are essentially a group activity, and there's a lot of fun to be had trying to out-fox your fellow players.

Unfortunately, it's often impossible to get your favourite group of players around a table whenever you fancy a game. This has inevitably led to the production of special "solo" games which can be played by a single player. Computers are ideal for this purpose, because they allow you to play out your favourite RPG from the comfort of your own living room. As yet, none of these games quite capture the flavour of the original role-playing systems. But some of the better games, such as Dungeon master, are now starting to come impressively close.

In recent years, role-playing games have managed to secure a respectable slice of the total games software market. This fact has now been belatedly acknowledged by the original producers of D&D (TSR), who have just released an "official" AD&D computer game for the ATARI ST. Maybe computer RPGs have finally come of age.

Incidentally, you may be wondering about the difference between a role-playing game and an adventure. A role-playing game can really be considered as a cross between an adventure and a war game. This lends a strong tactical element to an RPG which is generally lacking in an adventure.

If you've never played a role-playing game before, it's well worth searching around for game called "HACK!" which is now available from your favourite software library for the princely sum of £3.00. Although HACK! is incredibly crude by modern standards, and the graphics are practically non-existent, it remains an extremely enjoyable game, and can be highly recommended. I would also strongly suggest a look at FTL's incredible "Dungeon Master" program. This represents the current "state of the art" in computer-based RPGs, and has to be seen to be believed.

STOS Basic is ideally suited for the creation of these role-playing games. The combination of good sprite animation, along with the powerful map definer accessory makes RPGs well within the reach of most programmers. So providing you were prepared to invest enough time and energy into the project, there's no logical reason why you couldn't produce a game which compared favourably with Ultima IV or even Wizardry.

5.2 Anatomy of a Role-playing game

Before you can write a role-playing game for yourself, you will need to understand a little about how they work. The basic principles are exactly the same for computer- or human- generated RPGs. The game revolves around the activities a number of "characters". These characters can either be controlled by the player (player characters), or by the referee (Non-Player Characters or NPC's). Note that to avoid possible confusion, I'll start off by defining a couple of important terms:

RPG	From now on, this will refer to a computer game.
Real-RPG	Real-RPGs denote the original Role-playing systems which use human referees.

5.2.1 Character classes

Most games allow you to generate characters belonging to a number of different professions, known as classes. In a fantasy game like D&D, the typical classes include:

- ❑ Warriors;
- ❑ Magic Users;
- ❑ Priests;
- ❑ Assassins;
- ❑ Thieves.

Similarly, space games such as Traveller, split the characters up into the categories:

- ❑ Traders;
- ❑ Mercenaries;
- ❑ Troopers;
- ❑ Scouts;
- ❑ Navy.

5.2.2 Attributes

Each character is defined by a list of numbers known as attributes. These attributes determine the exact level of all a character's abilities. As with the classes, the precise nature of these statistics will vary from game to game.

Common attributes include:

Intelligence	Measures how clever the character is.
Endurance	Specifies the character's physical stamina. Affects how much damage the character can survive during combat.
Dexterity	How fast can the character move? How quickly can the character swing a blade?
Strength	How strong is the character? How hard are the character's blows?
Magical ability	Sets the overall power of spells a character is capable of casting.
Psionic strength	This measures a character's CURRENT magical ability. It will be temporarily reduced whenever a character casts a spell.

The weight or range of values each of these attributes can take will depend on the specific scoring system you are using. Normally, the higher the score, the better the attribute. The actual numbers are generally produced using a random number generator. Usually each character class is generated independently. This avoids the ridiculous possibility of having a magic user who is unable to cast any spells, or a fighter who is too weak to pick up his sword. I'll be discussing this problem in more detail later, when I'll be providing you with a simple character generator written entirely in STOS Basic.

Additionally, most other objects in the game such as weapons and armour will also possess attributes. The nature of these attributes will be specific to the object in question.

Assuming the values taken by an attribute could range from 1-20, I could define the character OLRIC as follows:

NAME:	OLRIC
CLASS:	Warrior
STRENGTH	10
ENDURANCE	14
DEXTERITY	15
INTELLIGENCE	5
MAGICAL ABILITY	3
PSIONIC STRENGTH	2

These numbers represent the sum total of the abilities of the warrior OLRIC. They are collectively referred to as statistics (or stats for short). Different numbers affect different things. The attributes for strength, endurance and dexterity can be combined to determine a character's ability for physical combat. This specifies the likelihood of a blow hitting Olric's opponent, and the amount of damage which would inflicted. Similarly, the attributes for psionics and magical ability determine Olric's ability to cast spells. As you can see, OLRIC is hardly suited for work as a magician.

Another type of attribute measures the performance of a specific skill, such as safe-breaking or engineering. These can be represented either as a percentage chance to succeed in an specific action, or as a numeric value which can be checked against a table. Here some typical skills for you to examine:

lock picking	This is a really useful talent in a fantasy game.
rifle shooting	If your game is based around crime, it might be a good idea to keep a separate measure of the character's shooting ability.
space craft repair	Essential for some space games!
invisibility	This is an ability which might well appear in a superhero type game.

5.2.3 Experience

It's a well known fact that practice often makes perfect. The same is true for the characters in a role-playing game. Characters start off relatively puny, but as the game progresses, their natural abilities develop over time. Eventually this experience leads to an improvement in the appropriate character attributes. This improvement is sometimes expressed in terms of the character's **level.**

All characters are initially given a level number of one, and an experience of zero. Every time a character is successful at something, this experience is slightly increased. When the character's experience exceeds a predetermined threshold, the level number is incremented by one, and the appropriate attributes improved accordingly.

Take the warrior OLRIC again. At the present time, his current statistics are:

STRENGTH	10
ENDURANCE	14
DEXTERITY	15
INTELLIGENCE	5
MAGICAL ABILITY	3
PSIONIC ABILITY	2

If Olric were to gain experience in fighting and progress to level two, each of the attributes of strength, endurance, and dexterity would be incremented accordingly. This could be achieved by multiplying each of the three attributes by a appropriate level factor.

Using a level multiplier of 1.25, Olric's statistics would now be increased to:

STRENGTH	12
ENDURANCE	17
DEXTERITY	18
INTELLIGENCE	5
MAGICAL ABILITY	3 (Not affected)
PSIONIC ABILITY	2 (Unchanged)

See how I've rounded the numbers down after the calculation. This is a just reflection of the fact that we will be using STOS Basic integers for all our calculations in the eventual program.

Note that if you decide to use this system, you will need to be very cautious about the factors you choose for each level. These need to be worked out by careful experimentation.

Some games simplify things further by assigning each level number with a name. e.g.

NOVICE	(Level 1)
APPRENTICE	(Level 2)
MASTER	(Level 3)
etc.	

It's also possible to keep a separate count of the success rate of every individual skill. So, in addition to their other attributes, a character could possess a range of optional skills like:

lock-picking	50%
starship navigation	30%
horse riding	5%

As the character learned from experience, the percentage chances of successfully using a skill could be gradually improved. This approach is used to great effect by role-playing games like RUNEQUEST™, or TRAVELLER™.

5.3 Scenarios

5.3.1 What is a scenario?

All Real-RPGs are split into two separate components. One component defines a detailed set of rules which form the backbone of the game. These rules specify the precise mechanics of the game-play, and are used to establish the outcome of the player's actions.

The other part of the game is the scenario. This is equivalent to the plot of a book, and provides full details about the particular story which will be enacted by the players. Because of the open-ended nature of a role-playing game, it is usually impossible to determine the final outcome of any particular scenario.

From any given set of rules, the number of possible scenarios is effectively limitless. The big difference between a Real-RPG, and the computer version, is that computer games are much more limited in scope. Unlike a human referee who can literally make things up as he goes along, the computer is forced to rely on a complete scenario which the programmer has carefully worked out in advance.

5.3.2 Practical considerations

Your first requirement is to choose a scenario for your game. Like books, scenarios can be grouped into a number of different genres. These include Fantasy (D&D and Bard's tale), Science fiction, Crime, and Superheroes. Once you've decided on the background, you must devise the individual plot of the game.

The best source of inspiration is to re-read some of your favourite novels in the area you have selected. If you haven't yet read any books in the genre then you have probably chosen the wrong subject.

Don't however, attempt to base your game too heavily on the work of a single author. Nowadays popular authors can naturally expect to sell the computer rights to their works for very respectable sums. They are therefore unlikely to welcome you stealing any of the characters and situations wholesale out one of their books, without prior written permission.

Comics in particular, are very sensitive about the names of their heroes being taken in vain. So any mention of a hero such as "Superman™" in one of your programs might be VERY unwise! There's also the question of originality. It's futile to attempt a rehash of someone else's work, hoping no-one will notice. Even if you choose something really obscure, there will always be at least one person who is familiar with it. This is particularly likely, in the field of science fiction, as many authors are now enthusiastic computer users.

But ignoring moral considerations, unless you invest the scenario with your own ideas, the game will be both derivative and utterly boring. So try to think of something really different, which makes you game stand out from the crowd.

The aim of scenario is to generate subtly the feeling that the player is really inside the game world you have created. It's important to work out the rationale behind the various characters extremely carefully. Who are they? Why are they participating in the adventure? What are their precise goals?

5.3.3 Some basic scenario ideas

Thankfully, all scenarios can be roughly divided into a relatively limited number of basic plots. Here is a list of the main possibilities:

1 The purpose is to retrieve one or more valuable artifacts which are hidden somewhere in the game. (Used in Dungeon Master, Lord of the Rings, etc..). There's often a pressing reason for this search, such saving the world or something, but this is normally incidental to the blood and gore!

2 A dastardly villain is threatening the safety of the player's world. The characters are given the thankless task of destroying this horrible creature before it wreaks havoc.

3 A beautiful princess has been kidnapped by an evil monster. The party of adventurers set out bravely to rescue her, against incredible odds. (This is a two-line precis of STARWARS)

4 The characters are a bunch of mindless psychopathic lunatics who want to kill as many monsters and amass as much treasure as possible. (Who said you had to be original?)

5 The characters are lost in the centre of a labyrinth. Their sole aim is to escape from their horrible predicament.

6 The purpose of the game is to solve a complex logical puzzle of some sort. (Used in Ultima IV).

None of these plots are restricted to a single genre. The same idea can be used equally well in a science fiction game, as in a sword and sorcery scenario.

Furthermore, it's perfectly acceptable to use any combination of these ideas in your finished game.

5.3.4 The game map

The next step is to produce a complete map of the world you will be using in your RPG. The standard method of generating this map is to make a rough sketch on a large piece of graph paper. This can be purchased at little expense from any decent stationery shop. The advantage of starting with the map on paper, is that it places you under no constraints whatsoever about the eventual nature of the graphics. It also allows you to see the whole design at once, which would be almost impossible if you attempted to draw the map directly with the Map definer.

You should now set up the obstacles which will be arranged against the players, and choose the ensuing rewards.

Sometimes, the only reward to the successful solution to a puzzle will be the satisfaction of beating the computer. Other times, the completion of a task will result in the discovery of an item of treasure or an increase in the abilities of the player's characters.

It is vital that you try to balance the risks taken by the characters with the possible rewards. If your game fails to achieve this balance, it will either be monotonously easy, or impossibly difficult. In order to work, a role-playing game must also include potential solutions to any traps which are to be encountered by the player.

The best human referees adopt a "hard but fair" approach. The fact is, any game which kills off the characters randomly without due cause is unlikely to capture the player's imagination for an appreciable length of time.

As a rough guide, I've briefly listed some of the more common hazards your players might encounter (Figure 5.1), along with a few of the possible rewards (Figure 5.2) on the next page. These lists can be used as a valuable source of ideas when you are creating your game.

You should now take your game map, and mark out the position of the appropriate objects/puzzles. The location of the monsters can either be random, or be worked out carefully in advance. If you're producing a set of rooms which will be encountered in a particular order, you should tailor the type and strength of your problems to the expected abilities of the characters. This keeps the game reasonably challenging whilst retaining its overall appeal.

After you have created your map, and designed the hazards and the treasure, your scenario will be complete. You will now be ready to produce a computer game based on this scenario.

Monsters
Hazards
- Pits
- Falling walls
- Booby-traps
- Cursed weapons/treasure
- Radiation

Logic puzzles
- Hidden doors
- Locked doors
  - Requiring specific key
  - Requiring brute force
  - Requiring a certain spell
- Teleport rooms
  (As the players enter a room, they are instantly transported to a completely different part of the map. Don't inform the players about this immediately. Let them work it out for themselves. It's much more fun!)
- Switches/Levers
  (Which need to be pulled in a particular order)
- Passwords
  (Which need to be typed in)
- Objects
  (Which need to be used in a certain way)

Figure 5.1 Obstacles to the players

Money

Weapons

Armour

Spells

Experience

Transportation (Anything from a horse to a spaceship!)

Special objects
- Treasure
- Keys
- Significant objects
  (These are objects needed to solve a particular puzzle)

Figure 5.2 Possible Rewards

5.4 Game plan of a Role-playing game

I'll now discuss the detailed mechanics of a role-playing game. I will begin with providing you with a description of the program using pseudo-code.

```
Initialise dungeon

If new game then
            Generate characters
        else
            Load saved game

Repeat
    Input action
    If action is ''save game'' then save current dungeon
    If action is movement
        then
            check if movement is allowed
            If movement is legal
                then
                    Move characters
                    Redraw screen
    Check for an encounter
    If enemy encountered
        then Resolve combat
    Check for a trap
    If trap discovered
        then Spring trap
    Check for objects
    If action is ''Pick''
        then Get object
    If action is ''Use''
        then Use object
Until Party is killed or Quest is completed
Terminate game
```

Figure 5.3 Break-down of a role-playing game

If you examine this description carefully, you should be able to isolate a number of the more important activities These include:

- ❑ Initialise game;
- ❑ Generate characters;
- ❑ Load game;
- ❑ Input Action;

- ❑ Save game;
- ❑ Check for legal move;
- ❑ Redraw Screen;
- ❑ Resolve combat;
- ❑ Spring Trap;
- ❑ Get Object;
- ❑ Use Object.

I'll be expanding some of these requirements in a little more detail during the rest of this chapter.

5.5 Creating a character

5.5.1 Selecting the attributes

The choice of the possible character attributes can have far reaching consequences for your game. Most RPGs have the following three attributes in common:

Endurance (or Stamina)	Resistance to attack
Dexterity	Speed of attack
Strength	Force of a physical blow

Any other attributes can be invented completely at your own discretion. Here are few simple guidelines. Fantasy games, such as D&D need some measure of the character's magical ability. This results in attributes such as WISDOM, or PSIONIC strength. Similarly, Space games often require an indicator of a character's intelligence.

The nature of your scenario may make certain skills essential for the completion of a game. If the adventure is futuristic, you may decide to include skills like engineering or astronavigation. Unlike a character's attributes, these skills are entirely optional. Different characters can have completely different ranges of skills.

You can also choose a number of more unusual attributes. These can be used to ''flesh out'' the character's personality, and can add a whole new dimension to your games.

Supposing your game involves several characters controlled by a single player. It is normally assumed implicitly that these characters will obey the player's orders without question. But what will happen if one of the characters is a coward? This character is liable to ignore any commands which place him in unnecessary risk. So if the player tells him to attack a fire breathing dragon with his bare hands, he is likely to run away, terribly fast. You can implement this idea by adding an attribute like Bravery. This can either be displayed on the screen along with the character's statistics, or sneakily concealed for the internal use of your program.

This technique is particularly effective if the party can grow during the game. Some RPGs such as ULTIMA IV, commence with a single character who can "recruit" help as the game progresses. In this situation, you can add an attribute denoting the trustworthiness of any character the player attempts to recruit. Whenever the party encountered some really valuable treasure, one of the characters might independently decide to steal it from the rest of the group. You could also envisage the party splitting up into several warring factions. This could have potentially hilarious results, especially if the baddies had hold of all the parties most potent weapons!

Obviously, this type of nastiness needs to be used with a little caution. If the honour of a character is crucial to the games solution, you need to include some way for the player to work this out in advance. This might involve a magical artifact such as a jewel which turns a different colour depending on a character's trustworthiness.

5.5.2 Generating a character

Whenever a game is played, a set of characters will need to be allocated to the player. The easiest possibility is to restrict the player to a list of characters which have been prepared in advance. The appeal of this idea, is that it avoids having to bother with a separate character generator. It also guarantees that the object of the game is achievable with any set of characters which has been selected by the player.

Whilst there is nothing inherently wrong with this approach, it is recommended that you give each character a distinct personality. Each character should be discussed separately in the documentation, which should explain precisely who they are, and why they are available and willing to embark on the current adventure. Careful use of this technique can add a feeling of atmosphere which is often lacking in randomly generated characters.

Alternatively, you can generate your characters anew every time the scenario is played. This allows each player to create their own unique set of characters for the game. It also enables someone to adapt their favourite characters from a completely different game.

If each attribute could range from 1-100, you could generate the statistics of a character using a line like:

```
100strength=rnd(100):stamina=rnd(100):dexterity=rnd(100)
```

Unfortunately, this would produce a very poor spread of numbers indeed. Any character would be equally likely to get a strength of 99 as one of 9. So it would also be perfectly possible for a character to be generated with ridiculously low values in all three characteristics. Similarly, the program could accidentally bring forth a god-like character who could effortlessly destroy even the toughest monster with just a single blow.

A better approach would be to add an appropriate offset of some sort to the raw number.

```
100 strength = rnd(10) +5: stamina = rnd(10) +5: dexterity = rnd
(10) +5
```

This would limit the initial stats of the character to numbers between 5 and 15.

See how I've initially kept the attributes small. This allows plenty of scope for them to be increased as the character gains experience.

You can also combine several calls to the random number generator at once. e.g.

```
100 strength = rnd(5) + rnd(5) + rnd(5) + rnd(5) + 4
```

This line is the exact equivalent to rolling four dice in a Real-RPG. Most numbers produced by this function are clustered around an average of 14. The chances of getting an unusually high number such as 24 or an excessively low value are relatively small. The big danger of this approach is that the random number generator used by STOS Basic is not completely random. If you're not careful, you can therefore generate some very strange results with this system.

Here is a listing of a simple character generator for you to type in. Don't bother to enter the REM statements, as they are only included for documentation purposes.

Example 5.1 Character generation in STOS Basic.

```
10   rem Character Generation in STOS Basic
20   rem Assumes the character has the following 5
attributes
30   rem Strength, Dexterity, Stamina, IQ, Magic
40   rem Each attribute can range from 1-100
50   rem Also assumes a maximum of 10 characters
60   C=1 : rem current character
70   dim STR(10),DEX(10),STA(10),IQ(10),MAG(10),NAME$(10)
80   dim TYPE(10),TYPENAME$(4),SPECIES(10),SPECNAME$(4)
90   for I=1 to 3 :read TYPENAME$(I),SPECNAME$(I) :next I
100  mode 0 : cls physic : cls back : curs off
110  rem set up menus
120  rem Character menu
130  menu$ (1)=" Character "
140  menu$ (1,1)=" Create character "
150  menu$ (1,2)=" Examine character"
160  menu$ (1,3)=" Quit"
170  rem Species
180  menu$ (2)=" Species "
190  menu$ (2,1)="Human"
200  menu$ (2,2)="Dwarf"
210  menu$ (2,3)="Troll"
220  rem Class menu
```

```
230 menu$ (3)=" Class "
240 menu$ (3,1)="Fighter"
250 menu$ (3,2)="Wizard "
260 menu$ (3,3)="Priest"
270 rem activate menu
280 menu on
290 gosub 620 : rem draw main display
300 on menu goto 340,740,700
310 on menu on
320 goto 320
330 rem character menu
340 M=mnselect : if M=0 then goto 300
350 on M gosub 380,480,1090
360 goto 300
370 rem Create a character with current settings
380 if C>10 then boom : return
390 locate 13,2 : input NAME$(C)
400 if SPECIES(C)=0 then SPECIES(C)=1
410 on SPECIES(C) gosub 810,780,840
420 if TYPE(C)=0 then TYPE(C)=1
430 on TYPE(C) gosub 910,980,1040
440 gosub 630 : gosub 560
450 inc C
460 return
470 rem examine characters
480 locate 12,2 : input N$
485 rem find characters
486 rem I can't use MATCH because the names must be
sorted
487 rem Sorting the names loses the relationship between
488 rem the names and the statistics
490 N=1 : FOUND=false
500 repeat
510 if NAME$(N)=N$ then FOUND=true else inc N
520 until FOUND=true or N>10
530 if FOUND=false then boom : N=1
540 swap N,C : gosub 630 : gosub 560 : swap C,N
550 return
560 if NAME$(C)="" then return
565 rem Print out statistics
570 locate 12,0 : print C; : locate 13,2 : print
NAME$(C);
580 locate 13,3 : print TYPENAME$(TYPE(C))
585 locate 13,4 : print SPECNAME$(SPECIES(C))
590 locate 12,6 : print STR(C); : locate 12,7 : print
DEX(C)
```

```
600 locate 12,8 : print STA(C); : locate 12,9 : print
IQ(C)
610 locate 12,10 : print MAG(C) : return
615 rem print out titles
620 windopen 1,5,5,30,15,5 : title "Statistics"
630 clw : curs off : locate 0,0 : print "Character :";C
640 locate 0,2 : print "Name :";
645 locate 0,3 : print "Class :";
646 locate 0,4 : print "Species :";
650 locate 0,6 : print "Strength :"; : locate 0,7
655 print "Dexterity :";
660 locate 0,8 : print "Stamina :";
665 locate 0,9 : print "IQ :";
670 locate 0,10 : print "Magic :";
680 return
690 rem class menu
700 CM=mnselect : if CM=0 then 300
710 TYPE(C)=CM
720 goto 300
730 rem species menu
740 S=mnselect : if S=0 then 300
750 SPECIES(C)=S
760 goto 300
770 rem Generate dwarves
780 STR(C)=rnd(5)+2 : DEX(C)=rnd(10)+8 :
STA(C)=rnd(10)+7
790 IQ(C)=rnd(10)+5 : MAG(C)=rnd(8)+8 : return
800 rem Generate Humans
810 STR(C)=rnd(10)+5 : DEX(C)=rnd(10)+5 :
STA(C)=rnd(10)+5
820 IQ(C)=rnd(10)+5 : MAG(C)=rnd(5)+5 : return
830 rem generate trolls
840 STR(C)=rnd(10)+10 : rem trolls are strong
850 DEX(C)=rnd(3)+2 : rem trolls are slow
860 STA(C)=rnd(10)+10 : rem trolls are also VERY tough!
870 IQ(C)=rnd(3)+2 : rem trolls are thick
880 MAG(C)=rnd(2) : rem lousy magicians
890 return
900 rem Generate Fighter
910 STR(C)=STR(C)*1.5:DEX(C)=DEX(C)*1.5:STA(C)=STA(C)*
1.5
920 rem Fighters make lousy wizards
930 MAG(C)=MAG(C)/3
940 rem Fighters are generally thick
950 IQ(C)=IQ(C)/2
960 return
```

```
970  rem Generate Wizard
980  IQ(C)=IQ(C)*1.5+1 : MAG(C)=MAG(C)*2+1
990  STR(C)=STR(C)/1.5
1000 DEX(C)=DEX(C)/1.5
1010 STA(C)=STA(C)/1.2
1020 return
1030 rem priests
1040 IQ(C)=IQ(C)*2 : rem priests are very well educated
1050 MAG(C)=MAG(C)*1.5+1 : rem priests are also fair
magicians
1060 STR(C)=STR(C)/1.2 : rem not too strong
1070 return
1080 rem quit
1090 pop : menu off : on menu off : default : stop
1100 data "Fighter","Human","Wizard","Dwarf","Priest",
"Troll"
```

I've divided the possible characters into three species, Humans, Dwarves, and Trolls. But you could quickly modify these races for use with a SF game. All you would need to do, would be to omit the magic, and change the species names to something really alien. So the trolls might by called QVORN instead.

Each race has its natural advantages and its inherent disadvantages. This preserves the balance of the game and avoids generating characters which are too powerful to play realistically.

It's best to start off with a good idea about the type of races your are trying to produce. Here are some potted descriptions of the races I defined in Example 5.1

HUMANS – are the most flexible of the character types. They are powerful enough to reasonably good at magic, yet if they have the inclination they make formidable fighters.

DWARVES – are magic experts. They are very tough and fast, but they are not particularly strong. So a dwarf would have to work very hard to become a successful fighter.

TROLLS – on the other hand, the fantasy equivalent of tanks. These people are natural born killers. They may not be too bright, but they a VERY hard to kill.

The generation system for these using can be found in the routines at 770, 800, and 830.

Once the players have chosen a race for their character, they need to select a profession. In Example 5.1, I've provided there possible classes, Fighter, Wizard, and Priest. Again, you could easily change these to reflect any scenario you had in mind. You would simply need to change some of the attributes, and alter the figures.

As with races, every class is generated by a separate piece of code. These modify the raw attributes to reflect the result of years of training in a particular skill. I've implemented this alteration using a system of multipliers. So the more talents an individual has in a certain profession, the higher their eventual abilities will reach after training.

A wizard might be generated using the lines:

```
980  IQ(C)=IQ(C)*1.5+1 : MAG(C)=MAG(C)*2+1
990  STR(C)=STR(C)/1.5
1000 DEX(C)=DEX(C)/1.5
1010 STA(C)=STA(C)/1.2
```

This would normally produce a physically weak character with low dexterity and high magical ability. Perfect for a wizard. Similarly, a fighter would need high values for the strength, dexterity, and stamina. Look at the routine at 900 for an example of this type of system.

Note that I derived the numbers used by this generation system purely by experimentation. There's no guarantee that the same values will be especially suitable for a specific game. So it's important to experiment with these generators for yourself, in order to produce a character creation system which is just right for your own game.

5.6 Drawing the map

Unlike adventure games, a map of the current surroundings of the party is essential in any true RPG. This is because all role-playing games incorporate a strong tactical element, which necessitates a display of the type and position of the various monsters.

Over the years, several approaches have been used for these displays. In this section, I'll briefly examine some of the more popular ones, and will briefly explain how they can be implemented using STOS Basic.

5.6.1 Displaying a map from above

This is the undoubtedly the easiest method of viewing the terrain around the party. Screens can be quickly generated using the STOS Basic map definer. You begin by creating a colourful set of sprites representing the various features of the terrain, such as walls, hills, and trees. You can then draw each screen in turn using the Map accessory. These screens can be combined to produce the complete map of the game.

Normally, this map will be consist of many different rooms. It is vital to keep track of the connections between the different rooms, otherwise your program will get totally lost. This can be done by arranging the rooms according to a logical pattern as shown in Figure 5.4 on the next page.

Room 1	Room 2	Room 3	Room4	Room 5
Room 6	Room 7	Room 8	Room 9	Room 10
Room 11	Room 12	Room 13	Room 14	Room 15

Figure 5.4 Room Maps

Supposing the party was currently inhabiting screen 8. If they were to move over the top of the screen, they would be entering room number 3. Similarly, if they were to move off the bottom, they would find themselves in room 13. By following a few simple rules, the appropriate rooms can be displayed on the screen automatically. If m is the number of the current room, then the number of the adjacent rooms can be seen from Figure 5.5.

m - 6	m - 5	m - 4
m - 1	m	m + 1
m + 4	m + 5	m + 6

Figure 5.5 Moving between rooms

Now for some pseudo-code to demonstrate how this movement technique could be implemented in practice. This is listed in Figure 5.6 on the next page.

Obviously, this is a very crude system indeed and lacks a couple of features found in more sophisticated routines. It does however aptly demonstrate the basic principles of screen management.

5.6.2 Displaying part of a map

One minor problem with this technique, is that the output from the map utility automatically assumes that the entire screen will be used for the room display. Since you usually need to restrict your graphics to just a section of the screen, this can be a real headache. Fortunately, it's fairly easy to modify the standard drawing routines to display any STOS map in several successive parts.

```
if party exits left-hand edge
     then
          if current_room>1 then
               subtract one from current room
               redraw current_room
          endif

if party exits right-hand edge
     then
          if current_room<last_room then
               add one to current room
               redraw current_room
          endif

if party exits upper edge
     then
          if current_room>rooms_per_row then
               subtract rooms_per_row from current room
               redraw current_room
          endif

if party exits bottom edge
     then
          if current_room+rooms_per_row<last_room then
               add rooms_per_row to current room
               redraw current_room
          endif
```

Figure 5.6 Moving the party across the screen

In order to use this approach, you will have to limit the size of the game screens to an integral number of sprite widths. Otherwise some sprites will disconcertingly seem to disappear of the edge of your display. You also need to divide the game screens into a fixed number of maps which can be subsequently produced from the map definer. e.g.

```
load "back.mbk":rem from the accessories disc
```

Example 5.2 Displaying maps in a small section of the screen

```
10   rem Example 5.2
20   rem draw a map on a section of the screen
30   mode 0 : hide on
```

```
40  rem number of full sized maps per horizontal and
vertical row
50  MAPS_PER_ROW=2 : MAPS_PER_COLUMN=2
60  HEIGHT=8 : WIDTH=12 : rem width of screen in sprites
70  rem number of game screens per horizontal and
vertical row
80  VIEWS_PER_ROW=3 : VIEWS_PER_COL=3 :
VIEW_COUNT=VIEWS_PER_ROW*VIEWS_PER_COL
90  dim C(16),SEG$(62),MAP(80,60) : rem dimension map
array
100 gosub 150 : rem get palette data
110 gosub 180 : rem load sprite data into segment string
120 gosub 260 : rem load map data in map array
130 locate 0,15 : print space$(39); : locate 0,15 :
input "Input the Map number (0-8)";MAP_NO : if
MAP_NO>VIEW_COUNT-1 or MAP_NO<0 then boom : locate 0,15 :
print " This map does not exist" : wait 20 : goto 130
140 fade 1 : wait 7 : gosub 450 : fade
1,C(0),C(1),C(2),C(3),C(4),C(5),C(6),C(7),C(8),C(9),C(10)
,C(11),C(12),C(13),C(14),C(15) : wait key : goto 130
150 rem Find pallete for sprites
160 X=hunt(start(1) to start(1)+length(1),"PALT") :
X=X+4
170 for A=0 to 15 : C(A)=deek(X+A*2) : next A : return
180 rem load segment array with sprite data
190 cls physic : cls back
200 for I=1 to 30
210 cls physic,0,0,0 to 16,16
220 sprite 1,0,0,I : put sprite 1 : wait vbl
230 SEG$(I)=screen$(physic,0,0 to 16,16) : next I
240 sprite 1,-100,-100,1
250 return
260 rem load map array from data statements
270 rem read data
280 restore 590 : read NL : rem number of lines per map
290 rem calculate constants
300 read N : rem number of maps
310 read W : rem number of sprites per line
320 read H : rem number of lines per screen
330 NO_OF_COLS=320/W : NO_OF_ROWS=199/H
340 rem ignore partially hidden lines
350 if 199 mod H<>0 then inc NO_OF_ROWS : HIDDEN=1
360 TOTAL_ROWS=MAPS_PER_ROW*NO_OF_ROWS :
TOTAL_COLS=MAPS_PER_COL*NO_OF_COLS
370 for C=0 to MAPS_PER_COLUMN-1 : rem number of screens
380 for R=0 to MAPS_PER_ROW-1
```

```
390 if C<>0 or R<>0 then read DW,DH : rem ignore size
data
400 for J=0 to NO_OF_COLS-1
410 for K=0 to NO_OF_ROWS-1-HIDDEN
420 read MAP(R*NO_OF_COLS+J,C*(NO_OF_ROWS-HIDDEN)+K) :
rem read sprite data
430 next K : if HIDDEN=1 then read DUMMY : rem ignore
unused line at end
440 next J : next R : next C : return
450 rem display a map
460 VIEWX=MAP_NO mod VIEWS_PER_ROW : VIEWY=MAP_NO/
VIEWS_PER_ROW
470 MAP_POS_X=VIEWX*WIDTH : MAP_POS_Y=VIEWY*HEIGHT
480 rem Starting coordinates of map display
490 rem change in sixteen pixel increments (for SCREEN$)
500 XPOS=1 : YPOS=1
510 XSIZE=W*WIDTH+XPOS : YSIZE=H*HEIGHT+YPOS : rem
bottom corners of map window
520 rem clear map area
530 cls physic,0,XPOS,YPOS to XSIZE,YSIZE : cls
back,0,XPOS,YPOS to XSIZE,YSIZE
540 for Y=0 to HEIGHT-1 : rem number of rows
550 for X=0 to WIDTH-1 : rem number of columns
560 XV=X+MAP_POS_X : YV=Y+MAP_POS_Y : if MAP(XV,YV)>0
then screen$(physic,X*W+XPOS,Y*H+YPOS)=SEG$(MAP(XV,YV))
570 next X : next Y : return
580 rem map data
590 data 25,4
600 data16,16,10,10,10,10,10,10,10,10,10,10,10,10,10,10,
0,0,0,0,0,0
610 data10,10,0,0,0,0,10,0,13,13,13,13,0,10,10,0,13,13,
13,10
620 data0,13,6,0,13,0,10,10,0,13,0,0,10,0,13,0,0,13,0,10
630 data10,0,13,0,0,10,0,13,0,0,0,0,10,10,0,13,0,0,10,0
640 data13,0,0,0,0,10,10,0,13,0,0,10,0,13,0,0,13,0,10,10
650 data0,13,0,0,10,0,13,0,0,13,0,10,10,0,13,0,0,10,0,13
660 data13,13,13,0,10,10,0,13,13,13,10,0,0,0,0,0,0,0,0,0
670 data0,0,0,10,10,10,0,0,10,10,10,10,10,10,10,10,10,
10,10,0
680 data0,10,10,10,10,0,0,0,10,10,0,0,0,0,0,0,10,10,0,0
690 data0,0,10,0,0,11,0,11,0,10,10,0,0,0,0,10,0,0,11,0
700 data11,0,10,10,10,10,10,0,10,11,11,11,0,11,0,10,10,
0,0,10
710 data0,10,11,0,0,0,11,0,10,10,0,0,0,0,10,11,8,0,0,11
720 data0,10,10,10,10,10,0,10,11,11,11,11,11,0,10,10,0,
0,0,0
```

```
730  data16,16,10,0,0,0,0,0,0,10,10,0,0,0,0,10,0,0,0,0,0,
0
740  data10,10,0,0,0,0,10,0,0,0,0,0,10,10,0,0,0,0,10
750  data10,0,10,0,10,0,10,10,0,0,0,0,10,0,0,0,0,0,10
760  data10,0,0,0,0,10,0,0,0,0,0,10,10,0,0,0,0,10,0
770  data0,0,0,0,0,10,10,0,0,0,0,10,0,0,0,0,0,10,10
780  data0,0,0,0,10,0,0,0,0,0,10,10,0,0,0,0,10,0,0
790  data0,0,0,0,10,10,0,0,0,0,10,0,0,0,0,0,10,10,0
800  data0,0,0,10,0,0,0,0,0,10,10,0,0,0,0,10,0,0,0
810  data0,0,0,10,10,0,0,0,0,10,0,0,0,0,0,0,0,0,0
820  data0,0,10,9,0,0,0,0,0,0,0,0,0,0,10,10,10,10,10
830  data10,10,10,10,10,10,10,0,0,0,0,0,0,0,0,0,0,0,0
840  data0,0,0,0,0,0,0,0,0,0,0,0,0,0,0,0,0
850  data0,0,0,0,0,0,0,0,0,0,0,0,0,0,0,0,0
860  data16,16,10,10,10,10,10,10,10,10,10,10,10,10,0,0,0,
0,10,0,10,0
870  data0,0,0,0,10,0,13,13,0,10,0,10,0,0,10,10,0,10,0,0
880  data13,0,10,0,0,0,0,10,10,0,10,0,0,13,0,10,0,0,10,10
890  data10,10,0,10,0,0,13,0,10,0,0,10,0,7,10,0,10,0,0,13
900  data0,10,0,0,10,0,0,10,0,10,0,0,13,0,10,0,0,10,0,10
910  data10,0,10,0,0,13,0,10,0,0,10,0,0,0,0,10,0,13,13,0
920  data10,0,0,10,0,0,0,0,10,0,0,0,0,0,0,10,10,10,10
930  data0,10,0,10,10,10,10,10,10,10,10,10,10,0,10,0,10,
10,10,10
940  data10,10,10,10,10,10,0,10,0,0,0,0,10,0,0,0,0,0,0
950  data10,0,0,0,0,10,0,0,0,0,0,0,10,0,0,0,0,10,0
960  data0,0,0,0,0,0,10,0,0,0,0,10,0,0,0,0,0,0,10
970  data0,0,0,0,10,0,0,0,0,0,0,10,0,0,0,0,10,0,0
980  data0,0,0,0,0,10,0,0,0,0,10,0,0,0,0,0,0,10,0
990  data16,16,0,0,0,10,0,0,0,0,0,0,10,0,0,0,0,10,0,0,0
1000 data0,0,0,0,10,0,0,10,0,10,0,0,0,0,0,0,10,0,0
1010 data10,0,10,10,10,0,10,10,10,10,10,0,0,10,0,10,0,10,
0,0
1020 data0,0,0,10,0,0,10,0,10,0,0,0,0,10,0,10,0,0,10
1030 data0,10,10,10,10,10,0,10,0,10,0,0,10,0,10,0,0,0,0,0
1040 data10,0,10,0,0,10,0,10,0,10,10,10,10,10,0,10,0,0,
10,0
1050 data10,0,10,0,6,10,0,0,10,0,0,10,0,10,0,10,0,10,10,0
1060 data0,10,0,0,10,0,10,0,10,0,0,0,0,0,10,0,0,10,0,10
1070 data0,10,0,0,0,10,10,10,0,0,10,0,10,0,10,10,10,10,
10,0
1080 data10,0,0,10,0,0,0,0,0,0,0,0,10,0,10,10,10,10,10
1090 data10,10,10,10,10,10,10,0,0,0,0,0,0,0,0,0,0,0,0
1100 data0,0,0,0,0,0,0,0,0,0,0,0,0,0,0,0,0
1110 data0,0,0,0,0,0,0,0,0,0,0,0,0,0,0,0,0
```

This program can be readily modified to place your map displays anywhere on the ST's screen. Feel free to experiment with it as much as you like. Once you've stored the sprites in the map array, you can use this information for a variety of other purposes.

The routine in Example 5.2, for instance, assumes that you wish to display the entire area around the party. This corresponds to the situation when the party can see for a considerable distance. If each sprite represented a unit of 10 feet in the game world, displaying the full screen would be roughly equivalent to a visibility of about 60 feet in all directions. Whilst this might be true if the party of out in the open, on a sunny day, it is unlikely to be the case in a dark and gloomy dungeon. Many role-playing games therefore only draw the locations immediately adjacent to the party as they are moving. This can be demonstrated by the following small diagram:

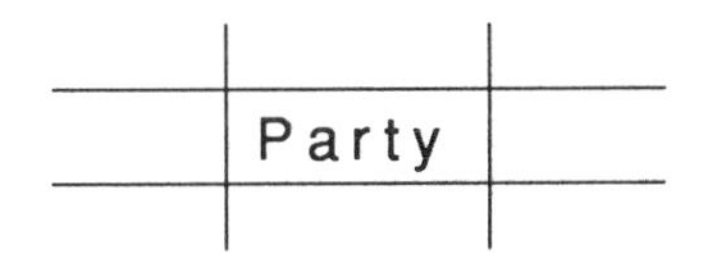

You can implement this effect with the following STOS Basic program.

Example 5.3 Visibility

```
5    rem Example 5.3
10   rem drawing a map around the character
20   mode 0 : hide on : pen 8 : curs off
25   CHAR=25
30   rem number of full sized maps per horizontal and
vertical row
40   MAPS_PER_ROW=2 : MAPS_PER_COLUMN=2
50   HEIGHT=8 : WIDTH=12 : rem width of screen in sprites
60   rem number of game screens per horizontal and
vertical row
70   VIEWS_PER_ROW=3 : VIEWS_PER_COL=3
75   VIEW_COUNT=VIEWS_PER_ROW*VIEWS_PER_COL
80   dim C(16),SEG$(62),MAP(80,60)  : rem dimension map
array
90   gosub 140 : rem get palette data
100  gosub 170 : rem load sprite data into segment string
110  gosub 250 : rem load map data in map array
130  fade 1,C(0),C(1),C(2),C(3),C(4),C(5),C(6),C(7),C(8),
C(9), C(10),C(11),C(12),C(13),C(14),C(15)
135  goto 1000 : rem control system
140  rem Find pallete for sprites
150  X=hunt(start(1) to start(1)+length(1),"PALT") :
X=X+4
```

```
160 for A=0 to 15 : C(A)=deek(X+A*2) : next A : return
170 rem load segment array with sprite data
180 cls physic : cls back
190 for I=1 to 30
200 cls physic,0,0,0 to 16,16
210 sprite 1,0,0,I : put sprite 1 : wait vbl
220 SEG$(I)=screen$(physic,0,0 to 16,16) : next I
230 sprite 1,-100,-100,1
240 return
250 rem load map array from data statements
260 rem read data
270 restore 50005 :read NL :rem number of lines per map
280 rem calculate constants
290 read N : rem number of maps
300 read W : rem number of sprites per line
310 read H : rem number of lines per screen
320 NO_OF_COLS=320/W : NO_OF_ROWS=199/H
330 rem ignore partially hidden lines
340 if 199 mod H<>0 then inc NO_OF_ROWS : HIDDEN=1
350 TOTAL_ROWS=MAPS_PER_ROW*NO_OF_ROWS
355 TOTAL_COLS=MAPS_PER_COL*NO_OF_COLS
360 for C=0 to MAPS_PER_COLUMN-1 : rem number of screens
370 for R=0 to MAPS_PER_ROW-1
380 if C<>0 or R<>0 then read DW,DH : rem ignore size
data
390 for J=0 to NO_OF_COLS-1
400 for K=0 to NO_OF_ROWS-1-HIDDEN
405 rem read sprite data
410 read MAP(R*NO_OF_COLS+J,C*(NO_OF_ROWS-HIDDEN)+K)
420 next K : if HIDDEN=1 then read DUMMY : rem ignore
unused line at end
430 next J : next R : next C : return
1000 rem moving through a map
1010 XPOS=0 : YPOS=0
1020 XSIZE=W*WIDTH+XPOS : YSIZE=H*HEIGHT+YPOS : rem
bottom corners of map window
1025 rem initial starting position relative to top left
corner of screen
1030 MAP_NO=0 : CHARACTER_X=1 : CHARACTER_Y=1
1040 locate 0,16 : print "Room number" : locate 12,16 :
print MAP_NO
1050 rem main loop
1060 gosub 1590 : rem load absolute coordinates of
character in CX,CY
1070 CX=CHARACTER_X+MAP_POS_X : CY=CHARACTER_Y+MAP_POS_Y
1075 rem get joystick info
```

```
1080 if jleft then gosub 1230
1090 if jright then gosub 1310
1100 if jdown then gosub 1400
1110 if jup then gosub 1490
1115 rem did character move
1120 if CHARACTER_X=OLD_X and CHARACTER_Y=OLD_Y then 1060
1130 OLD_X=CHARACTER_X : OLD_Y=CHARACTER_Y
1140 rem display area around character
1150 for XP=OLD_X-1 to OLD_X+1
1160 for YP=OLD_Y-1 to OLD_Y+1
1170 if XP=OLD_X and YP=OLD_Y then sprite
1,XP*W+XPOS,YP*W+YPOS,CHAR : goto 1210
1180 if XP<0 or YP<0 or XP>WIDTH-1 or YP>HEIGHT-1 then
1210
1190 XV=XP+MAP_POS_X : YV=YP+MAP_POS_Y : rem ate 0,18 :
print space$(30) : locate 0,18 : print XV,YV;
1200 if MAP(XV,YV)>0 then
screen$(physic,XP*W+XPOS,YP*H+YPOS)=SEG$(MAP(XV,YV))
1210 next YP : next XP : wait 1 : goto 1050
1220 rem move left
1230 if CX<=0 then return : rem player reached end of
world
1240 rem illegal move?
1250 if MAP(CX-1,CY)<>0 then return
1260 rem player is still in current map
1270 if CHARACTER_X>0 then dec CHARACTER_X : dec CX :
return
1280 rem player reached edge of map
1290 dec MAP_NO : gosub 1580 : rem clear screen
1300 CHARACTER_X=WIDTH-1 : gosub 1590 : return
1310 rem move right
1320 if CX>MAPS_PER_ROW*(320/W) then return
1330 rem illegal move?
1340 if MAP(CX+1,CY)<>0 then return
1350 rem player is still in current map
1360 if CHARACTER_X<WIDTH-1 then inc CHARACTER_X : inc CX
: return
1370 rem player reached edge of map
1380 inc MAP_NO : gosub 1580 : rem clear screen
1390 CHARACTER_X=0 : gosub 1590 : return
1400 rem move down
1410 if CY>MAPS_PER_ROW*(200/H) then return
1420 rem illegal move?
1430 if MAP(CX,CY+1)<>0 then return
1440 rem player is still in current map
```

```
1450 if CHARACTER_Y<HEIGHT-1 then inc CHARACTER_Y : inc
CY : return
1460 rem player reached edge of map
1470 MAP_NO=MAP_NO+VIEWS_PER_ROW : gosub 1580 : rem clear
screen
1480 CHARACTER_Y=0 : gosub 1590 : return
1490 rem move up
1500 if CY<=0 then return
1510 rem illegal move?
1520 if MAP(CX,CY-1)<>0 then return
1530 rem player is still in current map
1540 if CHARACTER_Y>0 then dec CHARACTER_Y : dec CY :
return
1550 rem player reached edge of map
1560 MAP_NO=MAP_NO-VIEWS_PER_ROW : gosub 1580 : rem clear
screen
1570 CHARACTER_Y=HEIGHT-1 : gosub 1590 : return
1575 rem clear screen
1580 cls physic,0,XPOS,YPOS to XSIZE,YSIZE : cls
back,0,XPOS,YPOS to XSIZE,YSIZE : locate 12,16 : print
MAP_NO : return
1585 rem update absolute coordinates of character in
CX,CY
1586 rem these are relative to the entire map (containing
all 9 views)
1590 VIEWX=MAP_NO mod VIEWS_PER_ROW : VIEWY=MAP_NO/
VIEWS_PER_ROW
1600 MAP_POS_X=VIEWX*WIDTH : MAP_POS_Y=VIEWY*HEIGHT
1610 CX=CHARACTER_X+MAP_POS_X : CY=CHARACTER_Y+MAP_POS_Y
: return
50005rem Add map data here. (Use the one included in
example 5.2)
```

It's also possible to add checks for the detection of walls or monsters directly into this routine. You could, for instance, place the locations of the various monsters into a 2D array in the following way:

```
10 dim monster(12,12)
```

Every location on the display would have one element in this array. If an element was zero, then the area would be free, and any other value would indicate the position of the occupiers statistics in the attributes table. This table could be loaded when reading in the map data.

You could now add the detection routine on the next page into Example 5.3.

```
85  dim MONSTER(80,60),ENCOUNTER(8)
410 read OBJECT : OX=R*NO_OF_COLS+J : OY=C*(NO_OF_ROWS-
HIDDEN)+K
415 MAP(OX,OY)=OBJECT : if OBJECT>5 and OBJECT <10 then
MONSTER(OX,OY)=OBJECT-5
1054 for M=0 to EN
1055 if ENCOUNTER(M)<>0 then bell: rem handle encopunter
1056 ENCOUNTER(M)=0 : next M : EN=0
1205 if MONSTER(XV,YV)<>0 then ENCOUNTER(EN)=MONSTER(XV,
YV) : inc EN
```

This routine loads an ENCOUNTER array with a list of "monsters" facing the party. Since there are no actual monsters in my current map, I've loaded the positions of the treasures into the monster array instead.

After the program has loaded the encounter table, it can then perform any required actions using a combat routine at the start of the control loop. In the case of Example 5.3, this routine would be called at line 1055.

5.6.3 3D effects

Another possibility is to draw your displays in glorious 3D. Providing you known a little mathematics, the illusion of 3D is not really difficult to produce, and if it is used properly, it can be incredibly effective. You can easily generate this type of routine using the techniques I will be discussing in Chapter 7.

Don't attempt to be over-ambitious however. Games such as FTL's Dungeon Master were certainly not written overnight. Frankly, you would have to work long and hard to achieve an effect which even vaguely approached this excellent game. Despite this, 3D graphics are certainly worth thinking about, especially for the combat sequences. It's quite possible to combine a standard 2D system for mapping the dungeon, with a powerful 3D combat sequence using animated sprites.

5.7 Controlling the character

After you've created your maps, and implemented them using STOS Basic, you will be ready to add the various puzzles and combat sequences. The nature of these routines will vary from game to game. One module which is crucial to all games, however, is the routine which reads and interprets the player's commands.

5.7.1 Using the keyboard

In spite of the availability of the complex input devices like the mouse and the joystick, the ST's keyboard is still a popular way of entering the commands in a RPG. This is because, unlike other input devices, there is no real limit to the amount of information which can be entered quickly and easily by the player.

Movement can be implemented using either compass directions, such as North, South, East, and West; or the standard ST's cursor keys. Other commands, like "fight" or "unlock" can be entered from the keyboard as in a normal text adventure. Each command will have its own particular key combinations. When you are designing these codes, you should attempt to make them as short as possible. This is especially true of the movement and combat options. Nowadays, few people will be happy to type in North or South every time they move.

If you are using single key commands, you should chose keys which will be easy for the player to remember. So the "Get object" command should be controlled using "g" or "p" rather than "z". You should also remember to make full use of the ST's function keys. These provide you with an ideal way of entering instructions. It's a good idea to display the entire list of instructions whenever the ST's <help> key is pressed. This can improve the effectiveness of your game considerably.

Example 5.4 Reading the <HELP> key

```
10   rem Fragment of code to read the ST's HELP key
20   x$=inkey$:if asc(x$)=0 then s=scancode
30   if s=98 then gosub 1000:s=0
40   goto 20:rem jump back to main keyboard loop
999  rem help routine
1000 print "You think you've got problems?":return
1010 rem this would usually be a little more helpful
```

You could now place a simple routine to print out the current commands at line 1000. This would take no time whatsoever to write, but it would be a godsend to the players.

One common problem which occurs, when reading the keyboard input, is entering the movement commands using the cursor keys. Here the difficulty lies in the fact than these keys do not normally return a value from the INKEY$ function. Like the <HELP> key, they can, however, be read using the SCANCODE function.

If your game requires you to input longer pieces of text, you may need to enter them using the STOS Basic INPUT or INPUT$ commands. Always use the LINE INPUT versions of these instructions, because they are much less fussy about the type of data they will accept.

You can use these commands in conjunction with MATCH, which searches a string array containing the allowable inputs and returns the position of the input string in the array. This number can then be used in your program. For further details of this technique, see Chapter 6.

5.7.2 Joystick input

The ST's joystick is very useful for entering movement commands and for controlling the character during combat. The only drawback with using the joystick, is that you are limited to 16 possible inputs.

These consist of the eight normal directions in conjunction with the fire button. For some games, 16 commands are simply not enough, and you are therefore forced to split the control between the joystick and the keyboard.

STOS Basic provides you with two separate sets of commands to read the joystick input.

The simpler set includes the instructions:

```
JLEFT
JRIGHT
JUP
JDOWN
FIRE
```

The problem with these instructions, are that they take no account of diagonals. These are best detected through the JOY function. This can read all sixteen of the possible positions: e.g.

```
100 rem Read joystick and jump to routine
110 j=joy(0):jump=j*1000:If jump>0 then gosub jump
120 goto 110
```

This code executes the subroutines at

```
1000,2000,3000...16000,
```

depending on the input from the joystick. It is particularly useful for arcade adventures which use complex animation sequences, as each action can be performed by its own individual routine.

5.7.3 Using the mouse

The ST's mouse pointer provides you with an extremely effective mechanism for controlling the activities of your party.

STOS Basic includes a powerful ZONE command, which makes it very easy to implement complicated dialogue boxes using the mouse pointer. These screen zones can be used to control everything from character generation to combat.

Furthermore, you can also use some of the many STOS menu commands to set the various game options. An example of this technique can be found in the combat simulator listed in Example 5.5 on page 131. This uses the Universal Control panel described in the previous chapter.

5.8 Multiple characters

Many role-playing games allow the player to control a party consisting of a number of individual characters. This is an attempt to simulate the action of the original RPGs which were played by several people.

In order to be really effective, the character in an RPG needs to be effectively an extension of the player's own personality. Because people are only able to directly relate to a single character at a time, multiple characters lose some of the flavour of original game. So why do most games still bother to provide them?

The answer is that, used properly, multiple characters can add an intriguing element of strategy to your game. The player now has the additional responsibility of selecting the mix of character types in the party.

Each character type has its own uses, and the player needs to weigh their advantages against their disadvantages. Furthermore, by choosing a different arrangement of characters, the same game can be played over and over again.

5.8.1 The leading character

If you were to ask to player to control the movements of four or five characters on the screen independently, then the action of the game would be reduced to a crawl. Because of this, it's normally easiest to nominate one character from the group as the leader. If the party starts off with a single character, the choice should be taken out of the player's hands. This will allow you to add a little autonomy to the rest of the characters. In real life, not all people are honest or trustworthy. The addition of realistic characters with their own "personality", can enhance the atmosphere of even the simplest game.

Games which display a view of the party from above can avoid a great deal of unnecessary complication by only representing the leader on the standard game map. A three dimensional display should also be assumed to show the surroundings entirely from the view point of the current leader.

5.8.2 Individual control

Individual control becomes important only during combat. Each character in the group needs to be given the specific orders for the attack. These orders need to be input at high speed to keep the action of the game running smoothly.

The ideal way of achieving this with STOS Basic, is to use the mouse. Some games utilise a separate screen for this purpose, and allow each player to be moved around independently. Experience has shown that the combat element of these games is often dangerously unwieldy. If you really want to use individual control, you would be better to allow the input of lists of orders to the character in advance. This would bring the RPG much closer to a genuine war-game.

5.9 Combat

It is the combat elements of a role-playing game which set it apart from the run-of-the-mill adventure. When you are writing your games, you should take particular care to make the fighting as fast and as furious as possible.

5.9.1 Mêlée rounds

All the action in the game is split into a number of separate **mêlée** rounds. Every mêlée round involves a single exchange of blows between two sets of fighters.

One set represents the characters controlled by the player and the other group comprises the monsters which are assumed to be opposing them.

The effect of a weapon is determined using two special attributes:

DAMAGE	This is a number representing the average amount of damage which will be done if the weapon hits an opponent.
HIT PROBABILITY	Determines the likelihood of any weapon actually hitting.

Note that, for the purposes of my discussion, a "weapon" can be taken as anything which is capable of inflicting damage on an opponent. This includes natural weapons like claws, teeth and fists. Like the character statistics, the weapon statistics are best stored in an array: e.g.

```
dim WEAPON(10),HIT_PROB(10):rem space for ten weapons
```

Every weapon which can appear in your game, will have need an entry somewhere in this table.

The attributes of a weapon can be further affected by the statistics of the person who is wielding it. Obviously, strong characters will inflict more damage than weaker ones. Similarly, dexterous characters will have a better chance of hitting their opponents. In order to reflect this fact, bonuses are normally added to the basic weapon statistics. The size and type of these bonuses vary depending on the weapon. So if a fighter was firing a gun, the strength bonuses would be minimal. The size of the bonus' in any particular instance, need to be worked out by experimentation. The damage inflicted on the characters will normally subtracted from one the attributes to determine their current state of health. There are two approaches you can take:

1 Subtract the damage from the character's stamina. If this becomes less than or equal to zero, then the character has been killed by one of the monsters.

2 Divide the damage evenly between the attributes STAMINA, STRENGTH or DEXTERITY. Only kill off the character when a couple of attributes reach zero. This is a more advanced system because it avoids the ridiculous possibility of a dying character jumping from the ground and chopping a monsters head off with a single blow.

Combat is performed in the following stages:

1 choose weapon

2 choose an opponent

3 check whether weapon hits the opponent

4 if hit is scored then
    determine damage
    check effect of damage

It's necessary to perform these steps for every character who is involved in the fighting. This includes all the monsters as well as the members of the adventuring party. The battle will continue until all members of one side are dead, or one group of combatants retreat.

Steps one and two can be controlled directly using the mouse. If you allowed each character to hold a single weapon ready for action, the first step could be removed. Also, the opponent could be selected automatically by your program, either randomly, or by taking account of the relative positions of the characters.

The third step, however, is a little more complicated. This is because members of the party can attempt to parry. This involves trying to place their weapon or their shield so as to deflect the blow.

The likelihood of a successful parry will largely depend on the relative dexterity of the two combatants. If an agile character tries to block a clumsy opponent, the defence will probably succeed. Similarly, a fast blow against a slow defender stands a very good chance of hitting. The best way of achieving this is to work out the ratio of the two DEX values as follows:

PARRY_CHANCE=(DEX of defending player)/ (DEX of attacker)

You then check for the success of a parry with the line:

```
R=rnd(100) :R=R+25*PARRY_CHANCE:if R<HIT_PROB(WEAPON)
then ? "hit" else ? "parried"
```

The final element a combat situation is the possibility of a fumble. Whenever several people are wielding weapons around, there's always the real danger that they will hit one of their allies by mistake. Many Real-RPGs assign a specific die roll such as a double zero for this purpose. If the player rolls this value, something disastrous is assumed to have taken place, and further dice are rolled to determine the final outcome. This can vary between the character accidentally shooting himself in the foot, or decimating his entire party!

The same technique can also be applied in one of your own games. All you need to do, is test for the possibility of a fumble, and then insert the appropriate IF..THEN statement to detect it. The result of the fumbles is entirely up to you.

Another complication is raised by the possibilities of armour. The net effect of this will be to reduce the impact of a blow by a fixed amount, depending on the strength of the armour. This can be implemented using a simple offset which can be subtracted from the damage inflicted on the player.

Different types of armour will absorb different amounts of damage. This can be represented by an attribute such as the DEFENCE factor. The higher the defence factor, the better the armour. You could store this information in an array such as:

```
100 dim ARMOUR(100)
```

The effect of an attack without a parry can be seen from the following fragment of code:

```
100 rem attack
110 rem Set weapon statistics
120 PROB=50:DAMAGE=10:BONUS=0
130 R=rnd(100):rem get a number from 1 to 100
140 rem check if attack successful
145 if R=0 then ? "You fumbled":stop
150 if R<PROB then HITS=RND(DAMAGE)+BONUS+1:print
"ATTACK DID ",HITS," Amount of damage":stop
160 print "attack failed
```

Note that the attack bonus is currently assumed to be zero.

Now for a larger example, which demonstrates a complete combat routine:

Exmple 5.5 A simple mêlée round

```
10   rem Example of a Mêlée round
20   rem initialise arrays
30   dim STR(10),DEX(10),STA(10),IQ(10),MAG(10),
DAMAGE(10)
35   dim HIT_PROB(10),WEAPON$(10)
40   mode 0 : cls back : cls physic
50   C=1 : rem current character
60   input "What is your characters Name ?";NAME$
65   if NAME$="" then boom : goto 60
70   cls : cls physic : cls back
80   gosub 660 : rem generate player character
90   pen 4 : locate 17,10 : print "Attack" : locate 17,14
95   Print "Parry ";
100 locate 12,18 : print "Axe" : locate 18,18 : print
"Club"
105 locate 24,18 : print "Sword" : pen 1
110 windopen 1,0,12,10,13,3 : title NAME$ : C=1 : gosub
620
120 gosub 710
```

```
130 windopen 2,30,12,10,13,3 : title "Tiger!"
135 C=2 : gosub 620
140 windopen 3,0,5,40,3,0 : windopen 4,0,8,40,3,0
150 restore 1070 : gosub 890
160 rem read weapons in array
170 for I=1 to 4
175 read WEAPON$(I),DAMAGE(I),HIT_PROB(I)
180 next I
185 SELECTED=4 : gosub 1050 : WEAPON=2:rem select club
189 rem main combat loop
190 repeat
200 wait 5
210 gosub 1000:rem read control panel
220 if Z<>0 then on Z gosub 740,760,780,820,860
230 rem Tiger attacks spontaneously
240 if timer=100 or rnd(100)>90 then gosub 410
250 until CHARACTER_IS_DEAD or TIGER_IS_DEAD
260 wait key : default : stop
270 rem handle players attack round
280 if DEX(1)=0 then PARRY_CHANCE#=4 : goto 320
290 PARRY_CHANCE#=DEX(2)/DEX(1):rem compare DEX's
300 HIT=0
310 rem now attack
320 rem check if tiger parries
340 TIGER_PARRY=rnd(3)
350 R=rnd(100) : rem roll a dice
355 rem does tiger attempt to parry
360 if TIGER_PARRY=3 then R=R+25*PARRY_CHANCE# : window
3 : clw : curs off : centre "<Tiger parries>" : return
365 rem check if blow hit
370 if R<HIT_PROB(WEAPON) then gosub 550:rem handle blow
380 if HIT=0 then qwindow 4 : clw : curs off : centre
">You missed<" : return
385 rem check if dead
390 if STA(2)<0 and DEX(2)<0 and STR(2)<0 then default :
centre "<The tiger is dead!>" : TIGER_IS_DEAD=true :
return
400 rem tiger attacks player
410 R=rnd(100) : rem get a number from 1 to 100
415 rem work out relative dexterities
420 if DEX(2)=0 then PARRY_CHANCE#=4 : goto 320
430 PARRY_CHANCE#=DEX(1)/DEX(2)
440 if PARRY then R=R+25*PARRY_CHANCE#
455 rem Does tiger successfully strike
460 if R<HIT_PROB(4) then gosub 590:rem Strike
successful
```

```
465 rem parry successful
470 if PARRY and HIT=0 then window 4 : clw : curs off :
centre "<You parried>"
475 rem attack failed
480 if ATTACK and HIT=0 then window 3 : clw : curs off :
centre "<The Tiger missed>"
485 rem update attributes
490 C=1 : window 1 : gosub 620 : C=2 : window 2 : gosub
620
495 rem Has tiger killed you?
500 if STA(1)<0 and DEX(1)<0 and STR(1)<0 then default :
centre "You died!" : CHARACTER_IS_DEAD=true
505 rem reset flags
510 if PARRY then PARRY=false : return
520 if ATTACK then ATTACK=false
530 return
540 rem hurt tiger
545 rem deduct hits equally from all attributes
550 HIT=rnd(DAMAGE(WEAPON)) : STA(2)=STA(2)-HIT/3
555 DEX(2)=DEX(2)-HIT/3 : STR(2)=STR(2)-HIT/3
560 window 4 : clw : : curs off
565 P$="<You inflicted"+str$(HIT)+" points of damage>"
570 centre P$:return
580 rem tiger got you
585 rem take damage
590 HIT=rnd(DAMAGE(4)) : STA(1)=STA(1)-HIT/3
595 DEX(1)=DEX(1)-HIT/3 : STR(2)=STR(2)-HIT/3
600 window 3 : clw : curs off
605 P$="<Tiger did "+str$(HIT)+" points of damage>"
610 centre P$:return
605 rem print out attributes
620 curs off : locate 0,3 : print "Str:";STR(C);" "
625 locate 0,4 : print "Dex:";DEX(C);" ";
630 locate 0,5 : print "Sta:";STA(C);" ";
635 locate 0,6 : print "Int:";IQ(C);" ";
640 locate 0,7 : print "Mag:";MAG(C);" ";
650 return
660 rem generate fighter
665 rem high strength,dexterity and stamina
670 STR(1)=rnd(10)+8 : DEX(1)=rnd(10)+8
675 STA(1)=rnd(10)+8
680 rem lousy magic
685 IQ(1)=rnd(5)+5 : MAG(I)=rnd(1)+3
690 return
700 rem generate a tiger
```

```
710 STR(2)=rnd(10)+15 : DEX(2)=rnd(10)+15 :
STA(2)=rnd(10)+15
715 rem how many tigers do YOU know are brilliant
magicians
720 IQ(2)=rnd(3)+2 : MAG(2)=0 : return
725 rem control system
730 rem read attack button
740 ATTACK=true : PARRY=false : SELECTED=1 : gosub 1050
745 timer=0 : gosub 280 : gosub 1050 : return
750 rem read parry
760 PARRY=true : ATTACK=false : SELECTED=2 : gosub 1050
765 timer=0 : gosub 410 : gosub 1050 : return
770 rem get axe
780 SELECTED=WEAPON+2 : rem get old box number
790 if SELECTED<>3 then gosub 1050 : SELECTED=3 : gosub
1050
800 WEAPON=1 : return : rem invert box
810 rem get club
820 SELECTED=WEAPON+2 : rem get old box number
830 if SELECTED<>4 then gosub 1050 : SELECTED=4 : gosub
1050
840 WEAPON=2 : return
850 rem get sword
860 SELECTED=WEAPON+2 : rem get old box number
870 if SELECTED<>5 then gosub 1050 : SELECTED=5 : gosub
1050
880 WEAPON=3 : return
890 rem initialise control panel
900 read NZ : reset zone
910 if NZ<0 or NZ>127 then stop
920 dim SWITCH(NZ,4),STATUS(NZ)
930 for I=1 to NZ
940 for J=0 to 3
950 read SWITCH(I,J)
960 next J
970 set zone I,SWITCH(I,0),SWITCH(I,1) to
SWITCH(I,2),SWITCH(I,3)
980 box SWITCH(I,0),SWITCH(I,1) to
SWITCH(I,2),SWITCH(I,3)
990 next I : return
1000 rem check zone
1010 Z=zone(0) : if Z=0 or mouse key=0 then Z=0 : return
1020 STATUS(Z)=not(STATUS(Z))
1030 if DEBUG then qwindow 0 : locate 0,15 : print
STATUS(Z),Z;
1040 return
```

```
1050 rem Invert a box
1060 wait 5 : gr writing 3 : ink 1
1065 bar SWITCH(SELECTED,0),SWITCH(SELECTED,1) to
SWITCH(SELECTED,2),SWITCH(SELECTED,3) : gr writing 1 :
return
1066 rem dialogue box data
1070 data 5
1080 data 80,100,240,132
1090 data 80,133,240,164
1100 data 80,165,132,195
1110 data 133,165,187,195
1120 data 188,165,240,195
1125 rem Weapon data
1126 rem NAME,Damage,Hit probability
1130 data "AXE",9,60
1140 data "CLUB",6,80
1150 data "SWORD",15,40
1160 data "CLAWS",12,50
```

Note that this example is intended purely as a demonstration. Without the underlying support provided by the rest of the RPG's graphics routines, it's a pretty uninspiring if you treat it in isolation. But the basic mechanics of the program are identical to the real combat systems found in many commercial games.

5.10 Magic

Magic is an integral part of many role-playing systems. The big problem with magic of course, is that it is totally confined to the player's imagination. Like it or not, in the real world, magic simply doesn't work. So whilst we may know a little about the swords part of "Swords and sorcery", the sorcery bit is completely outside our actual experience.

The only way to successfully apply magic in a game, is to carefully invent a logical and consistent system of rules. Although the laws of physics may be different in your game world, you should always try to keep within the bounds of common sense. The fact is, unless the players are provided with a convincing rationale which underlies your system, they will simply refuse to believe in it.

In practice, you will undoubtedly need to place real restrictions in the capabilities of your magic users. Otherwise there will be nothing to stop a powerful wizard zapping even your toughest monsters with just a casual wave of his hand.

There are several possible solutions to this difficulty:

1 Assume that all spells need a material component of some sort which is used up after the spell has been cast. Really powerful spells might need especially rare items in order to work.

An example of this technique can be seen in the excellent ULTIMA games. You could even use the same idea as the basis of the entire scenario.

2 Make wizards start off physically weak and limit their initial abilities ruthlessly. As the characters increase in power, you can progressively confront them against tougher and tougher monsters.

3 Keep an indicator of a character's current power rating, which can increase with experience. In order to cast a particular spell, the character needs temporarily to expend a certain amount of magical energy. By assigning the highest power requirements to the more effective spells, you can easily restrict the strongest magic to characters who have survived some way into your RPG. This is used in the vast majority of D&D type games, and works well.

4 Assign a cryptic code to each spell. If a character doesn't know the code, then it is impossible to cast the particular spell. You can place these codes on scrolls at appropriate points in your game as a reward for solving a especially difficult puzzle. This is the approach used in FTL's Dungeon master program.

It is perfectly possible to exploit any combination of these ideas in a single game. After all you're the boss of this world. So quite literally anything goes!

5.11 Conclusion

Creating a role-playing game can be an highly enjoyable pastime in its own right. I've personally refereed several Real-RPGs and I can assure you that they are terrific fun to organise. You can now capture the same feeling of satisfaction by writing your very own role-playing game on the Atari ST. With a little help from STOS Basic, and a lot hard work, you might well produce a game which is commercially viable. All you need are the ideas and the imagination. The rest is easy.

6

Adventure games

6.1 A little history

All modern adventure games are the direct descendants of a single computer program written in FORTRAN in the early seventies. This was the infamous "Colossal Cave Adventure", written by Crowther and Woods. When it was first produced, "Colossal Cave" was one of the largest computer programs ever written. Astonishingly enough, it's now perfectly possible to fit the entire game on a standard 520 ST! So we now quite literally have the power of an circa 1970 mainframe at our fingertips.

As you can imagine, the games software market for an early seventies mainframe was just a little limited. So the Colossal Cave Adventure was never actually sold commercially, and poor old Crowther and Woods never made a penny out of their creation.

The first commercial adventure games were the "Scott Adams adventure series" released around 1979 for the TRS-80 series of computers. These managed to capture the imagination of a whole generation of home computer enthusiasts. But despite the undoubted success of the Scott Adams adventures, they were undoubtedly crude by comparison with what was to come later.

For me, the modern adventure was initiated with a piece of artificial intelligence research into natural language systems. This culminated a program called "ZORK", which was designed as a demonstration of the way computer systems could be made to "understand" human sentences. ZORK had all the characteristics we now associate with an adventure, and included the ability to handle some very complicated instructions indeed.

Subsequently, some of the programmers behind this project decided to try to produce a version of this game for use on a home computer, and the INFOCOM company, as we now know it, was born. Eventually of course, they were forced to admit defeat. The final version of ZORK had to be split up into three complete adventures

It's impossible to over-emphasise the impact Infocom have had on the adventuring scene. Their product list includes classics like "ZORK", "Planetfall" and the amazingly funny "Hitch-hikers Guide to the Galaxy" adventure.

6.2 Adventurers start here

In this chapter, I'll be demonstrating how you can create one of these adventure games yourself using STOS Basic. But what actually is an adventure game? Well, the basic ideas are quite similar to those of a role-playing game. The crucial difference between the games lies in the nature of the challenges presented to the player.

The problems in an adventure game are essentially intellectual, and there's little scope for physical combat. Another factor, is that most adventures restrict themselves to just a single player character. This avoids the strong tactical element which is usually present in an RPG. The adventure takes place in an imaginary world in which practically anything is possible. The surroundings are described by a short piece of fulsome text which scrolls down towards the bottom of the screen. In the more modern adventures this text is often supplemented by a picture of the current scenery.

The player takes control of an intrepid explorer who is inhabiting the world of the adventure. This character can be commanded using simple English sentences which are usually entered directly from the keyboard.

The underlying appeal of adventures is that they allow you to temporarily abandon the frustrations of the real world, and embark on a realistic and satisfying journey into the realms of imagination.

The easiest way to familiarise yourself with these games, is to play one yourself. There are currently several adventure games on the public domain, including a complete version of the original Colossal Cave adventure.

Here is a short transcript from the start of the game to whet your appetite. I've typed the computer's responses in italics.

6.2.1 Sample transcript from Colossal cave

Somewhere nearby, is colossal cave where others have found fortunes in treasure and gold, though it is rumoured that some who enter are never seen again. Magic is said to work in the cave. I will be your eyes and hands. Direct me with 1 or 2 word commands...

You are standing at the end of a road before a small brick building. Around you is a forest. A small stream flows out of the building and down a gully.

>enter building

You are inside a building, a well house for a large spring.
There are some keys on the ground here.
There is a shiny brass lamp nearby.
There is tasty food here.
There is a bottle of water here.

>get lamp

OK.

>rub lamp

Rubbing the electric lamp is not particularly rewarding. Anyway, nothing happens.

What mysterious puzzle awaits you in this adventure? Where is that cave thing that was mentioned early on? I'm afraid you'll need to purchase a copy of Colossal cave to find out!

6.2.2 Why STOS Basic?

At this point, you might by wondering why anyone would wish to write an adventure in STOS Basic, when there are special adventure creators such as STAC available for the ST. Well, the reason is simply a matter of flexibility. If you write an adventure in STOS Basic, you are free to create your game without any restrictions whatsoever. You can therefore produce full blown graphic adventures which would be impossible in any other medium. Once you've written the core of your adventuring system, it's really no harder to write your games in STOS Basic as it is in a dedicated package like STAC. Since I'll be providing most of these routines for you, you will be able to concentrate on the ideas in your adventure, without having to worry about any messy implementation details at all.

6.3 Scenario design

In order to produce a truly playable adventure, it's vital to generate a believable atmosphere which captures the player's imagination completely. This is even more important for an adventure than for an RPG, as there are no combat sequences add spice to the game. In an adventure, the game play is centred completely on the world you have created.

You must therefore go to considerable lengths to make this as interesting and engrossing as possible.

The standard method of creating this atmosphere is to pack the room descriptions with adjectives. So a tree would be described like:

"A massive oak tree blossoming with the generous bounty of spring" rather than the more prosaic, but equally accurate

"A tall tree".

Don't however, allow yourself to go overboard with this idea. If you allow your descriptions to become too flowery, you are rather more likely to send your players to sleep than to inspire them to complete your adventure.

6.3.1 Creating a map

You should always start off by drawing a complete map of your game on paper. This should include full details of the connections between the various rooms, along with any ideas you may have about the expected contents. Try to keep the design of your game world consistent.

Every location and every object in your adventure should have been put there for a reason, even if it's just to confuse the player. If you forget about this, and attempt to match a set of logically unconnected locations together, you will produce an appalling jumble of fragmented ingredients which no-one will believe.

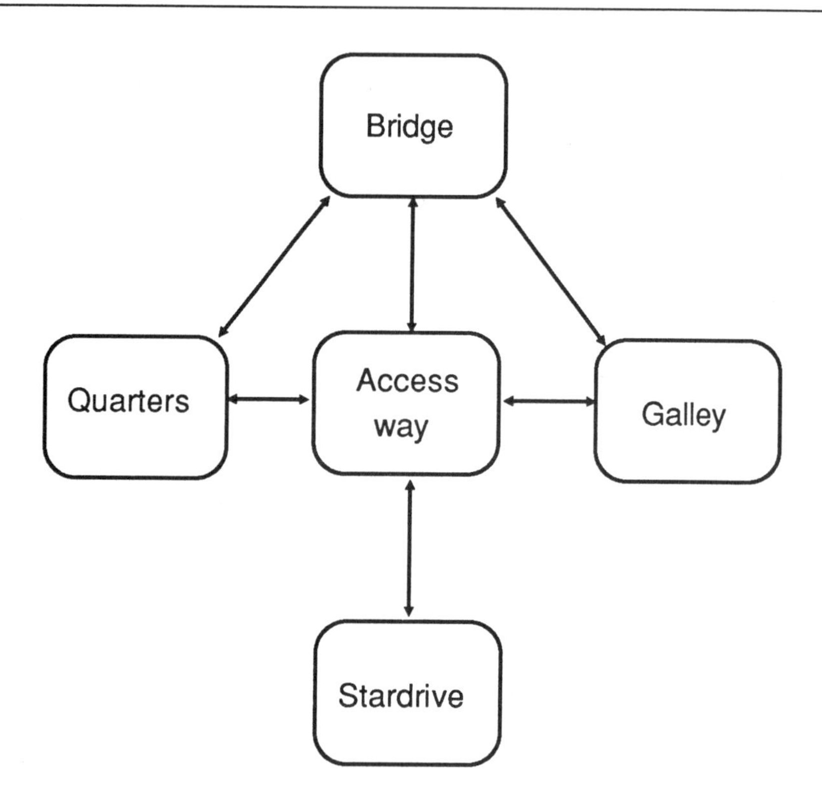

Figure 6.1 Section of a game map

You are now ready to invent the puzzles and traps which will be encountered in the adventure. For me, this activity is one of the most enjoyable parts of the entire process. Obviously all problems which are essential to the completion of the game need to be solvable, but it's important to keep these solutions within the context of the game world. So if you've set your adventure in a world of swords and sorcery, it's pointless to have problems requiring the player to fix a computer!

As you devise your puzzles, you should carefully mesh them into the background of the game world. Games which lack any form of consistent pattern, no matter how twisted or bizarre, invariably fail to engender the believable atmosphere which is so vital to a successful adventure.

The best puzzles have solutions which appear to be totally obvious in hindsight, but which are fiendishly difficult at the time. Remember, nobody enjoys a puzzle which is too easy, or ridiculously contrived. But if you can get the players to regularly kick themselves for their stupidity, then your scenario will be providing them with a real and exciting challenge.

One of the simplest examples of this technique, is subtly to alter a standard message to include some vital piece of information.

Completely different locations can be given almost identical descriptions. It's amazing how often the player will just skim through the text without totally reading it. Once the players finally realise the solution, they will be amazed to discover that the information has been in front of their eyes all the time!

You can also attempt to describe a commonplace object in an unfamiliar way. In a world of magic, you can have great fun adding mechanical devices such as cars or refrigerators. These can be explained through the eyes of the character experiencing the adventure, without reference to the assumptions of our modern-day world. So a car might be regarded as a gigantic metallic monster with horrible teeth and a fierce growl. Imagine the chaos which would ensue if your adventure attempted to rescue an unfortunate damsel who was being ''eaten'' by this monster. Rather than being actually grateful, the girl would be extremely upset at being dragged out of her car by some moronic barbarian with delusions of heroism!

It's normally advisable to start the adventure with simple puzzels, and then slowly increase the complexity of your problems during the progression of the game. This draws the players into the game world, without frustrating them unnecessarily at the beginning.

6.4 Game plan of an adventure

The overall mechanics of the adventure can best be summarised with a little pseudo-code as shown in Figure 6.2 on the next page.

Before you can understand this description, you'll need to be introduced to some new terms, as follows:

events include all possible occurrences in your adventure. These manage things such a door opening, a monster appearing, or even one of your characters legs falling off for no readily apparent reason.

A **high priority event** is one which must be performed immediately. A typical high priority event is the character's death. Whenever this occurs, the program should

```
repeat

perform high priority event
describe room
input a line of text
split text into individual words

check for valid words

if word is a system command then interpret system command
if word is a movement
     then
          if move is allowed
               then
                    enter new room
               endif
     endif

interpret local commands
perform local events
interpret global commands
perform low priority events

if word is not recognized then print ''I don't understand''

until player exits, wins, or loses
```

Figure 6.2 Pseudo-code description of an adventure

terminate at once, without bothering to read the keyboard, or display the room description. These events are rather like the "Go to jail" cards in Monopoly, as they take complete precedence of any other commands in the game

Low priority events are similar to the above, but are slightly less earth shattering in nature. These handle events such as hunger, which can often be avoided with a little action on the part of the player. (Eating some food would certainly help).

Local events. These are situations that can arise only if the character is occupying a particular location. Traps, for instance, will only be sprung when the character enters a certain room.

It's also possible to group the player's instructions into a similar set of categories, as follows:

Movement commands are instructions to the character to move in a certain direction. These include phrases like: GO EAST, WEST, ENTER SHIP,..etc.

System commands are used to control the actions of the adventure program itself. So instructions such as QUIT, SAVE, or INVENTORY are all system commands.

Finally there are the local and global commands. Local commands are like local events in that they can only be performed at a specific location. In contrast, Global commands can be executed anywhere in the adventure.

So "OPEN WINDOW" is a local command because it can only take place the room with the window. But "EAT FOOD" is global because it can be entered whenever the character is feeling a little peckish.

Here's a few more examples of these commands:

RAMSAVE	(System)
GET	(Global)
OOPS	(System)
PRESS SWITCH	(Local)
DROP	(Global)
CLIMB WALL	(Local)

6.4.1 Standard routines

If you examine the pseudo-code in Figure 6.2 carefully, you should be able to isolate a number of the key components of an adventure game.

These include:

- ❑ perform high priority event;
- ❑ describe room;
- ❑ input a line of text;
- ❑ split text into individual words;
- ❑ check for valid words;
- ❑ interpret movement commands;
- ❑ interpret system commands;
- ❑ interpret local commands;
- ❑ perform local events;
- ❑ interpret global commands;
- ❑ perform low priority events.

I'll now take each of these routines and show you how they can be implemented in STOS Basic.

6.5 Understanding text

6.5.1 The text parser

The core of any adventure program is provided by the procedures which input the user's commands, and convert them into a form that can be directly understood by the computer.

These routines are commonly known as **parsers.**

But why do you need a complicated analysis routine in the first place? After all, it's perfectly feasible to enter the user's commands into a string variable, and simply test this using a successive set of IF..THEN statements in the following way:

```
100 input c$
110 if c$="get rock" then gosub 1000:rem get rock routine
120 if c$="kill dragon" then gosub 2000:rem kill dragon
```

The flaw with this simple-minded approach, is that it ignores the sheer richness of the English language. The single command "kill dragon" could also be expressed as:

- kill monster;
- attack dragon;
- destroy dragon.

If you were to limit your program to simple comparisons between the possible input strings, you would be forced to check each of the alternatives individually. Otherwise, it could take the player hours of effort to come across the exact phrasing which your game required. This would be agonisingly slow and would make it impossible for you to implement anything but the smallest adventures.

6.5.2 The Verb Noun parser

The solution is to allow each command to be entered using a number of common synonyms. Synonyms are just lists of words with the same or similar meanings. So destroy and attack are synonyms of the word "kill". Special dictionaries of these synonyms, called Thesauruses, are available. These contain the possible alternatives for most English words or phrases.

The job of your parser is to convert a complex English sentence into a form which can unambiguously recognised by the computer. This will involve converting any common synonyms of a word into a single unique identification number. You will now be able to perform the test for all combinations of a certain command with just a single IF..THEN instruction. e.g.

```
120 if verb=kill and noun=dragon then gosub 2000:rem kill
dragon
```

The easiest requirement of your parsing system is to split up a sentence into its individual words. Since most English words are separated by spaces, you can isolate the commands using the STOS Basic INSTR command like this:.

Example 6.1 Separating words

```
1000 rem Get line and split it into words
1010 line input ">";A$ : rem prompt can be anything
```

```
1020 COUNT=0 : CHAR=1 : rem word count and current character
1030 repeat
1040 TEST=instr(A$," ",CHAR)
1050 if TEST<>0 then L=TEST-CHAR else L=len(A$)-CHAR+1
1055 rem Note the 0 zero in WRD (OR is reserved)
1060 WRD$(COUNT)=mid$(A$,CHAR,L) : CHAR=TEST+1 : inc COUNT
1070 until TEST=0 or COUNT=11
1080 return
```

Note the use of LINE INPUT at 1010. Unlike the standard input command, LINE INPUT allows you to input sentences containing commas and periods (.). Occasionally this can be quite useful.

WRD$ is an array which will be used to hold your words. This will need to be dimensioned at the start of your program. You can't use a name like WORDS incidentally, because "OR" is a STOS Basic instruction. So WORDS is translated by STOS Basic as:

```
W or DS
```

Here's a small program which can be used to test this routine:

```
10  dim WRD$(10)
20  gosub 1000
30  for W=0 to COUNT-1 : print WRD$(W) : next W
999 stop
```

Don't forget to enter the lines in Example 6.1 before trying to run this program.

Once the words have been separated, your program can now begin to interpret them. The simplest form of parser uses the verb-noun system, which allows the user to enter sentences of up to two words in length.

The verb specifies an action to be taken, and the noun indicates the object which is to be manipulated. A valid sentence can begin with either a verb or a direction. So the following phrases are legal in this system:

>run
>east
>get carrot

As it is completely ridiculous to start off a sentence with a noun, this needs to be automatically rejected by the parser. Therefore a command such as:

>carrot

should generate a response from your adventure like:

I'm sorry, but you are not allowed to "CARROT" something.

The action of a verb-noun parser can be summarised by the pseudo-code in Figure 6.3 below.

```
split sentence into words
if number of words>2 then output ''sentence too complicated''
if word one is a direction then move character
if word one is a verb
     then
          if number of words=1 or word two is noun or direction
          then
               perform action
          else
               print ''I don't understand''
          endif
     else
          print ''you can't '';word one;'' something''
     endif
```

Figure 6.3 Pseudo-code expansion for a verb-noun parser.

You are strongly recommended to keep the computer's responses to improper English as polite as possible. Don't fall into the trap of using phrases which are sarcastic or rude. No matter how funny or clever these seem when you are writing them, they will quickly get under the player's skin. After the fourteenth occurrence of "Learn to type DUMMY!", even the most patient player is likely to feel justly aggrieved!

I've already shown you how a phrase can be split into words in Example 6.1. The other routines which will be required by the parser are:

check if word is a noun
check if word is a verb
check if word is a direction
perform action

STOS Basic contains a number of powerful string search commands which make it very easy for your program to check through a list of synonyms.

The best of these is the INSTR command which tests the words against of range of possibilities held in a string variable. Each type of word, will have its own individual search string, which will contain all allowable responses. It's common practice to restrict the string to the first few letters of each word. This speeds up the checking process considerably.

The number of significant letters in a word is entirely up to you, but the more letters you use, the more space which will be wasted by the shorter words. In practice, a good word size is six, as this combines a reasonable measure of accuracy with only a minimal memory overhead.

You can search these word lists using the INSTR statement as follows:

```
verb=instr(verb$,word$(1)):verb=verb/6:rem get verb number
```

Unfortunately, the above instruction produces a different number for every instruction. What your program needs, is some way of grouping words with the same meaning together.

The solution is to store a separate identification number for each possible synonym in an array. e.g.

```
dim action(100)
```

The contents of the ACTION array might look rather like this:

Element number	*Action number*	*Verb*
1	1	GET
2	2	DROP
3	3	ATTACK
4	3	KILL
5	4	INVENTORY
6	5	SAVE

Elements three and four of this array both have exactly the same action number. They therefore represent a single command from the player.

Similarly, all the synonyms used to describe an object will need to be held in an ITEM array. The format of this array will be identical to ACTION.

Example 6.2 Complete VERB-NOUN parser using INSTR

```
1100 rem Simple verb noun parser
1105 D=0 : NOUN=0 : VERB=0
1106 rem search for an exit
1110 D=instr(EXIT$,WRD$(0)) : if D<>0 then D=EXIT(D/7) :
return
1112 rem if word is not an exit, then try for a verb
1115 V=instr(VERB$,WRD$(0))
1120 if V=0 then ? "I don't know how to ";WRD$(0);"
something" : ER=1 : return
1125 VERB=ACTION(V/7):rem get action number
1126 rem verb=GO
1130 if VERB=1 then D=instr(EXIT$,WRD$(1)): : if D<>0 then
D=EXIT(D/7) : return
```

```
1131 rem first word if not a verb of a direction
1135 if COUNT=1 then return
1136 rem search through nouns
1140 N=instr(NOUN$,WRD$(1))
1145 if N=0 then ? "I can't see a ";WRD$(1);" here" : ER=1 :
return
1150 NOUN=ITEM(N/7):rem get item number
1155 return
```

This routine expects a list of words to be held in the WRD$ array before use. You can generate this list using the word-splitter given in Example 6.1

I've introduced, in this example, a separate mechanism for checking whether a word is a direction. This uses the EXIT$ and EXIT arrays. EXIT$ is just a list of the possible directions i.e

```
EXIT$="NORTH N SOUTH S"
```

The EXIT array holds the direction number for each word in this string. So NORTH and N both have exactly the same direction number as they represent a single movement for the player.

Before you can test Example 6.2, you need to define the arrays NOUN$, and VERB$ using lines like:

```
NOUN$="CARROT DOG ORANGE HAT "
VERB$="GET DROP KILL"
```

See how I've spaced them out so they are always exactly seven characters apart. If you pad the user's input with spaces, you can eliminate the possibility of your parser accidentally interpreting a noun such as CAR as CARROT. You will also need to define the synonym lists for ACTION, ITEM and EXIT.

You may be wondering why I've neglected the STOS Basic MATCH command in my discussion. This would allow you to check all the letters in a word, rather than the first five or six.

The big drawback of course, is that MATCH will only work using a sorted array. This makes it very difficult for you to generate a single identification number for a particular word, without tediously sorting the whole list in advance.

You can't sort the data in the ACTION, ITEM, and EXIT arrays using SORT because the identifiers are not in step with the appropriate strings. So the whole process needs to be performed by hand whenever you add a new word to the adventures vocabulary.

6.5.3 Expanding the parser

Although verb-noun parsers are undoubtedly useful, they do seem quite primitive by the standards we have come to expect from a modern adventure. Most popular adventure games now incorporate far more advanced text recognition systems, which can interpret a wide range of common English expressions. I'll now examine a number of simple techniques which can be used to enhance the standard verb-noun process.

Prepositions

A preposition is a word which is used to specify either the location of a noun, or the means used to manipulate it. Common English prepositions include:

- inside;
- under;
- with;
- by;
- at.

The ability to recognise phrases which contain prepositions increases the apparent intelligence of a parser dramatically. All the following phases could now be interpreted successfully by the computer:

- get gun from pocket;
- look around corner;
- kill monster using axe;
- open safe with key.

The typical phrase now includes 1 verb, 2 nouns, and a preposition. The first noun in this phrase is known as the subject, and the second as the object. Figure 6.4 on the next page shows a new version of the original pseudo-code which demonstrates how one of these parsers might work.

Well, it's not exactly pretty is it? Fortunately it's much easier to implement than it seems. Anyway, here's one I prepared earlier for you. If it still looks complicated, don't worry, because you can freely use it your own adventures without needing to understand any of it.

Example 6.3 Extended noun verb parser

```
1100 rem verb noun preposition parser
1105 DONE=0 : D=0 : NOUN(1)=0 : NOUN(2)=0 : VERB=0 : PREP=0
1106 rem check for a direction
1110 D=instr(EXIT$,WRD$(1)) : if D<>0 then D=EXIT(D/7) :
return
1112 rem check word one for a verb
1115 V=instr(VERB$,WRD$(1))
1116 rem word one must be a verb or a direction
1120 if V=0 then print "I don't know how to ";WRD$(1);"
something" : ER=1 : return:rem set error flag
```

(continued on page 151)

```
split sentence into words
if number of words>4 then output "sentence too complicated"

if word one is a direction
     then
          perform movement
     endif
if word one is a verb
     then
          if number of words=1 then
               perform action
          endif
          if number of words=2 then
               if word two is a noun or direction
                    then
                         perform action
                    else
                         print "I don't understand"
               endif
          endif
          if number of words=3 then
               if (word two is a preposition and word three is a
               noun)
                    then
                         perform action
                    else
                         print "I don't understand"
                    endif
               endif
          if number of words=4
               then
               if  (word  two  is  a  noun  and  word  three  is  a
               preposition and word four is a noun)
                    then
                         perform action
                    else
                         print "I don't understand"
                    endif
               endif
else
    print "you can't ";word one;" something"

endif
```

Figure 6.4 Pseudo-code expansion for an extended parser

```
1125 VERB=ACTION(V/7) : rem get action number
1126 rem handle go
1130 if VERB=1 then D=instr(EXIT$,WRD$(2)) : if D<>0 then
D=EXIT(D/7) : return
1132 rem about if not a verb or a direction
1135 if COUNT=1 then return
1136 rem check second word for a noun
1140 if COUNT=2 then WD=2 : NOUN_NUMBER=1 : gosub 1190 :
return
1142 rem if three words then check word 2 for a preposition
1143 rem then check word three for noun
1145 if COUNT=3 then WD=2 : gosub 1220 : WD=3 : NOUN_NUMBER=1
: gosub 1190 : return
1150 if COUNT<>4 then return
1151 rem four words entered
1155 rem is word two a noun
1160 WD=2 : NOUN_NUMBER=1 : gosub 1190
1165 WD=3 : gosub 1220 : rem Is word 3 a preposition
1170 rem is word four a noun
1175 WD=4 : NOUN_NUMBER=2 : gosub 1190
1180 return
1185 return
1190 rem Check for noun
1200 N=instr(NOUN$,WRD$(WD))
1205 if N=0 then print "I can't see a ";WRD$(WD);" here" :
ER=1 : return
1210 NOUN(NOUN_NUMBER)=ITEM(N/7)
1215 return
1220 rem check preposition
1300 P=instr(PREP$,WRD$(WD))
1305 if P=0 then print "I don't recognise the word ";WRD$(WD)
;" here" : ER=1 : return
1310 PREP=HOW(P/7)
1315 return
```

This parser should prove more than adequate for most of your adventures. It's certainly infinitely preferable to a verb- noun system. But if you enjoy experimenting, there are many further improvements you could make to improve it still further. You might decide to extend it to understand sentences involving more than two nouns. e.g.

```
attack monster inside room with axe
```

You could also include the ability to interpret lists, adverbs, and adjectives.

Don't however, fall into the trap of concentrating too much effort into the text recognition system. Although software reviewers seem to love the advanced parsers, many users quickly fall back to the original verb-noun system. One reason for this, is simply that short sentences are quicker to enter from the keyboard. Also, the verb-noun system is superbly direct. Seasoned adventures quickly realise that the chances of an adventure misinterpreting your commands is reduced enormously if you keep your instructions as straightforward as possible.

Despite having played some of the latest adventures from INFOCOM and RAINBIRD, I've yet to encounter a parser which could understand absolutely everything I threw at it. So don't be ashamed to restrict yourself to just the simplest text parser in your game. The really important part of an adventure is the scenario. Providing you can capture the player's imagination and include interesting and challenging puzzles in your adventure, the quality of the parser is probably irrelevant.

6.6 Picturing the scene

6.6.1 Choosing the graphics

The question of whether graphics and adventures actually mix is subject to fierce debate amongst adventuring enthusiasts.

The traditional view is that pictures take up valuable storage space which would be better used in creating fuller descriptions and more complicated puzzles. It's perfectly true that unless the graphics are superbly drawn, they can often destroy the atmosphere of a game rather than enhancing it.

Other people however, rightly point to the success of companies like RAINBIRD, whose games include some marvellous graphics while still being fiendishly challenging. The decision whether or not to use graphics in your game will depend entirely on which side of the argument you personally favour. But it's probably safest to start off with a completely text-based adventure, and then incorporate your graphics later when the program is finished.

This forces the original descriptions to stand independently from the graphics, and allows diehard Infocom addicts to turn off the pictures without destroying the appeal of the adventure. It also lets you freely modify the room descriptions until they are perfect, without having to worry about redrawing any of the associated pictures.

6.6.2 The screen compactor

The STOS Basic screen compactor is capable of quickly compressing any part of the ST's screen into just a fraction of its normal size. These screens can be created using any drawing package which supports either Degas or Neochrome screen formats.

Using the compactor, you will be able to pack around 30 of these screens onto a single-sided 3.5 inch disk.

It's preferable to store each game screen in its own individual file. Whenever a picture is needed, it can then be accessed directly using the LOAD instruction, and expanded into the screen with UNPACK.

The following example illustrates this process: place the STOS accessory disk into current drive, and enter the program in Example 6.4.

Example 6.4 Loading a screen

```
10  rem Loading a compacted screen
15  rem Enter a compressed screen saved in bank 5
20  load "backgrnd.mbk"
30  mode 0:flash off
40  reserve 5 as screen:rem Reserve screen for picture
50  unpack 5,6:rem Unpack screen
60  appear 6,30:rem Display screen
70  wait key
```

It's pointless to attempt to produce a piece of graphics for every location in the adventure. If you concentrate your efforts on the more interesting locations, you can use the same overall effort to produce a much higher standard of graphics.

6.7 Graphic adventures

Recently, a number of games have been developed which depart strongly from the standard text-based adventure.

The internal mechanics of these games are exactly the same as a normal adventure, but instead of entering words from the keyboard, the user is able to select an action directly from the screen using the mouse.

STOS Basic is ideally suited for this type of game, since it allows you to create control panels and menus effortlessly. The control panel can be generated using the Universal Control panel system demonstrated in Chapter 4. Once the actions have been input, they may be interpreted using the same techniques as used in other adventures. But there's absolutely no possibility of ambiguity, so the parser can be replaced with a simple call to the ZONE command.

Example 6.5 Simple screen input system

```
10  rem Example 6.5
20  mode 0 : cls physic : cls back
30  locate 0,0 : centre "Alternative Adventure example"
40  curs off
50  rem dimension arrays
60  dim WRD$(127),TYPE(127),MEANING(127),SWITCH(127,3)
70  NOUN=1 : VERB=2 : EXIT=3 : rem set up constants
80  gosub 140 : rem generate dialogue box and define screen
zones
90  gosub 350 : goto 90 : rem call Universal Control panel
```

```
100 stop
110 rem generate grid and set up zones
120 reset zone
130 rem define size and position of various buttons
140 XPOS=0 : YPOS=143 : NO_OF_ROWS=4 : NO_OF_COLS=5
150 LINE_LENGTH=10 : rem eight characters per button
160 WIDTH=xgraphic(LINE_LENGTH) : rem width of button in
pixels
170 HEIGHT=8 : rem height of button in pixels
180 rem draw dialogue boxes and install zones
190 for ROW=0 to NO_OF_ROWS-1
200 for COL=0 to NO_OF_COLS-1
210 Z_NUMBER=ROW*NO_OF_COLS+COL+1 : rem get zone number
220 rem Calculate position of zone
230 SWITCH(Z_NUMBER,0)=ROW*WIDTH+XPOS :
SWITCH(Z_NUMBER,1)=COL*HEIGHT+YPOS
240 SWITCH(Z_NUMBER,2)=(ROW+1)*WIDTH+XPOS-1 :
SWITCH(Z_NUMBER,3)=(COL+1)*HEIGHT+YPOS
250 rem read word's name,it's type (verb,noun or string) and
it's word number
260 read WRD$(Z_NUMBER),TYPE(Z_NUMBER),MEANING(Z_NUMBER)
270 rem print out text for the various buttons
280 locate ROW*LINE_LENGTH+1,COL+ytext(YPOS+1) : print
WRD$(Z_NUMBER)
290 rem draw a box around the text
300 box SWITCH(Z_NUMBER,0),SWITCH(Z_NUMBER,1) to
SWITCH(Z_NUMBER,2),SWITCH(Z_NUMBER,3)
310 rem set up screen zone
320 set zone
Z_NUMBER,SWITCH(Z_NUMBER,0),SWITCH(Z_NUMBER,1) to
SWITCH(Z_NUMBER,2),SWITCH(Z_NUMBER,3)
330 next COL
340 next ROW : return
350 rem check zone
360 Z=zone(0) : if Z=0 or mouse key=0 then return
370 gosub 440 : rem invert
380 rem display chosen word
390 if TYPE(Z)=NOUN then locate 0,5 : print space$(39) :
locate 0,5 : print "Noun number ";MEANING(Z)
400 if TYPE(Z)=VERB then locate 0,5 : print space$(39) :
locate 0,5 : print "Verb number ";MEANING(Z)
410 if TYPE(Z)=EXIT then locate 0,5 : print space$(39) :
locate 0,5 : print "Direction number ";MEANING(Z)
420 wait 10 : gosub 440
430 return
440 rem Invert a box
```

```
450 wait 5 : gr writing 3 : ink 1 : bar
SWITCH(Z,0),SWITCH(Z,1) to SWITCH(Z,2),SWITCH(Z,3) : gr
writing 1 : return
460 rem define words making up the control panel
470 rem actions
480 data " Get ",VERB,1," Drop",VERB,2," Look",VERB,3,"
Say",VERB,4
490 data " Attack",VERB,5," Throw",VERB,6,"
Drink",VERB,7," Eat",VERB,8
500 data " Search",VERB,9," Feel",VERB,10
510 rem objects
520 data " Room",NOUN,1," Knife ",NOUN,2," Wine",NOUN,3,"
Cat ",NOUN,4
530 data " Letter",NOUN,5
540 rem directions
550 data " North",EXIT,1," South",EXIT,2," East",EXIT,3,"
West",EXIT,4," Up",EXIT,5
```

Another idea might be to use the STOS sprites to provide a graphical representation of the objects found in the current location. These could be displayed over a background screen produced from NEOCHROME or DEGAS. The user could then pick up or drop objects directly from the screen using the mouse pointer. This could be implemented using the COLLIDE function to check for a collision between the mouse cursor and the relevant sprite.

6.8 The rooms

Every room in the adventure needs to be lovingly portrayed in a considerable amount of detail. Normally, each room will have two separate descriptions. The long description will be displayed the first time the player enters the room, and whenever the LOOK or DESCRIBE commands are entered.

There will also be a shorter description which will be printed on any subsequent visits.

6.8.1 The long room description

This is a complete word picture of the current room which includes vital information needed to solve the adventure, whilst still stimulating the player's imagination. It is vital that you provide the players with enough information to be able to completely visualise the room, as this will encourage the feeling that they are actually experiencing the adventure. As I mentioned earlier, this is often achieved by packing your description with plenty of adjectives and adverbs. Look at the following portrayal of two identical rooms.

1 *You are in a thirty feet high chamber. There are exits to the chamber to the east via a canyon and to the west through a small passage. A bird is singing.*

2 *You are in a splendid chamber thirty feet high. The walls are frozen rivers of orange stone. An awkward canyon and a good passage exit from the east and west sides of the chamber. A cheerful little bird is sitting there singing.*

The second piece of text is taken directly from the original Colossal cave adventure. Maybe the quality of some of the English is rather strained, but there's no doubt about which of the two descriptions is the more atmospheric.

Another thing to consider is humour. Used sparingly, this can add a nice element of fun to the adventure. But don't be too heavy handed about this. Repeated and unnecessary sarcasm can get very irritating after a while, and there's nothing so unfunny as a really bad joke. Unless you regard yourself as the next Douglas Adams, it's risky to try to base your game totally around humour. On the other hand, if you have a really terrific idea, maybe it's worth the risk.

6.8.2 The short room description

This is a one line summary of the current location. It is used to briefly describe a room which the player has already seen. The room in the previous example could have a short description like:

SPLENDID CHAMBER

6.8.3 Storing the room descriptions

Once you have written out the descriptions for each room, you will need to enter them in the ST's memory. Each room in your adventure will be assigned an individual identification number. I'll be showing you shortly how this number can be used to print out the descriptions as the player enters a room.

There will also be a STATUS array which will hold the list of rooms which has been visited by the player. This will be used to choose between the short or long room descriptions.

Whenever a room is entered, the relevant numbers in the array can be set to one. Your program can now automatically select the required mode with just a single test, e.g.

```
if  STATUS(ROOM)=0 then print long$ else print small$
```

As with many aspects of games programming, there are literally dozens of possible storage strategies.

Here are a few ideas.

1 Store each description in a string array. This could be defined using a line like:

```
10 dim desc$(100),sum$(100)
```

These strings can be loaded during initialisation, either from a file on the disk or from a list of data statements in your program. The appropriate descriptions could then be printed out using a line like:

```
1000 print desc$(current_room)
```

In practice there are a couple of inherent problems with this approach. If you load your descriptions from the disk, then you will be forced edit the appropriate file from outside STOS Basic in order to change a single line of your text.

So it's very hard to modify your adventure once you have created the original data file. Alternatively, if you store the description as a list of data statements, then you will be permanently stuck with two separate copies of your text in the ST's memory.

2 Access the descriptions directly from a set of DATA statements. Providing you arrange the data statements used for each location to start a specific distance apart, you can print out your room descriptions with the following code.

```
1000 restore 30000+100*current_room:read D$:print D$
```

This works by assuming that the line numbers containing the data for each successive room descriptions always are exactly 100 units apart, starting from line 30000, e.g.

```
30000 data "room 1"
30100 data "room 2"
```

You could also store all the short descriptions using the exactly the same system. These might be placed in the data statements from lines 40000 onwards.

The appeal of this second technique is that it makes it extremely easy to edit the room descriptions using the standard STOS Basic editor. Furthermore, this system is ideal for magazine publication, as it's possible to input the adventure directly from a printed page.

On the other hand, the first method is much faster, and can be recommended if you wish to sell your game commercially.

6.8.4 Displaying your descriptions

The STOS Basic windowing system allows you to divide up the game screen effortlessly between text and graphics. It also lets you create custom designed character sets for use with your adventure. These can be produced using the FONT definer program supplied with the STOS Basic package.

Here is a small example which illustrates this technique. Insert the STOS accessories disk into drive A and load a set with:

```
load "font2.mbk"
10  rem Using windows.
15  rem Open a window using the character set
20  rem See page 164 of the STOS manual for a full explanation
30  windopen 1,1,1,39,20,0,4
40  window 1:rem Activate window
50  home
60  print "Enter some text >";a$
70  if a$<>"" then 60
80  default
```

It's important to restrict the number of windows on the screen to the absolute minimum needed by the game. If you try to pack too much information onto the screen at once, the user will end up totally confused.

The prime consideration when designing a font should always be readability. It's ridiculous wasting your time and effort to create a fancy character set which is difficult for the player to actually read.

6.8.5 Moving between rooms

So far, I haven't included any mechanism to allow the player to move between the various rooms. Generally, this will be implemented by creating a map in memory of the connections between each room in the adventure. This map will contain a list of all the rooms which are accessible from a given location.

Supposing you had defined eight possible movement directions in your adventure. Each direction would be associated with a number. North might be represented by direction number one, south by direction two, etc.

You could now store the entire map in an array like:

```
dim map(no_of_locations,8)
```

After this array had been initialised, you could then find the result of moving the player's character in any direction simply by checking one of the elements in MAP. This element would be set to either zero (for no exit) or to the number of the room which could be reached in the chosen direction, e.g.

```
1000 exit=map(room,direction):if exit=0 then print "You
can't go that way" else room=exit
```

The map array will require 32 bytes for each room in your adventure. Unfortunately, most of this space will be completely wasted, as few locations have the maximum of eight different exits.

If your adventure is really large, it's possible to reduce some of this overhead by only holding the exits from the current room in your map array. The rest of the map can be held in a similar way to the room descriptions, either in a the form of a data statements or on a file on the disk.

This simplified system is much slower than the first approach because the map needs to be updated constantly after the player's movements. It can, however, save your program a great deal of memory.

The easiest way to understand about these maps is to create one yourself. So I'll demonstrate the process with a little worked example. Look at the map in Figure 6.5 on the next page.

We begin by defining the list of allowable directions in our adventure.

Direction	*Identifier*
north	1
south	2
east	3
west	4
north east	5
north west	6
south east	7
south west	8

We will now produce the connection list for Figure 6.5. Each location will be associated with several pairs of numbers. The first number will represent an allowable movement direction, and the second will indicate a room that can be reached in that direction.

After a few minutes work, you should be left with the following table of numbers:

Table 6.1 Typical Connection list

Location	*Name*	*Connections*
1	Bridge	1,4 4,2 3,3 2,6 7,5
2	Airlock	3,1
3	Rec Area	4,1
4	Obs Deck	2,1
5	Quarters	8,1 4,6
6	Gangway	2,7 1,1 3,5
7	Engine room	1,6

The obvious problem with this type of list is that it is impossible to read directly. This would cause you serious difficulties when you were entering the map definitions, as it would be disconcertingly easy to make a mistake. It would also be very hard to extend your adventure once it had been written. Luckily, there's a really neat way of entering this data into the computer which can simplify your table enormously.

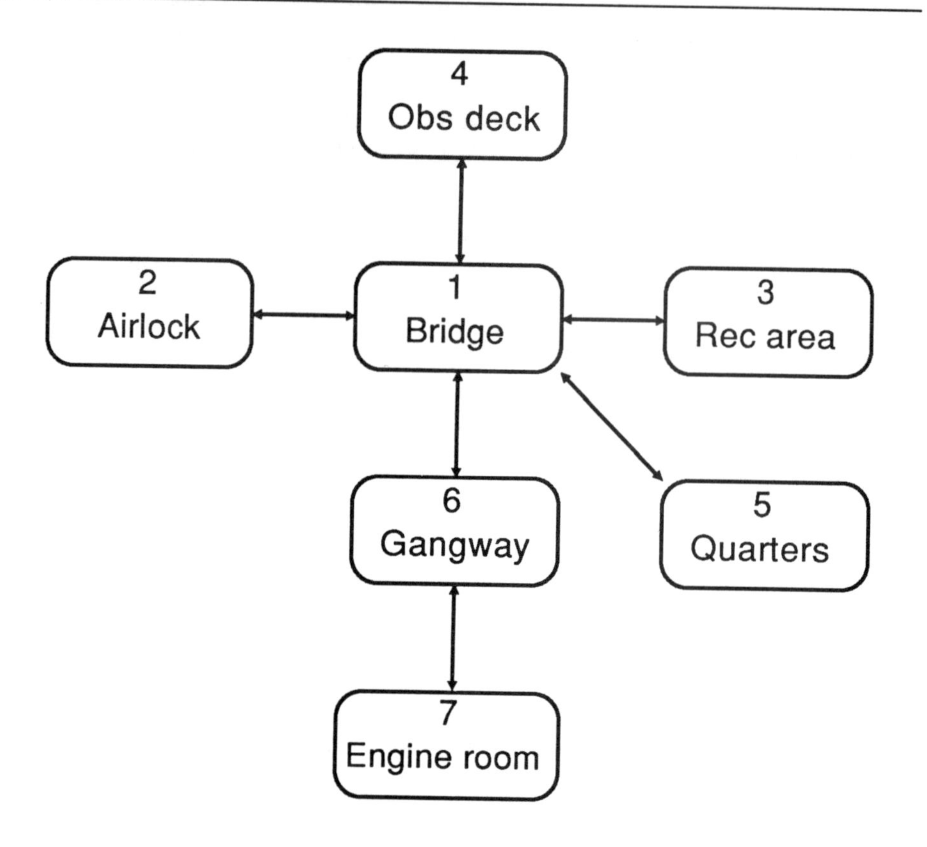

Figure 6.5 A typical room map

You start off by defining a list of constants for the various possible directions at the beginning of your program, e.g.

```
50 n=1:s=2:e=3:w=4:ne=5:nw=6:se=7:sw=8
```

You can now type the entire table directly into the computer in the following way:

```
50000 data N,4,W,2,E,3,S,6,SE,5:rem room 1
50001 data E,1:rem room 2
50002 data W,1:rem room 3
50003 data S,1:rem room 4
50004 data NW,1,W,6:rem room 5
50005 data S,7,N,1,E,5:rem room 6
50006 data N,6:rem room 7
```

As you can see, this data is much easier on the eye. If you subsequently wanted to connect room five to room three, you could now modify lines 50001 and 50002 to something like:

```
50002 data W,1,S,5:rem room 3
50004 data NW,1,W,6,N,3:rem room 5
```

Note that if you need to encrypt this data prior to publication in a magazine, you can replace these constants with the actual numbers using a series of CHANGE instructions from the editor, e.g.

```
CHANGE "N," to "1,":rem the comma avoids confusion with
CHANGE "S," to "2,":rem variables like NOTICE
```

Certain adventures also allow the player to move in unusual directions such as IN or OUT. Instead of defining a whole new direction for just a couple of locations, it's normally advisable to interpret these directions using the local command system I will be showing you a little later.

6.9 The objects

6.9.1 Choosing the objects

The next step in the creation of your game, is to decide on the nature and position of the **objects** you will be including in your adventure. These form the tools which will be used by the player to solve the puzzles, and survive the cunning traps you are eagerly preparing for the adventure.

It's important to realise that when I'm referring to an object, I'm actually talking about a vast range of possible entities. For the purposes of my discussion, an object can be treated as literally anything that can be manipulated by the player. Some objects can be picked up and examined, but others are much more intangible. Here is a list of the common objects which can be found in an adventure:

keys	Can be used to unlock doors
doors	Doors may be opened
holes	May be fallen into, or just looked in!
spells	Cannot be examined or picked up but may be CAST
buttons	Which can be pressed
red herrings	Intended simply to waste the player's time.

Whilst you are choosing your objects it's a good idea to jot down a few of the possible verbs which could be used to manipulate them. This will prove very helpful when you finally start generating the list of words required for the parser.

Each object in your adventure will be assigned it's own unique identification number. This will be used to refer to the object in the program. When you are starting your adventure, it's best to assign these numbers to a list of constants. This allows you to refer to an object directly, without having to look up its number in a table, e.g.

```
10000 CARROT=1:rem carrot is object 1
10010 WATCH=2:rem watch is object 2
```

You can now test for the presence of the carrot using a like like:

```
if NOUN=CARROT then print "What's up doc!"
```

6.9.2 The current location

In order to manage the objects in your adventure successfully, it's necessary to store a number of pieces of information. These include:

The **current location**. This is simply the room number where the object can be currently found. It is normally stored in a location array as follows:

```
1010 DIM OBJECT_LOC(1000):rem Where there are a maximum of
1000 objects.
```

Depending on the nature of your adventure, there will usually be several special locations:

Uncreated	The object has yet to be discovered or created in the adventure. It is effectively in limbo until your program assigns it to a specific location
Carried	The object is carried by the player
Worn	This means that the object is currently worn by the character.
Part	The object is part of another object. It cannot therefore be manipulated directly

These locations can be assigned numbers outside the allowable range of locations.

Depending on the nature of your adventure, there may well be other special locations which I haven't mentioned. So don't feel inhibited about extending these definitions to fit the needs of your adventure precisely.

Not all of the objects in your adventure can be carried by the character. You therefore need to treat any immovable objects separately in your program. One idea, is to define an array to store the weight of every object which appears in the adventure. Alternatively, you can use some sort of coding scheme to distinguish movable from fixed objects.

It's also important to have some way of storing the text which describes how each object will be seen by the player. Since these descriptions are usually rather short, it's easiest to keep them in an normal array, for example:

```
dim object$(1000)
```

Finally, there is the ITEM array which I mentioned earlier. This holds the object number which is associated with any particular word. It is used to convert a raw word number into a reference to a specific object in the adventure.

6.9.3 The inventory

When the character moves through the adventure, any objects being carried will need to be moved accordingly. This can be accomplished the storing the identification numbers of the required objects in an array.

```
dim INV(20)
```

The size of this array determines the maximum number of objects that can be carried by the player. This inventory can be printed out at any time using the following code:

Example 6.6 Inventory command

```
4000 rem INVENTORY
4001 APPARENT=0 : print "You are carrying"
4002 if CARRIED=0 then print "nothing" : return
4005 for I=1 to 20
4010 O=INV(I) : rem Get object number carried
4011 rem if object is carried then describe object
4015 if OBJECT_LOC(O)=CARRY then print OBJECT$(O) :
APPARENT=1
4016 next I : if APPARENT=0 then print "nothing"
4017 print
4020return
```

6.10 Handling the events

All the events in your adventure will be controlled through a set of variables known as **flags.** Flags store all the various pieces of information needed to determine the outcome of an event, or the fulfilment of a condition.

Here are a few examples of how these flags might be used in practice:

SAFE_OPEN	Set to 1 if the safe was open, otherwise 0.
ALIVE	Set to 0 if the player is killed. Normally 1.
TORCH	Stores the number of turns the current torch will last.
HUNGER	Set when the player is hungry.

It's theoretically possible to store these flags using normal Basic variables. Were you to attempt this approach in reality, you would be forced to save each variable by name during your SAVE game option. This would be unbelievably tedious, and it would be easy to miss out an essential variable from the list during development. It is much safer to hold the main variables in a single array. This could be defined from your Basic programs as follows:

```
dim v(1000)
```

You could now refer to each flag using the index; then the FOOD flag might correspond to V(1), the TORCH flag to V(2), etc.

You can simplify this notation considerably by substituting a previously defined basic variable for some of these numbers. This clarifies your program by allowing you to refer to the flags using an actual name, eg.

```
v(torch)=10:rem torch=1
```

Each of these variables would need to be defined separately during the initialisation process:

```
10000 torch=1:safe_open=2:alive=3:hunger=4
```

You could later remove these variables using the STOS CHANGE command. This would stop an unscrupulous player searching through the program text for hints.

As I stated earlier, the possible events which can happen to the adventurer can be divided into three different categories:

- ❑ High priority – Performed at the start of the control loop.
- ❑ Low priority – Executed at the end of the control loop.
- ❑ Local – Local to a specific room.

Here is a simple example of how a high priority event could be implemented:

```
5000rem DEATH
5010if v(alive)=1 then return:rem Player's character is
alive
5015rem If character dies, jump out of routine
5020pop:goto 20000:rem Another Game?
```

The "alive" flag might be set by a global event as follows:

```
6000rem HUNGER
6010dec v(hunger)
6020if v(hunger)<0 then print "I'm Hungry":v(hunger)=0
6030if v(hunger)<-5 then print "I'm starving"
6040if v(hunger)<-10 then print "If I don't eat something
soon I'll probably die!"
6050if v(hunger)<-15 then "I've starved to DEATH!":
v(alive)=0
6060return
```

Remember that the only essential difference between a high priority event and a low priority event is the order they are executed in the program. Otherwise, the programming techniques required to generate them are exactly the same. Both events can be implemented directly in your program as part of the main control loop.

Local events are best dealt with by assigning a separate subroutine to each location in the adventure. These subroutines will normally also include the program statements needed to interpret any local commands.

Here's a typical local event:

```
10000 rem Local event
10010 rem The pit
10015 rem leg and fallen are variables defined
10016 rem during initialisation
10020 if v(fallen)=1 then return:rem player already fallen
10030 v(fallen)=1:? "Arrgh! I've fallen down a pit!"
10040 If v(leg)=0 then ? "I think I've broken my leg!" else
"My leg really hurts"
10050 v(leg)=v(leg)+1:return:rem Break a leg
```

Alongside this routine, there would need to be a global event called OUTSIDE, which reset v(fallen) to zero if the player had managed work out some way of escaping from the pit.

6.11 Acting on the user's commands

In order for an adventure to work, there has to be some way of interpreting the player's commands, and choosing the relevant action. I've already shown you how you can convert these instructions into a numerical format using the parser. Assuming the VPN system from Example 6.3, the following information will be available to your interpretation routines.

VERB	Contains the number of the verb which has been input by the user
NOUN(1)	First noun
NOUN(2)	Second noun. 0 if it doesn't exist
PREP	Preposition
D	Direction number. This is set to zero if the user hasn't entered a direction.
COUNT	Number of words in the line

6.11.1 Global commands

Global commands may be entered at any point in the adventure. Each global command is executed using a single STOS Basic subroutine. GET, and DROP are typical of these global commands. Here are their definitions:

Example 6.7 GET and DROP

```
4025rem GET
4030if NOUN(1)=ALL then gosub 4150 : return
4035 rem GET object
4040 OBJECT=NOUN(1) : rem Get object number
4045 if OBJECT_LOC(OBJECT)<0 then ? "You can't pick up
";OBJECT$(OBJECT) : return
4050 if OBJECT_LOC(OBJECT)=CARRY then ? "But you are already
carrying ";OBJECT$(OBJECT) : return
4055 if OBJECT_LOC(OBJECT)=WEAR then ? "You'll need to
remove it first" : return
4060 if OBJECT_LOC(OBJECT)=0 then ? "But there isn't a
";WRD$(2);" here" : return
4065 if OBJECT_LOC(OBJECT)<>ROOM then ? "I can't see
";OBJECT$(OBJECT) : return
4070 rem Object is really here
4075 inc CARRIED : rem increase number of items carried
4080 if CARRIED>20 then print "It's too heavy" : return
4085 rem Get object
4090 print "You picked up ";OBJECT$(OBJECT) : return
4090 if NOUN(1)=ALL then gosub 4170 : return
```

If you examine this example carefully, you will probably be wondering why I bothered to sort the INV array at line 5080. This is necessary to allow you to search through it using the MATCH command

```
4100 rem Drop
4105 OBJECT=NOUN(1) : rem Get object number
4110 O=match(INV(0),OBJECT)
4112 if O<0 then print "But you don't have a ";WRD$(2) :
return
4115 rem Object is really carried
4120 rem Object worn
4125 if OBJECT_LOC(OBJECT)=WEAR then ? "You'll have to
remove ";OBJECT$(OBJECT);" first" : return
4130 INV(O)=0 : rem Set item to zero
4135 rem Sort inventory and push the current item to the
4140 sort INV(0) : dec CARRIED
4144 ? "You dropped ";OBJECT$(OBJECT) :
OBJECT_LOC(OBJECT)=ROOM
4145 return
4150 rem GET ALL
4150 APPARENT=0
4155 for I=1 to NO_OF_OBJECTS
```

```
4160 if abs(OBJECT_LOC(i))+ROOM then NOUN(1)=i : gosub 4035
: APPARENT=1
4165 next I
4166 if APPARENT=0 then print "There's nothing here!"
4167 return
4170 rem DROP ALL
4175 for I=1 to 20
4180 if INV(I)<>0 then NOUN(1)=INV(I) : gosub 4100
4185 next I : return
```

The standard way of calling a global command is to load an array with the locations of the various subroutines. You can now execute all global commands using a single line:

```
IF GLOBAL(VERB) then gosub GLOBAL(VERB)
```

Obviously you would need to remember that the GLOBAL array would need to be defined at the start of your program.

Finally, I'll provide you with a LOOK command which prints out a description of the current room:

Example 6.8 LOOK

```
7000rem LOOK
7005 rem G is a flag set to 1 when the use types LOOK
7006 rem But when the routine is called automatically G=0
7010 if V(VERBOSE)<>1 and STATUS(ROOM)=1 and G<>1 then
restore 40000+ROOM-1 : read D$ : print D$ : return
7015 rem long description
7020 restore 30000+100*(ROOM-1) : read DS : for L=1 to DS :
read D$: print D$ : next L : STATUS(ROOM)=1
7030 for I=1 to NO_OF_OBJECTS
7040 if abs(OBJECT_LOC(I))=ROOM then ? "There is
";OBJECT$(I)
7050 next I : return
```

6.11.2 Local commands

Some commands only make sense when the adventurer is occupying a specific location. A safe, for instance, can only be opened if the player is actually standing in front of it.

It's simplest to use the same subroutine to handle both local events and commands. This reduces the complexity of your program by performing all local operations in one place. Each location in your adventure will have its own individual routine. The starts of these routines will be held in an array like the GLOBAL array I showed you earlier.

You can now call up any local commands at the current room using a line in the control loop like:

```
if LOCAL(ROOM) then gosub LOCAL(ROOM)
```

Where LOCAL is assumed to have been defined during your programs initialisation section.

Note that this instruction includes an allowance for the fact that not all rooms need individual handler routines. It only tries to execute a subroutine if the appropriate element has been loaded into the local array. This enables you to pad out your adventure with many similar rooms without having to write a specific subroutine for each new location.

Remember that the local events are usually controlled using flags, and that commands are interpreted using the variables VERB, NOUN, and PREP. Here is an example of one these routines:

```
11000 rem Airlock
11005 rem open,spacesuit,air,out,go,door, alive
11006 rem are variables defined earlier
11010 if verb=open and (noun(1)=d00r or noun(1)=lock) then
v(air)=1:v(d00r)=1
11020 if v(air)=1 and v(spacesuit)=0 then ? "The air rushes
out of the airlock leaving you to die horribly.":? "You'll
never destroy that koala now!":v(alive)=1:return
11035 if v(air)=1 and v(d00r)=1 then "The door opens
smoothly. There is a meteor outside":v(door)=0:return
11040 if v(air) and verb=out or (verb=go and noun(1)=out
then room=5:return:rem move out
11045 return
```

6.11.3 System commands

System commands provide the user with the ability to interact directly with the program. Common system commands are LOAD, SAVE and VERBOSE. Here are a few useful definitions for your game:

```
170 rem call high priority event routines here
185 gosub 1000 : rem split up words
186 rem Check for system command
187 X=instr(SYS$,WRD$(1)) : rem search through list
188 if X=0 then 200 : rem word not found
189 X=X/6+1 : rem get command number
190 on X gosub 8070,8000,8140,8200,4000:rem jump to routine
200 rem call low priority events here
300 return
```

Example 6.9 SAVE, LOAD, and VERBOSE

```
8000rem Save game
8005F$=file select$("*.ADV","Save an adventure")
8010if F$="" then print "Save game aborted" : return
8011if len(F$)<4 then boom : goto 8005
8015if right$(F$,4)<>".ADV" then boom : goto 8005
8020open out #1,F$
8025rem save position and status
8030print #1,ROOM : print #1,SCRE
8035rem save flags
8040for I=0 to NO_OF_FLAGS : ? #1,V(I) : next I
8045rem save object locations
8050for I=0 to NO_OF_OBJECTS : ? #1,OBJECT_LOC(I) : next I
8065 print "Ok" : close #1 : return : rem that's all
8070 rem Load game
8075 F$=file select$("*.ADV","Load a game")
8080 if F$="" then print "Loading aborted" : return
8081 if len(F$)<4 then boom : goto 8075
8085 if right$(F$,4)<>".ADV" then boom : goto 8075
8090 open in #1,F$
8095 rem load position and status
8100 input #1,ROOM : input #1,SCRE
8105 rem load flags
8110 for I=0 to NO_OF_FLAGS : input #1,V(I) : next I
8115 rem load object locations
8116 CARRIED=0
8117 for I=0 to 20 : INV(I)=0 : next I : rem zero inventory
8120 for I=0 to NO_OF_OBJECTS : input #1,OBJECT_LOC(I)
8125 rem load inventory
8130 if OBJECT_LOC(I)=CARRY then INV(CARRIED)=I : inc
CARRIED
8135 next I : sort INV(0) : print "Ok" : close #1 : return
8140 rem Quit
8145 input "are you sure (Y,N) ";A$
8150 if A$<>"Y" and A$<>"y" then return
8155 print "You scored ";SCRE;" points" : pop : stop
8200 rem verbose
8210 V(VERBOSE)=not(V(VERBOSE))
8220 if V(VERBOSE)=0 then ? "Verbose off" else ? "Verbose on"
8230 return
```

6.11.4 Movement commands

The movement commands allow the player to move through the various locations in the adventure. Depending on the storage strategy you have chosen, a list of the possible exits will be found either in the MAP array or on the appropriate data statements in the program.

You can now interpret the player's movements using a routine such as:

```
3000 rem Move
3040 if MAP(ROOM,D)<>0 then ROOM=MAP(ROOM,D) : DONE=1 else
print "You can't go that way"
3050 return
```

6.12 Conclusions

If like me, you're a fan of adventures, it's well worth the effort involved to write one of your own. You'll probably find that the process of creating an adventure is actually even more fun than playing someone else's.

I've already provided you with all the elements you need to generate your own adventure in a matter of hours. Many of these routines compare favourably with those included in dedicated adventure creators costing over thirty pounds. So there's now no reason why you can't produce a perfectly commercial adventure directly within STOS Basic. After all, it's not often you get a perfectly legitimate chance to play God!

7

3D Techniques

7.1 Introduction

One day in the not-too-distant future, it's possible that we will be able to play our computer games using some sort of three-dimensional "holographic" display. Despite decades of accumulated research on this project however, the immediate prospects for such a development look depressingly bleak. This causes a severe difficulty for anyone trying to write a flight simulator game for the Atari ST. These games need to capture the illusion of movement through three-dimensional space. How can we possibility generate this type of display on a flat computer screen?

Fortunately for us, computer scientists have had to live with this problem for a long time, and have developed a vast repertoire of potent solutions to most of the more pressing requirements. These enable the skilled programmer to produce a good visual representation of any three-dimensional object on a standard display.

The amount of material which has been amassed on this subject is literally awesome, and a comprehensive explanation of the entire field could easily take up several books in its own right. Furthermore, much of the available information is highly technical and would prove unpalatable to the vast majority of potential readers.

I'll therefore restrict myself to a brief discussion of some of the more important concepts, without worrying about any of the complicated technical details. The intention is to concentrate on the practical aspects of the subject, giving only a cursory explanation of the complex mathematics required for a complete understanding. If you wish to explore the subject in more depth, I can recommend Uwe Braun's in depth analysis of the subject in *"3D Graphics techniques on the ST"* (see Bibliography).

7.2 Creating an object in 3D

7.2.1 Coordinate systems

Coordinate systems allow you to produce a complete description of the position and size of any object in three-dimensional space using a simple list of numbers.

The position of an object is represented using three numbers, which roughly correspond to the grid references of a map.

All measurements are taken from an arbitrary reference point known as the **origin.** The distances from the origin to the object are taken in three directions which are at right angles to one another. These directions are normally indicated using the letters X,Y, and Z.

Think of the coordinates in terms of a map. The Y value specifies the distance of the object from the ground, and the Z and X values measure the distances in the directions north/south and east/west respectively. Depending on the scale of the map, the units used for the coordinates can be anything from an inch to a light year.

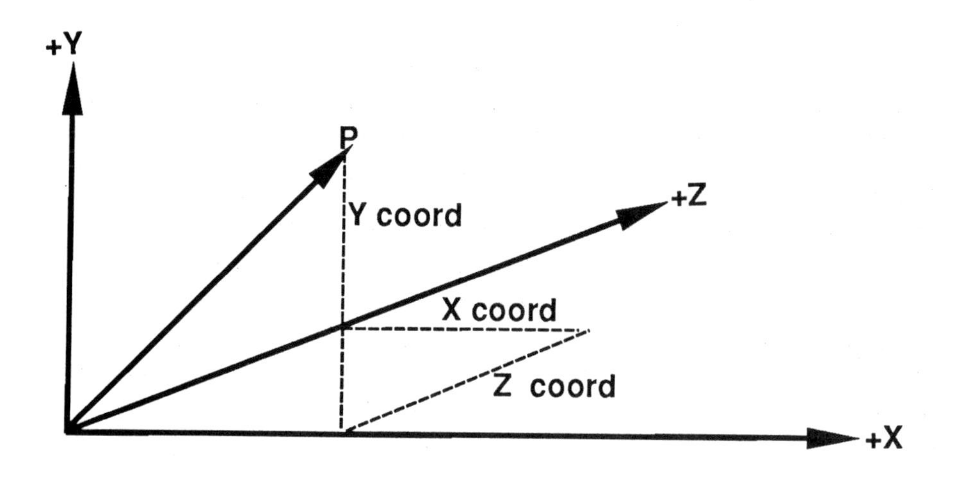

Figure 7.1 The position of a single point in 3D

The scale of these units can be set independently for each of the three directions. So you could measure the height of an object in units of a thousand feet, but its horizontal coordinates in miles.

You can also arbitrarily choose the directions in which the measurements will be taken. These directions would usually be selected during the planning stages of your game to simplify your calculations as much as possible. It's common practice to obey the following conventions:

- X values to the right of the origin are considered to be positive and distances to the left are treated as negative.
- Positive values of Y usually measure a point which is above the origin, with negative values being reserved for the points below.
- There is no fixed rule for the measurement of the Z-coordinate. For the purposes of my discussion, the Z-axis will form a line at right angles to your TV screen

pointing inwards. So a positive value will represent a point behind the screen, and a negative value a point in front of it.

Since I'm intending to use the screen as a window to an imaginary game world, I'll only be dealing with objects occurring on the far side of the screen. The Z-coordinates of these objects will therefore always be positive.

The example in Figure 7.1 only dealt with a single point, but it's perfectly feasible to represent infinitely more complicated objects using exactly the same system. Each corner point in the object is specified using its own individual set of three coordinates.

Take the pyramid in Figure 7.2. This has five corners labelled A to E. A typical set of coordinates for this pyramid would be:

Corner	*X*	*Y*	*Z*
A	0	10	0
B	0	0	5
C	5	0	0
D	0	0	-5
E	-5	0	0

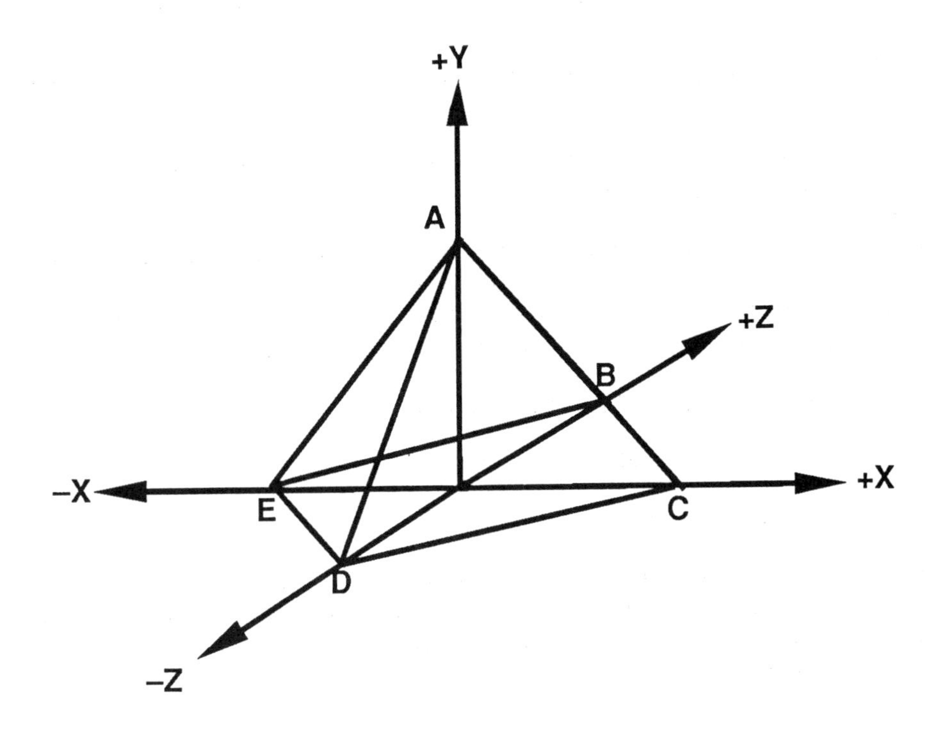

Figure 7.2 A simple 3D pyramid

These coordinates are usually abbreviated to a list of numbers enclosed between curved brackets. The standard format is:

(X,Y,Z)

So the coordinates describing the points of the pyramid could be represented as simply:

(0,10,0),(0,0,5),(5,0,0),(0,0,-5),(-5,0,0).

7.3 General techniques

I'll now briefly discuss a couple of general techniques which can be used to manipulate these sets of coordinates. These will form the groundwork for many of the 3D graphics routines I will be introducing in this chapter.

7.3.1 Moving the origin

As I've said before, the origin of your coordinates is completely arbitrary. You can change this reference point at any time, without affecting the relationships between any of the points which make up your object. This can be done using a process known as transformation. All transformations can be accomplished using the following stages:

1 Find the distances between the old origin and the new one in each of the three directions.

2 Subtract these distances from the appropriate values of every point you have defined in your coordinate system.

It's easiest to demonstrate this technique with an example. Look at the triangle in Figure 7.3 on the next page. This has been subjected to a transformation of the origin from (0,0,0) to (0,100,0). Before the transformation was performed, the coordinates of the points A and B were (50,50,0) and (100,50,0) respectively.

These coordinates have now been transformed into:

A=(50-0,50-100,0-0)=(50,-50,0)

B=(100-0,50-100,0-0)=(100,-50,0)

Note that although the coordinates may have changed, the distances between any two points such as A and B are remain exactly the same. The transformation hasn't actually moved anything. It's merely changed the reference point used for the measurement of the coordinates.

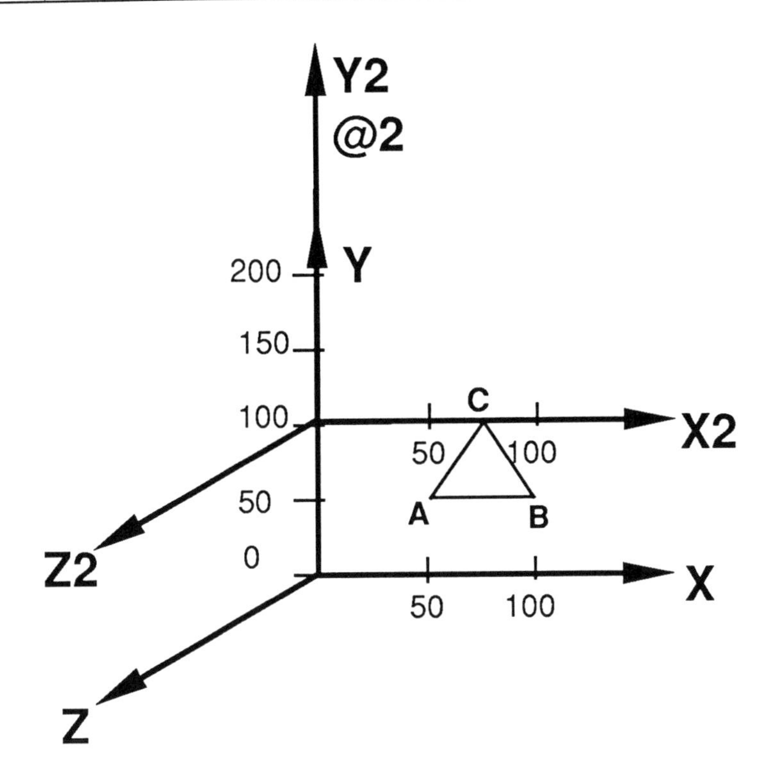

Figure 7.3 Transformation of coordinates

7.3.2 Scaling an object

Scaling is a simple process which allows you to enlarge or reduce the size of an object. This can be done by multiplying the coordinates by a known as a scaling factor. If the absolute value of this number is greater than one then distances between the various points in the object will expand. This will lead to an increase in the size of the object. Similarly, a scaling factor which lies in the range between zero and one, will produce a reduction effect.

Figure 7.4 on the next page shows the result of scaling a pyramid by a factor of two. After the scaling operation, the coordinates would be changed as follows:

Old coordinates:

(0,10,0),(0,0,5),(5,0,0),(0,0,-5),(-5,0,0)

New coordinates:

(0,20,0),(0,0,10),(10,0,0),(0,0,-10),(-10,0,0).

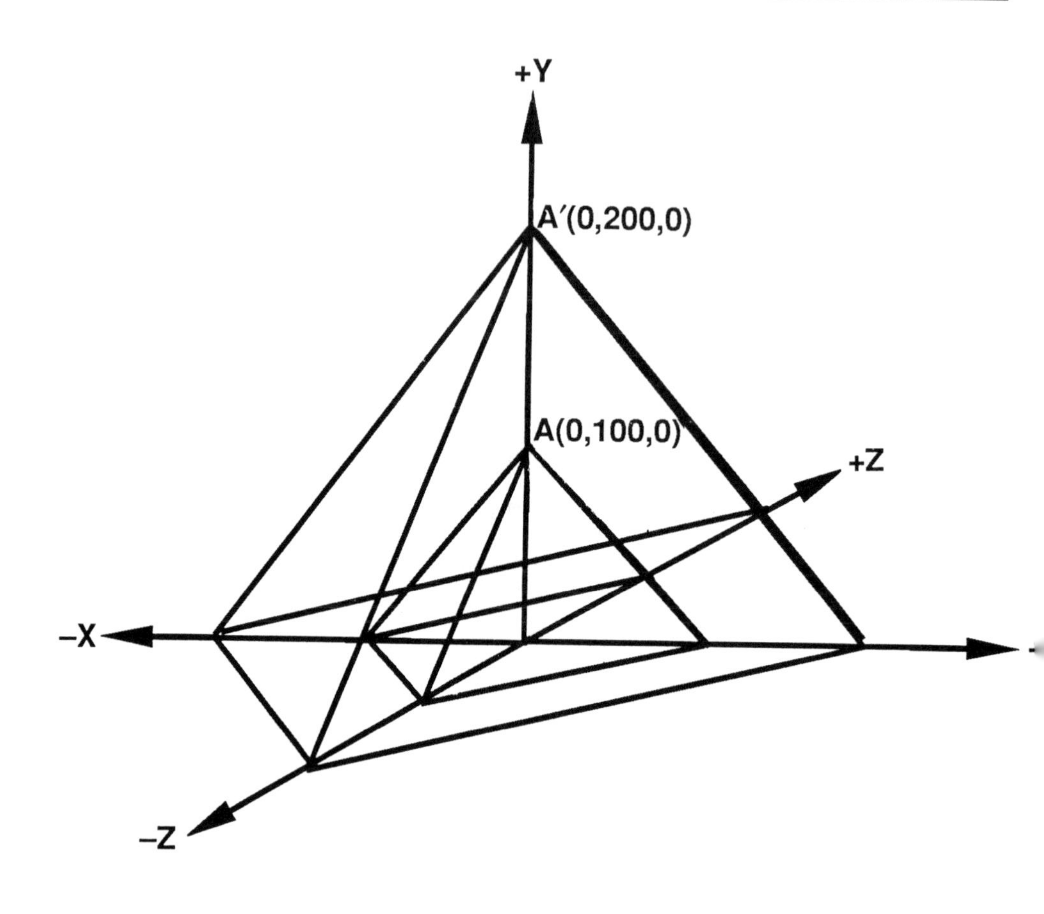

Figure 7.4 Scaling a pyramid

You could now reduce this pyramid back to its original size by multiplying it by a scaling factor of 0.5.

The example in Figure 7.4 was centred on the origin. If you were to scale an object some distance away from this point, the object would appear to jump away from the centre. Far from being an annoyance, this feature, shown in Figure 7.5 on the next page, is actually useful, because it forms the basis of the perspective calculations I will be discussing presently.

If you want to avoid this movement, you need to transform the coordinates of the origin to the centre point of the object before you perform the scaling operation. You can then scale your object as required, and reverse the process to move it back to its original starting point. This results in the object changing in size, while apparently staying fixed in space.

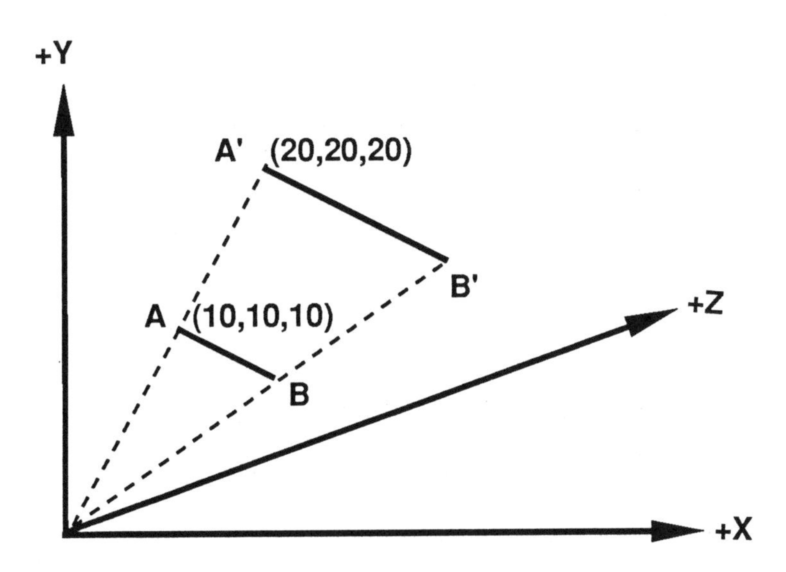

Figure 7.5 Scaling an object apart from the centre

7.4 Displaying an object in 3D

I'll now show you how some of these techniques can be applied to produce an accurate representation of a three-dimensional object on your computer screen.

7.4.1 Perspective

The drawing process relies on an effect called perspective, which has been tacitly understood by artists for centuries. The basic idea can be summarised by the following rule:

The apparent size of an object varies in proportion to its distance from the observer.

This means that the further away you are from an object, the smaller it will appear. If you move twice as close to an object, then the object will seem to double in size. But as you move away, the object will gradually fade into the horizon.

This fact is of course, intuitively obvious. It's used by our brains to judge the relative distances of objects in the world around us, and this is an ability which we pick up during early infancy.

There are however, a number of peculiar side effects. If you look at a three-dimensional object such as a cube, the face which is further from you will look slightly smaller than the face which is nearest to your eye. The edges of the cube will therefore apparently converge somewhere in the centre of your field of vision. Look at the cube in Figure 7.6 below.

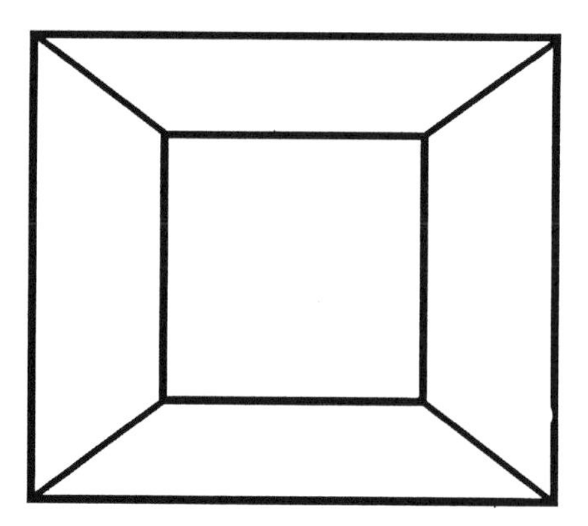

Figure 7.6 Representation of a cube in three dimensions

Because the lines in this figure converge according to the rules of perspective, our brains automatically assemble it into a realistic three-dimensional cube.

The point at which the horizontal lines in a picture meet is known as the **vanishing point.** You can see this convergence more clearly from the parallel railway tracks in Figure 7.7 on the next page. The vanishing point occurs when the two tracks merge together into the distance.

Artists have long applied this idea to produce their landscapes and room interiors. They would start their picture by marking the vanishing point somewhere in the centre of the canvas. They would then sketch in several lines stretching from the vanishing point to the edges of the frame. These lines could be used as guidelines for the perspective effect. Any lines in the picture which were parallel to the ground (along the Z-axis) could now be drawn by following the guidelines. This would generate a convincing illusion that the picture was set in a real three-dimensional world.

Particularly clever artists, like M.C Esher, even played tricks with the rules of perspective, and painted seemingly sensible pictures which bent reality in strange and impossible ways. These resulted in the complete confusion of the viewer's sense of perspective, which were totally mindboggling. Literally. When you examine these pictures, your brain is unable to cope with the contradictory visual information. It therefore keeps switching back and forth between several impossible viewpoints. This is disconcertingly weird.

In order to harness the perspective effect on a computer, it's necessary to condense some of these ideas into a comprehensive set of mathematical equations. Since the

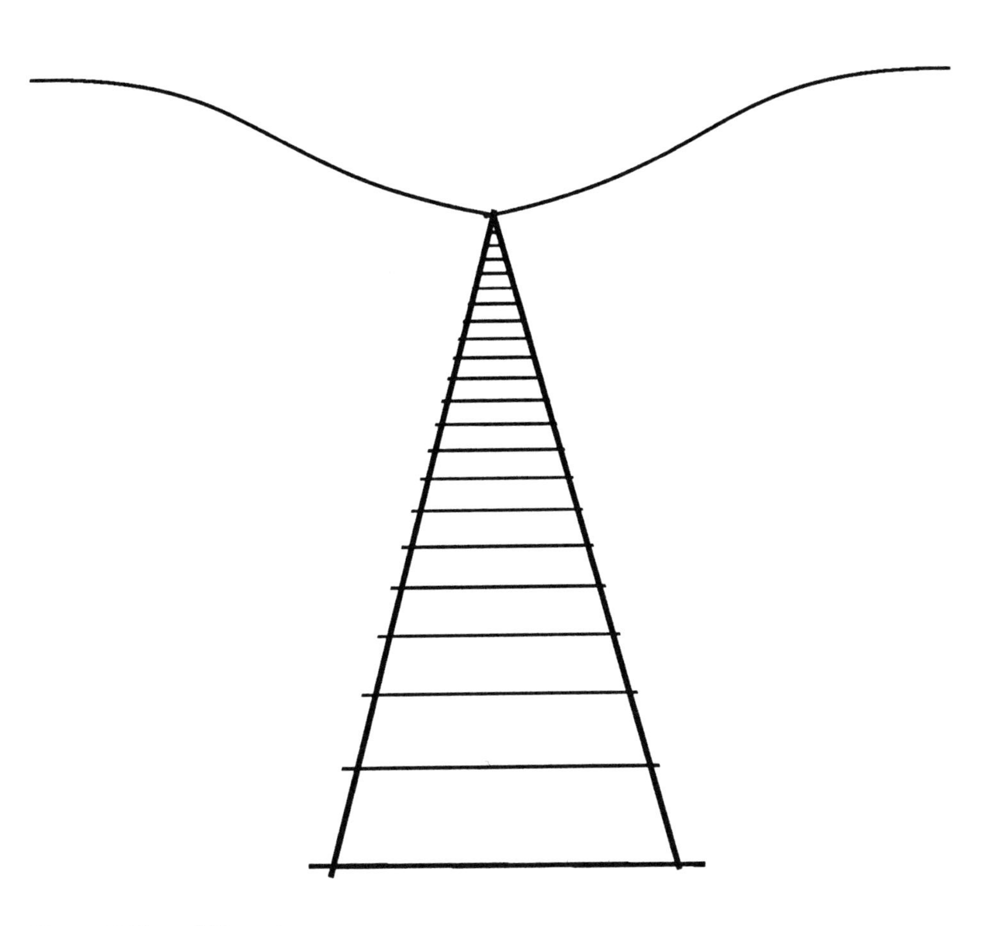

Figure 7.7 The vanishing point

images seen by the eye are focused using an organic lens mechanism, it's possible to derive these formulae directly from an understanding of the physics of lenses. Rather than present you with yet another slice of boring O-level physics, I'll limit myself here the results of these calculations.

The apparent size of an object displayed on a computer screen can be found by the following equation:

apparent size = real size * perspective factor

The perspective factor is a just multiplier used to change the visible size of the object. The magnitude of this factor depends on the relationship between the distance of your eye from the screen, and the total distances between the eye and the object. This is shown in Figure 7.8 on the next page.

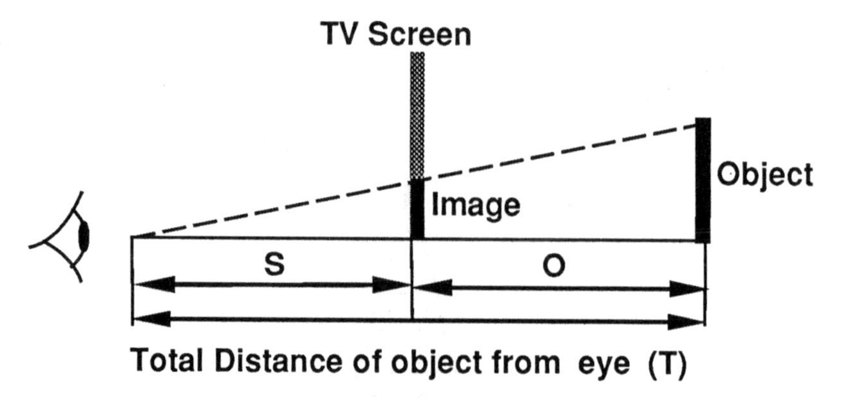

Figure 7.8 Perspective

The perspective factor can be computed from the formula:

perspective factor = S/T

Where:

S = The distance from the eye to the screen, and
T = The total distance from the eye to the object

From the diagram in Figure 7.8, it can be seen that T is the distance from the eye to the screen (S) added to the distance of the object behind the screen (O).

So:

perspective factor = Real size * S/(S+O)

It's vital to realise that the viewing distance S is just an imaginary figure. If S is very small relative to O, then the image will look unnaturally expanded. The effect of this is very similar to that of a wide-angle lens on a camera. Conversely, if S is proportionally large compared to O then the display will seem to be compressed into the distance.

The number you use for the viewing distance depends only on the effect you want to create. It does NOT depend on the actual distance of the viewer from the ST's screen. This will vary according to the user's personal preferences, and is largely irrelevant to your calculation. Otherwise you would be forced to include a ruler with your game with instructions to the players to position their heads correctly. This would be very silly, although it would certainly provide your players a little harmless amusement!

If you assume that the centre of the viewing screen lies at the origin of the coordinate system, and that the positive part of the Z-axis extends directly into the screen, then the following equations can be derived:

X=X*S/(S+Z)	Perspective correction for X coord	(1)
Y=Y*S/(S+Z)	Perspective correction for Y coord	(2)

Notes:

1 These equations can be used to convert a set of three game world coordinates into the X, Y coordinates used by the ST screen. Since the screen is at the origin, the distance of any point from the screen (O) will be given directly by its Z coordinate.

2 These equations only strictly apply if the origin lies at the centre of the screen. Unfortunately, the ST's drawing operations work using an origin at the top left hand corner. The formulae therefore need to be modified slightly using the transformation techniques I showed you earlier.

If your program held the centre point of the screen the variables CX and CY, equations (1) and (2) can be extended to:

VX=CX+X*S/(S+Z) (3)

The directions of measurement in the Y-axis used by the screen coordinates and the game coordinates are completely opposite. You can correct for this by multiplying the Y-coordinates by minus 1. (This is effectively a rotation of 180 degrees. See later)

VY=(Y*S/(S+Z)-CY)*-1

or

VY=CY-Y*S/(S+Z) (4)

VX and VY are the coordinates required by the STOS Basic drawing commands. The appropriate points can now be plotted directly on the screen using PLOT.

In a computer game, the corner points in the object would be connected with straight lines. All objects would need to be represented using two arrays. One array would contain a list of the three game world coordinates for each point. The other array would hold a list of the lines connecting these corners to form the finished object. I'll now demonstrate these techniques with an example program:

Example 7.1 3D drawing routine

```
10  rem Simple 3D drawing routine
20  auto back off : rem See optimization techniques in C 1
30  CX#=320/divx : CY#=200/divy : rem get centre of screen
40  OX#=0 : OY#=0 : OZ#=100 : rem Object coords in game world
50  read NP : rem Read number of points in object
60  dim OBJECT#(NP,3),VIEW#(NP,3),VX(NP),VY(NP)
70  rem load points
80  for I=1 to NP
```

```
90  for J=0 to 2
100 read OBJECT#(I,J)
110 next J : next I
120 read NL : rem read number of lines
130 dim LINES(NL,2) : rem dimension line array
140 for I=0 to NL-1
150 read LINES(I,0),LINES(I,1)
160 next I
170 rem main program
180 input "Viewing distance";S#
190 if S#<1 then print "Viewing distance must be >0 " : goto
180
200 input "Ship coordinates X,Y,Z";SX#,SY#,SZ#
210 input "Object coordinates X,Y,Z";OX#,OY#,OZ#
220 if OZ#<50 then print "That's much too close" : goto 210
230 rem Copy object definition into view array
240 for I=1 to NP
250 VIEW#(I,0)=OBJECT#(I,0)+OX#-SX#:rem transform origin
260 VIEW#(I,1)=OBJECT#(I,1)+OY#-SY#:rem to screen centre
270 VIEW#(I,2)=OBJECT#(I,2)+OZ#-SZ#
280 next I
290 rem calculate perspective
300 for P=1 to NP
310 O#=VIEW#(P,2) : rem get Z coordinate of point
320 PERS#=S#/(S#+O#) : rem get perspective factor
330 VX(P)=CX#+VIEW#(P,0)*PERS# : rem Get screen coordinates
340 VY(P)=CY#-VIEW#(P,1)*PERS#
350 next P
360 rem Draw lines
370 cls physic : cls back
380 hide on
390 for I=0 to NL-1
400 rem get starting ending points of line
410 X1=VX(LINES(I,0)) : X2=VX(LINES(I,1))
415 Y1=VY(LINES(I,0)) : Y2=VY(LINES(I,1))
420 draw X1,Y1 to X2,Y2 : rem draw line
430 next I
440 screen copy physic to back : show on
450 goto 180
700 rem define corner points of a cube
705 rem This can be changed for any other object
706 rem number of coordinates in the object
710 data 8
715 rem corner point 1
720 data-50,-50,50
725 rem corner point 2
```

```
730 data 50,-50,50
740 data 50,-50,-50
750 data-50,-50,-50
760 data-50,50,50
770 data 50,50,50
780 data 50,50,-50
790 data-50,50,-50
800 rem define the connecting lines
805 rem Number of lines in the figure
810 data 12
812 rem pairs of points to be connected
820 data1,2,2,3,3,4,4,1,5,6,6,7,7,8,8,5,8,4,7,3,6,2,5,1
```

Since this program is rather complicated, it's worth spending a little time explaining some of the various features.

On startup you will be asked to input the viewing distance S. This is needed by the perspective calculations. A good value to start with is about a hundred. Try playing with larger or smaller viewing distances to see the effects.

The program makes use of four separate coordinate systems. One set is held in the OBJECT array, and contains a list of coordinates measured relative to the centre point of the object. The OBJECT coordinates enable you to define an object without having to worry about its eventual position in space. It also allows you to generate several similar objects from just one set of coordinates. This is very useful for games like Elite, because it allows you to create a large game world out of a few simple components.

The second set of coordinates refer to the absolute position of the object in a three-dimensional map of the game world. These "game world" coordinates are used by your program to determine the relative positions of several objects in three-dimensional space. The example program prompts you for the starting coordinates of both the cockpit and the object. These are entered in the order X,Y,Z and are loaded into the variables SX#, SY#, SZ# and OX#, OY#, OZ# for the ship and the object respectively.

Start with a set of coordinates like:

```
0,0,0  (For the ship)
0,0,50 (For the object)
```

Keep the value of OZ# greater than fifty, otherwise the program may try drawing the cube from a viewpoint behind the screen!

Note that to simplify the program, I've been forced to assume that the view port always points in the positive direction of the Z-axis. I'll be showing you how this can be changed in the section on 3D rotations.

The VIEW array holds a copy of these points after they have been transformed to an origin at the centre of the cockpit's screen. It's needed as a temporary copy of the game world for the perspective calculations. You are recommended to recreate the view coordinates from scratch every time the object is redrawn. This will avoid the risk of rounding errors in the ST's calculations which can reduce your display to a hopeless jumble.

Finally, there are the arrays VX and VY which hold the actual screen coordinates. These hold the list of actual points which will be plotted on the screen after the perspective calculations have taken place. The starting and ending points of the lines are held in the LINES array. These lines can be plotted directly using the DRAW command from STOS Basic.

Summary of the coordinate systems

Object coordinates – These are used to define the size and shape of the objects in your game.

Game world coordinates – Specifies the position of an object in the game world.

View-port coordinates – These are measured relative to the cockpit's centre and are needed for the perspective calculations.

Screen coordinates – Hold the final coordinates of the points on the ST's two dimensional screen after the perspective calculation.

If you play around with this program, you'll probably find that it occasionally terminates with an "ILLEGAL FUNCTION CALL" error. This is caused by an attempt to display an object which was too large to fit on the ST's screen. The solution to this problem is to perform an activity known as clipping.

7.4.2 Clipping

A clipping routine checks whether a line will fit on the screen before drawing it. If the line is too big, it truncates it to fit in the available space.

Don't be mislead by the STOS Basic CLIP instruction. This is only intended for use with windows, and has no facilities for handling objects larger the total screen area.

Surprisingly enough, there has been a great deal of research into these clipping techniques. As the majority of clipping systems are extremely complicated, I'll restrict myself here to just a brute force approach. If you want to explore more advanced clipping routines, I can recommend Data Becker's *3D graphics programming*, as it contains a full description of the popular "Cohen and Sutherland" technique.

The easiest clipping method is to check each coordinate explicitly with an IF THEN statement. In my previous example, this could be accomplished by the following code:

```
410 gosub 470:rem call clipping routine
415 rem Draw line if one or more points lie inside screen
420 if VPX<2 and VPY<2 then draw X1#,Y1# to X2#,Y2#
455 rem note that I've assumed a mode 0 screen
456 rem you'll need to change some of the constants
467 rem for other resolutions
460 rem perform clipping
470 VPX=0 : VPY=0 :rem Set visible point checks
475 G#=0:rem set gradient of a line
480 X1#=VX(LINES(I,0)) : X2#=VX(LINES(I,1)):rem coords
490 Y1#=VY(LINES(I,0)) : Y2#=VY(LINES(I,1)):rem are REAL
495 rem calculate gradient
500 if X2#-X1#<>0 then G#=(Y2#-Y1#)/(X2#-X1#) else 610
510 if G#=0 then 610
515 rem check whether a point lies outside the screen
516 rem and calculate the intersection point with the screen
520 if X1#<0 then Y1#=Y1#-X1#*G# : X1#=0 : inc VPX
530 if X2#<0 then Y2#=Y2#-X2#*G# : X2#=0 : inc VPX
540 if X1#>319 then DX#=X1#-319 : X1#=319 : Y1#=Y1#-DX#*G# :
inc VPX
550 if X2#>319 then DX#=X2#-319 : X2#=319 : Y2#=Y2#-DX#*G# :
inc VPX
560 if Y1#<0 then X1#=X1#-Y1#/G# : Y1#=0 : inc VPY
570 if Y2#<0 then X2#=X2#-Y2#/G# : Y2#=0 : inc VPY
580 if Y1#>199 then DY#=Y1#-199 : Y1#=199 : X1#=X1#-DY#/G# :
inc VPY
590 if Y2#>199 then DY#=Y2#-199 : Y2#=199 : X2#=X2#-DY#/G# :
inc VPY
600 return
605 rem Gradient = 0 or infinite so line is horizontal or
vertical
610 if X1#<0 then X1#=0 : inc VPX
620 if X2#<0 then X2#=0 : inc VPX
630 if X1#>319 then X1#=319 : inc VPX
640 if X2#>319 then X2#=319 : inc VPX
650 if Y1#<0 then Y1#=0 : inc VPY
660 if Y2#<0 then Y2#=0 : inc VPY
670 if Y1#>199 then Y1#=199 : inc VPY
680 if Y2#>199 then Y2#=199 : inc VPY
690 return
```

As you can see, even a simple-minded approach looks unpleasantly messy when it's actually implemented! The basic idea of my routine is to check each corner point in the line to see if it lies on the screen. If the program is dealing with just a simple vertical or horizontal line, this can be safely truncated at the edge of the screen.

For other lines your program is required to calculate the coordinates of the point where the line overruns the ST's screen. This can be performed by getting the slope of the line using the equation of a straight line:

Slope = (Y2-Y1)/(X2-X1)

It is now possible to compute the required intersection point needed by your routine. The result is by no means perfect, but the routine does produce an acceptable effect in the majority of cases, without the overhead of a really fancy clipping algorithm. Suffice it to say, you may make full use of this routine in your own programs.

The variable VPX holds the number of X coordinates in the line which have been clipped, and VPY holds the number of Y coordinates. If either VPX or VPY is greater than 2, both the starting point and the ending point of the line will lie outside the screen. In this case, it's safe to ignore the line completely.

7.5 3D rotation

Most flight simulators require you to fly an aeroplane through a complicated series of manœuvers in the game world. The attitude of the craft is often controlled using the joystick. As the joystick is pulled back, the angle of flight will be altered accordingly.

7.5.1 Rotation directions

When dealing with these angles, it's common practice to measure all rotations parallel to one of the three axes. Rotations in an anti-clockwise direction are considered positive, and clockwise rotations are negative.

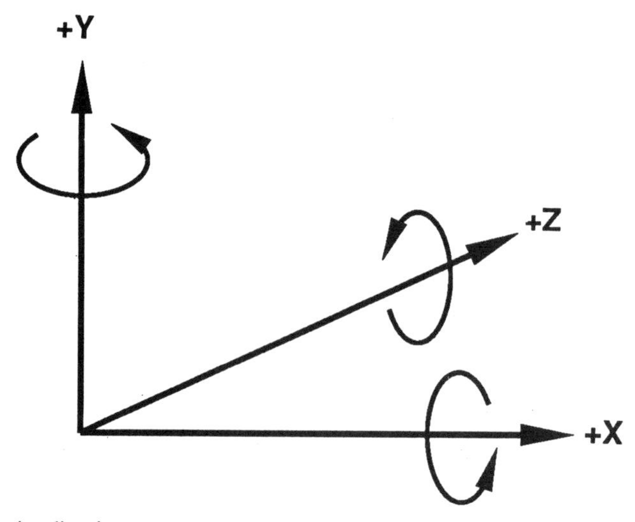

Figure 7.9 Rotation directions

If the ST's joystick is pulled up or down, then the heading will usually be rotated parallel to the X-axis. The effect of moving the joystick to the left/right direction will however, vary from game to game. Sometimes it controls the heading parallel to the Z-axis, and other times it changes the current heading along the Y-axis.

7.5.2 The 3D rotation formulae

All of these rotation effects can be generated using the same set of simple formulae. As in the case of the perspective equations, I'll produce these equations out of thin air, avoiding the problem of derivation completely. Frankly, the derivation isn't complicated, and should only prove an minor challenge to anyone with an A-level in mathematics. (Hint, use the addition formulae for SIN and COS to get the new rotated coordinates).

Here are the equations for these rotations:

Rotation parallel to the X-axis

All X coordinates are unchanged. The Y- and Z coordinates need to be computed using the formulae:

```
new z =(Old Y)*SIN(XA)-(Old Z)*COS(XA)          (5)
new y = (Old Y)*COS(XA)+(Old Z)*SIN(XA)         (6)
```

Where:
XA is the angle of rotation parallel to the X-axis

Rotation parallel to the Y-axis

```
new Y = Old Y (Unchanged)
new X = (Old X)*SIN(YA)-(Old Z)*COS(YA)         (7)
new Z = -(Old X)*COS(YA)-(Old Z)*SIN(YA)        (8)
```

Where:
YA is the angle of rotation parallel to the Y-axis

Rotation parallel to Z-axis

```
new Z = Old Z (Unchanged)
new X = (Old X)*COS(ZA)-(Old Y)*SIN(ZA)         (9)
new Y = (Old X)*SIN(YA)+(Old Y)*COS(ZA)         (10)
```

SIN and COS describe ratios between the various sides of a right angled triangle. The relations can be seen in Figure 7.10. If you're still slightly unsure, it's worth mentioning that both of these functions are included as part of the STOS Basic system. So you can happily use them in the rotation equations without worrying how they actually work.

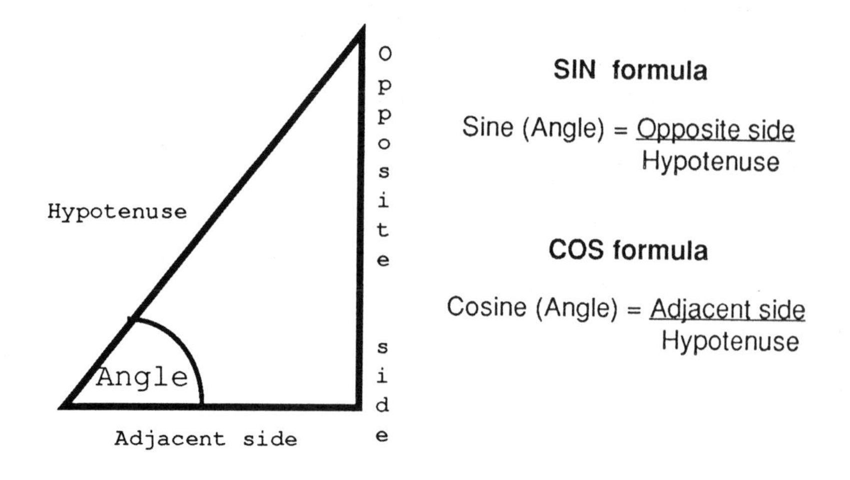

Figure 7.10 (SIN and COS)

The use of these equations in can be seen in Example 7.2.

Example 7.2 (3D rotation)

```
10  rem 3D experimenter program
15  rem By Stephen Hill
16  rem See optimization techniques in Chapter 2
20  auto back off
30  mode 0 : cls physic : cls back : curs off : hide on
35  rem title screen
40  windopen 1,10,5,20,18 : curs off
50  print : centre "3D Experimenter" : print : print
55  centre "By Stephen R Hill"
60  locate 0,5 : centre "Press:"
65  locate 0,7 : centre "<RETURN> to run" : locate 0,9
66  centre "<HELP> for options"
70  X$=inkey$ : if scancode=98 then windel 1 : gosub 1440 :
goto 80
75  if X$="" then 70 else windel 1
76  rem get centre of screen
80  CX#=160 : CY#=100 :rem change for modes 1 or 2
90  OX#=0 : OY#=0 : OZ#=100 : rem Object coords in game world
100 read NP : rem Read number of points in object
110 dim OBJECT#(NP,3),VIEW#(NP,3),VX(NP),VY(NP)
120 rem load points
130 for I=1 to NP
140 for J=0 to 2
```

```
150 read OBJECT#(I,J)
160 next J : next I
170 read NL : rem read number of lines
180 dim LINES(NL,2) : rem dimension line array
190 for I=0 to NL-1
200 read LINES(I,0),LINES(I,1)
210 next I
220 rem main program
230 gosub 900 : rem position ship and object
240 gosub 380 : gosub 450 : gosub 530
250 XA=0 : YA=90 : ZA=0
260 rem main loop
270 repeat
280 ROTATED=0 : COZ#=OZ#:rem Save centre coordinate
290 X$=inkey$ : SK=scancode:rem get keypress
300 if SK=98 then gosub 1450:rem call help menu
305 rem Handle function keys VIEW coords
310 if SK>58 and SK<=68 then FK=SK-58 : on FK gosub
980,1000,1020,1040,1060,1080,1100,1120,900,1140
314 rem if rotated then copy OBJECT to VIEW (gosub 380)
315 rem perform X rotation (gosub 1160)
316 rem perform Y rotation (gosub 1260)
317 rem perform Z rotation (gosub 1260)
318 rem determine perspective (gosub 450)
319 rem draw lines (gosub 530)
320 if ROTATED then gosub 380 : gosub 1160 : gosub 1260 :
gosub 1360 : gosub 450 : gosub 530
325 rem display status
330 locate 0,19 : print "Distance =";OZ#-SZ#
340 locate 0,20 : print "X-angle=";XA;" Y-angle =";YA;
345 print " Z-angle=";ZA;
350 until true=false:rem repeat loop forever
360 curs on:rem just in case
370 stop
380 rem Copy object definition into view array
390 for I=1 to NP
400 VIEW#(I,0)=OBJECT#(I,0)+OX#-SX#
410 VIEW#(I,1)=OBJECT#(I,1)+OY#-SY#
420 VIEW#(I,2)=OBJECT#(I,2)+OZ#-SZ#
430 next I
440 return
450 rem calculate perspective
460 for P=1 to NP
470 O#=VIEW#(P,2) : rem get Z coordinate of point
480 PERS#=S#/(S#+O#) : rem get perspective factor
```

```
490 VX(P)=CX#+VIEW#(P,0)*PERS# : rem G#et screen
coordinates
500 VY(P)=CY#-VIEW#(P,1)*PERS#
510 next P
520 return
530 rem Draw lines
540 cls physic
550 rem check if object is behind ship
560 if COZ#<0 then return
570 for I=0 to NL-1
580 rem perform clipping
590 gosub 660
595 rem if at least one point is visible then draw line
600 if VPX<2 and VPY<2 then draw X1#,Y1# to X2#,Y2#
610 next I
620 return
640 rem perform clipping
650 rem change clip coordinates for modes 1 and 2
660 VPX=0 : VPY=0 : G#=0
665 rem get starting and end points of line
670 X1#=VX(LINES(I,0)) : X2#=VX(LINES(I,1))
680 Y1#=VY(LINES(I,0)) : Y2#=VY(LINES(I,1))
685 rem is slope positive
690 if X2#-X1#<>0 then G#=(Y2#-Y1#)/(X2#-X1#) else 800
695 rem is slope zero
700 if G#=0 then 800
705 rem get intersection point
710 if X1#<0 then Y1#=Y1#-X1#*G# : X1#=0 : inc VPX
720 if X2#<0 then Y2#=Y2#-X2#*G# : X2#=0 : inc VPX
730 if X1#>319 then DX#=X1#-319 : X1#=319 : Y1#=Y1#-DX#*G# :
inc VPX
740 if X2#>319 then DX#=X2#-319 : X2#=319 : Y2#=Y2#-DX#*G# :
inc VPX
750 if Y1#<0 then X1#=X1#-Y1#/G# : Y1#=0 : inc VPY
760 if Y2#<0 then X2#=X2#-Y2#/G# : Y2#=0 : inc VPY
770 if Y1#>199 then DY#=Y1#-199 : Y1#=199 : X1#=X1#-DY#/G# :
inc VPY
780 if Y2#>199 then DY#=Y2#-199 : Y2#=199 : X2#=X2#-DY#/G# :
inc VPY
790 return
795 rem horizontal or vertical line
800 if X1#<0 then X1#=0 : inc VPX
810 if X2#<0 then X2#=0 : inc VPX
820 if X1#>319 then X1#=319 : inc VPX
830 if X2#>319 then X2#=319 : inc VPX
840 if Y1#<0 then Y1#=0 : inc VPY
```

```
850 if Y2#<0 then Y2#=0 : inc VPY
860 if Y1#>199 then Y1#=199 : inc VPY
870 if Y2#>199 then Y2#=199 : inc VPY
880 return
890 rem set initial conditions
900 cls : ROTATED=true
910 input "Viewing distance";S#
920 if S#<1 then print "Viewing distance must be >0 " : goto
910
930 input "Ship coordinates X,Y,Z";SX#,SY#,SZ#
940 input "Object coordinates X,Y,Z";OX#,OY#,OZ#
950 if OZ#<50+SZ# then print "That's much too close" : goto
940
960 curs off : return
970 rem Add 10 to X angle
980 XA=XA+10 : ROTATED=1 : return
990 rem Subtract 10 from X angle
1000 XA=XA-10 : ROTATED=1 : return
1010 rem Add 10 to Y angle
1020 YA=YA+10 : ROTATED=1 : return
1030 rem Subtract 10 from Y angle
1040 YA=YA-10 : ROTATED=1 : return
1050 rem Add 10 to Z angle
1060 ZA=ZA+10 : ROTATED=1 : return
1070 rem Subtract 10 from Z angle
1080 ZA=ZA-10 : ROTATED=1 : return
1090 rem move ship forwards
1100 SZ#=SZ#+10 : ROTATED=1 : return
1110 rem move ship backwards
1120 SZ#=SZ#-10 : ROTATED=1 : return
1130 rem stop
1140 pop : curs on : show on : clear key : stop
1150 rem rotate object along X-axis
1160 RXA#=rad(XA) : rem Trig functions work in radians
1170 SN#=sin(RXA#) : CS#=cos(RXA#)
1175 rem Get distance of object centre from cockpit
1180 COZ#=-COZ#*CS#+(OY#-SY#)*SN#
1185 rem rotate the object data in VIEW
1190 for I=1 to NP
1200 Y#=VIEW#(I,1) : Z#=VIEW#(I,2)
1210 NZ#=Y#*SN#-Z#*CS# : rem new z coord
1220 Y#=Z#*SN#+Y#*CS# : rem new y coord
1230 VIEW#(I,1)=Y# : VIEW#(I,2)=NZ#
1240 next I : return
1250 rem rotate object along Y-axis
1260 RYA#=rad(YA) : rem Trig functions work in radians
```

```
1270 SN#=sin(RYA#) : CS#=cos(RYA#)
1275 rem Get distance of object centre from cockpit
1280 COZ#=-(OX#-SX#)*CS#-COZ#*SN# : rem get z coord of
centre
1285 rem rotate the object data in VIEW
1290 for I=1 to NP
1300 X#=VIEW#(I,0) : Z#=VIEW#(I,2)
1310 NX#=X#*SN#-Z#*CS# : rem get new X coor
1320 Z#=-X#*CS#-Z#*SN# : rem get new Y coord
1330 VIEW#(I,0)=NX# : VIEW#(I,2)=Z#
1340 next I : return
1350 rem rotate object along Z-axis
1360 RZA#=rad(ZA) : rem Trig functions work in radians
1370 SN#=sin(RZA#) : CS#=cos(RZA#)
1375 rem rotate the object data in VIEW
1380 for I=1 to NP
1390 X#=VIEW#(I,0) : Y#=VIEW#(I,1)
1400 NX#=X#*CS#-Y#*SN# : rem get new x coord (9)
1410 Y#=X#*SN#+Y#*CS# : rem Get new y coord (10)
1420 VIEW#(I,0)=NX# : VIEW#(I,1)=Y#
1430 next I : return
1440 rem help menu
1450 windopen 1,10,5,20,18 : curs off
1460 print : centre "Function keys" : print : print
1470 print "F1 : Increment XA"
1480 print "F2 : Decrement XA"
1490 print "F3 : Increment YA"
1500 print "F4 : Decrement YA"
1510 print "F5 : Increment ZA"
1520 print "F6 : Decrement ZA"
1530 print "F7 : Move closer"
1540 print "F8 : Move away"
1550 print "F9 : New position"
1560 print "F10: Exit program"
1570 locate 0,14 : centre "<RETURN> to resume" : wait key :
wait 10 : windel 1 : cls physic : cls back : clear key : return
1575 rem a rectangular block
1580 data 8:rem eight points
1590 data-50,-50,50
1600 data 50,-50,50
1610 data 50,-50,-50
1620 data-50,-50,-50
1630 data-50,50,50
1640 data 50,50,50
1650 data 50,50,-50
1660 data-50,50,-50
```

```
1670 rem lines
1680 data 12:rem twelve lines
1690 data1,2,2,3,3,4,4,1,5,6,6,7,7,8,8,5,8,4,7,3,6,2,5,1
```

As this program is rather involved, I'll provide you with a complete pseudo-code description of its main activities.

Table 7.1 Breakdown of the 3D experimenter program

Action	*lines*	*Comments*
Initialise program	10	Load object array
	120	Loads object coordinates into OBJECT
Load line array	170	Loads LINES with connections between corners
Set viewing position	230	Calls routine at line 900
Set position of ship	930	
Set position of object	940	
Copy OBJECT data into VIEW	240	Calls subroutine at 380
Calculate perspective	240	Calls subroutine at 450
Draw object	240	Calls subroutine at 530
Set initial conditions	250	See Note 1
Repeat	270	Main loop
Reset ROTATED flag	280	if user changed anything ROTATED=true
Load COZ# with OZ#	280	COZ# is used by the check for visibility, see Note 2
Get a keypress	290	
Test <HELP> key	300	Help menu at 1440
Input command	310	See Note 3
If heading is changed	320	
Then		
Copy OBJECT to VIEW	380	
Perform X-rotation	1160	
Perform Y-rotation	1260	
Perform Z-rotation	1360	
Compute perspective	450	
Draw object	530	
Endif		
Print status	330	
Until true=false	350	Do forever

Notes:

1 YA# is measured anti-clockwise from the Y-axis. A viewpoint along the Z-axis therefore corresponds to a heading of 90 degrees.

2 This variable is used to determine the relative distance from the ship to the object along the Z-axis. If this value is negative, then the object is currently behind the ship, and should not be drawn. (See section 7.6)

3 The reason I'm using SCANCODE rather than ON FKEY is that I need the scancode for the <HELP> menu. Alas, the ON FKEY command will not work in conjunction with the INSTR function. I am therefore forced to read the function keys directly using SCANCODE.

Here are few ideas for possible modifications to this program:

1 Add the ability to handle several objects at once. This could be done by extending the object# and view# arrays into another dimension. e.g.

```
dim object#(no,points,3),dim view#(no,points,3)
```

You could then extend the rotation routines to rotate all objects in the current view point.

2 Draw the object on a separate logical screen, and flick between the logical and physical screens. See Chapter 8 on animation.

3 View the object from a range of viewpoints. This can be best accomplished using the following rotations:

Effect	*Rotation*
Back view	Rotate view by 180 degrees on X-axis
Left view	Rotate view by 270 degrees on Y-axis
Right view	Rotate by 90 degrees on Y-axis
Over view	Rotate by 270 degrees on X-axis
Under view	Rotate by 90 degrees on X-axis

7.6 Checking for visibility

If you are writing a full-blown flight simulator, then it's vital to determine quickly which objects will be visible from the current position. This will allow you to reveal the new elements of the game world as they become visible from the player's ship.

If you attempted to individually check each object in your entire game whenever the ship moved, you would be faced with a mammoth task. Most flight simulators contain literally hundreds of objects. Of course, only a few of these objects will be in view at any one time; the vast majority will be too far away to be seen.

The first stage of your visibility check is to split the game world into a number of rectangular zones. This allows you to restrict your tests to the objects in the immediate vicinity of the player's ship, which simplifies things enormously. The sizes and nature of these areas will naturally depend on your game. A genuine flight simulation would set each zone to a particular grid reference on a real map. Other games, like Elite use playing areas the size of an entire solar system.

In order to manage these areas, you need to keep track of the position of every object in a specific area. You might decide to calculate these positions in advance during the creation of your game. It's also possible to allocate the positions randomly whenever a player enters a specific zone. All coordinates will be measured from the centre of the zone to the centre point of your object.

Providing you use the same format to keep track of the coordinates of your spaceship, you can easily determine which objects will be visible from the player's cockpit.

Let's assume, for the purposes of argument, that the coordinates of the object and the player's ship are held in the variables OX, OY, OZ, and SX, SY, SZ.

The object will only be visible if it satisfies the following conditions:

1 The object is in front of the ship. This condition is only true if OZ-SZ is positive.

2 The object is close enough to the ship to be seen. The apparent size of the object depends on the perspective factor. If the perspective factor is negligible, then the object will be too small to be seen from the ship.

3 The object lies within the field of vision enclosed by the cockpit.

Your visibility routine would need to test all these conditions for every object in the current area. This might be accomplished within a small FOR/NEXT loop.

A good demonstration of the first type of check can be found in Example 7.2. This rotates a COZ# along with the coordinates. If COZ# becomes negative, then the object is not drawn on the screen.

Note that the coordinates used in these calculations are relative to the cockpit's centre rather than the current zone. That's why I'm subtracting SX# and SY# in the appropriate formulae.

As the centre point of the object is only an average, it's still possible that some of the points in the object might have a negative Z coordinate, despite the fact that the centre value is positive. In this case, the ship and the object may have collided, and your program should check for this condition accordingly. e.g.

```
425 if O#<=0 then vis(i)=0:goto 510 else vis(i)=1
```

Where:

vis is an array containing one element for each object in the area.
O# holds the current Z coordinate in the perspective calculations.

This line neatly checks for a collision whilst keeping the value of O# positive.

If you try this approach, you need to remember to prevent the drawing operations displaying an invisible object. This can be accomplished using a simple test at the start of the drawing routine.

The second visibility condition is also quite easy. If you restrict the maximum size of the object to the physical dimensions of the ST screen, then the object will disappear from view when the perspective factor reduces each screen coordinate to a number less than one. This occurs when the factor is less than about (1/screen_width).

Every time you multiply this number by an X or Y coordinate, the result will be smaller than one, and the point will not be plotted. You can check for the perspective factor using the centre coordinate OZ. So:

```
if S/(OZ+S)>(1/320) then vis(i)=1 else vis(i)=0
```

Incidentally, if you increase this minimum value, you will reduce the range of visibility of your objects accordingly. This could be very useful for certain types of games.

I'll now show you how you can check for the final visibility condition. The field of vision of your craft is obviously limited to the size of the ST's screen. If the centre point of the object lies outside this area, then part or all of the object will be hidden.

Providing you have assumed that the maximum size of the object in any dimension is less than the maximum screen width, you can test for this condition using the following procedure:

Start off by calculating the perspective values from OX and OY and placing them in PX,PY

```
if (PX<-screen_width) then object to left
if (PX>screen_width*2) then object to right
if (PY<-screen width) then object above
if (PY>screen width*2) Then object below
```

This check is only not completely accurate, and it will inevitably flag some invisible objects as being visible. Fortunately, these objects will be safely handled by your clipping routine without problems.

The same conditions can be extended to check whether an object has crashed into the ship. If the conditions are satisfied when the VIS variable has been set to one, then the object must be immediately in front of the ship, at a distance of zero or less. The only way this condition could be satisfied would be if the two objects had collided!

7.7 Flight simulators

I'll now conclude this chapter with a few ideas about how you could apply some of these techniques to a practical problem such as a flight simulator. These games generally allow several objects to be in the current game area at one time. You would therefore need to expand the OBJECT, VIEW and LINE arrays accordingly:

```
dim objects(total_objects,points_per_object,3)
dim view(objects_per_area,points_per_object,3)
dim line(total_objects,lines_per_object,2)
```

Each object in the game would be defined by its own set of coordinates held in the array OBJECTS. The LINE array would contain the lines used to connect these points into a coherent shape. As I've said before, you would normally split the game world into a number of rectangular zones. Every zone would contain a list of the objects present, and the coordinates of these objects relative to its centre point. This data would be stored in a two-dimensional array which could be created with the lines:

```
dim area(objects_per_area,3)
dim local objects (objects_per_area)
```

The coordinates stored in the area array would be relative to the centre point of the current zone. These coordinates could be added to the coordinate definitions in OBJECT to produce a complete map of each point in 3D space.

Whenever the ship arrived in a new area, the VIEW array would be loaded with the coordinates of every point making up the objects in the zone. The view point would then be transformed to the centre of the cockpit by subtracting the coordinates of the ship from each value in this VIEW array.

The player's ship could now be moved through the area as required. After every movement, the distance travelled would be subtracted from the coordinates in the VIEW array. Similarly, if the objects around the ship moved, then the new distance could be added to the VIEW coordinates.

In real life, changing your viewpoint can be achieved by simply turning your head. If you turn your head to the right, the entire world seems to creep away from the left. Of course, you know that this effect is only an illusion. The real world is fixed, and it's only your field of vision which is being rotated. But in a computer, it's easiest to rotate the actual world, whilst keeping your viewpoint steady. This allows you to use all the perspective calculations I showed you earlier.

When the player changed the heading of the craft, all the points in the VIEW array will be rotated in the opposite direction. This would provide the illusion of a shift in the cockpit's viewpoint. Remember that the VIEW array is completely separate to the object arrays which hold the absolute position of the object. The information it holds is required solely for the creation of the view outside the cockpit's window.

Finally, your program would need to perform the perspective calculations and check for each object's visibility. The screen could now be cleared, and the visible objects redrawn after clipping.

The entire process can be summarised by the pseudo-code listed in Figure 7.11 below.

```
initialise object arrays
load first area
load VIEW array from object definitions
choose a position for the ship
transform coordinate in VIEW relative to cockpit centre
repeat
    if ship moves outside current area
        then
            find new area
            get position of ship relative to area
            load VIEW array from OBJECT definitions
            transform coordinates in VIEW relative to
            cockpit centre
        endif
    update ship's position
    if ship's position changes
        then
            subtract distance moved in all three directions
            from the VIEW coordinates
        endif

    update object's position
    get first object
    Repeat
        if current object has moved
        then
            add distance moved to object data in VIEW
        endif
        if ships heading has changed
        then
            rotate all VIEW coordinates by new heading
        endif
        get next object
    until no more objects

    calculate perspective
    load screen coordinates into VX and VY arrays
    isolate visible objects
    clip screen coordinates
    redraw visible objects
until game over
```

Figure 7.11 Breakdown of a simple 3D flight simulator

7.8 Practical considerations

The necessity to perform many calculations before and after each movement places a considerable burden on your program. However, there are a number of optimization tricks you can use to keep the game moving reasonably quickly.

The best of these is to splash out some money on the STOS Basic compiler. Since I wrote the manual of this package, it's hard to free myself completely from any accusations of bias. But I honestly believe that it is an indispensable part of any STOS Basic development system. Like the rest of the STOS Basic package, there are a number of free extras. The most interesting, is the new STOS version 2.4. This uses single precision mathematics which lead to a dramatic improvement in the execution speed of the SIN and COS functions. Typical speed increases are of the order of twenty times, so you'll probably notice the difference even in your interpreted programs.

And once you've compiled you routines into machine code, you can expect the rest of the program to run considerably faster.

7.8.1 Sine tables

Sine tables allow you to perform many of your calculations in integer arithmetic. The idea is to precalculate all the sine and cosine functions in advance and convert them into integers. These integers are placed in a look-up table which can be accessed from your program, almost instantaneously.

The conversion process starts by calculating the sine of the angles from one to ninety degrees. You now multiply each value by a number which is a power of two, such as 32768. This gives you a result between 0 and 32768 which is placed in a table.

You can now find the sine of a number by simply looking up the value from the table and dividing by 32768. Once you've got the sine table, the cosine of an angle can be derived using the formula:

    cos(angle)=sin(90-angle)

You could incorporate this technique directly into the rotation routines in Example 7.2. Here's a fragment of code which demonstrates this for a rotation parallel to the X-axis.

```
420 s=st(XA)/32768:c=st(90-XA)/32768
430 for i=0 to np-1
440 y#=view(i,2):z#=view(i,3)
450 nz# = Z#*C-Y#*S
460 y*= Z#*S+Y#*C
```

For further information on this system, see the section on look-up tables in Chapter 1.

7.9 Conclusions

By now, you should be well on your way to appreciating the type of problems you will need to solve in order to write your own flight simulator in STOS Basic. I appreciate that this is not the simplest of subjects to comprehend. It's the type of topic which makes even the most hardened computer scientists cringe in their seats. So I do hope I've managed to shed a little light on the topic, and removed some of the mystery from it.

When I first played Elite, I was restricted to a 48K Spectrum. With a little help from the STOS Basic compiler and a great deal of hard work, I'm sure it's possible to beat that original program comfortably using the techniques I've shown you in this chapter. Even if you decide not to attempt to write a simulation game yourself, do have fun playing around with my experimenter program.

8

Animation techniques

STOS Basic provides the games programmer with a host of powerful instructions which greatly simplify the creation of animated screens. This chapter will be explaining how you can exploit some of these features for use in your own games.

8.1 Colour scrolling

8.1.1 Basic principles

The Atari ST allows you to use up to sixteen colours on the screen at any one time. Each colour can be individually selected from a grand total of 512 possible shades. The values for these colours are stored in a set of memory locations known as the colour registers. Whenever one of these registers is updated, the appropriate colour on the screen is altered immediately.

STOS Basic refers to each register by a number from 0 to 15. This number can be used to set one of the registers to a particular colour value using the COLOUR instruction in the following way:

```
colour 1,$700:rem load index one with $700 (RED)
```

Supposing you were drawing a rectangle on the screen using the colour held in register 1. This could be accomplished by the instructions:

```
10 ink 1:bar 100,50 to 200,150
```

What would happen if you were to load one of the other registers with the same shade and then attempted to overwrite the bar with a circle? Well, you can now test this by entering the lines:

```
15 rem Copy colour 1 into register number 2
20 colour 2,colour(1)
30 ink 2:circle 150,100,25
```

When you run this program, the screen seems to be empty except for a large red block near the centre. But appearances are deceptive. This can be seen when you add the following to the program.

```
40 wait key:colour 2,$777
```

Suddenly, a filled circle appears from out of nowhere. This is the circle which was drawn by line 30. Up until now, the circle has been impossible to see, because it was displayed in the same colour as the rectangle underneath. The colour statement at line 40 then loaded colour number two with $777 (white). This made the circle drawn in colour two stand out against the red rectangle.

As far as the ST is concerned, anything drawn using a different colour register is displayed on the screen totally separately. So if two objects are drawn on top of each other using registers containing identical colour values, they will seem to merge together completely. If you subsequently update one of the colour registers, one object will appear to wink into existence above the other. Here's a larger example which demonstrates this idea.

Example 8.1 A moving box

```
10 mode 0 : cls physic : cls back : flash off
11 auto back off : hide on
12 rem Set all colours to black
15 for C=0 to 15 : colour C,0 : next C
20 for I=0 to 2
30 for J=0 to 5
40 ink I*5+J : rem Set ink used for block
50 bar J*50,I*60 to (J+1)*50,(I+1)*60 : rem draw a BAR
60 next J
70 next I
80 rem Animate bar
90 colour 1,$770 : rem first block=yellow
100 for C=2 to 15
110 colour C-1,0 : colour C,$770 : rem Switch block
115 wait 3
120 next C
125 colour 15,0:goto 90
```

Example 8.1 draws fifteen boxes on the screen. Each box is drawn using a different colour index. These registers are all set to zero at the start of the program. So the boxes are indistinguishable against the black background. The program then successively makes each box appear on the screen by manipulating the colour registers using the COLOUR instructions at 110. The result is the illusion of a single box jumping back and forth across the ST's screen.

The same process can be applied to animate any sequence of objects you wish. Remember that when you change a colour, you affect all the objects painted with it.

If you want to animate an object against a colourful background, you will therefore need to keep the colours in the object entirely separate from those in the rest of the display. Also, it is vital to ensure that none of the objects overlap. Otherwise the animation effect simply won't work.

One limitation in Example 8.1, was that your program has to manage all the colour cycling by itself. STOS Basic includes three useful instructions which allow you to perform the entire process automatically.

8.1.2 FLASH

The FLASH command successively changes the value held in any single colour register using an interrupt routine. This can be used to generate a vast range of effects. Try adding the following lines to Example 8.1:

```
12  dim F$(16)
13  rem Save colours
14  for C=1 to 15 : F$(C)=hex$(colour(C))-''$'' : next C
99  rem Set up flash
100 C$=''(0,10)(''+F$(C)+'',''+str$(rnd(10)+1)+'')''
110 flash C,C$
115 wait 3
120 next C
125 colour 15,0
```

The same process can also be used to add a little life to your background screens.

Imagine you were displaying a picture of a computer bank. Each button on the control panel could be made to flash through several different colours. So as you looked at the computer, the display would appear to be continually changing in front your eyes. Since FLASH works independently of your Basic programs, once you have initialised the display, you can forget about the animation completely. Another possible use for this feature would be to create the alert screens found in games such as "Star Trek (TM)".

8.1.3 SHIFT

SHIFT consecutively rotates the values held in the palette through each of the sixteen colour registers. This can be used to produce some stunning effects, which can be glimpsed from the program in Example 8.2.

Example 8.2 The shift command

```
10  hide on : mode 0 : auto back off : cls physic : cls back :
flash off
20  shift 2
40  I=1 : for X=0 to 319 step 2
50  inc I : if I>15 then I=1
```

```
60  ink I : draw 160,100 to X,0
70  next X
80  I=1 : for X=0 to 199 step 2
90  inc I : if I>15 then I=1
100 ink I : draw 160,100 to 319,X
110 next X
120 I=1 : for X=319 to 0 step-2
130 inc I : if I>15 then I=1
140 ink I : draw 160,100 to X,199
150 next X
160 I=1 : for X=199 to 0 step-2
170 inc I : if I>15 then I=1
180 ink I : draw 160,100 to 0,X
190 next X
200 wait key : show on : cls : shift off
```

Example 8.2 generates a beautiful moiré pattern which would look great as your program is loading. It's produced by drawing successive lines in the colours 1 to 15, from the centre of the screen to the edges. When you shift these colours through the available possibilities, you end up with something which looks like a whirling kaleidoscope. SHIFT is perfect for creating the "hyperspace" sequences found in games like "Captain Blood". It can also be used to produce impressive explosion effects.

If you wish to keep part of your display static, you can optionally add a starting colour to the SHIFT instruction. This is especially useful if you need a specific area on the screen to be visible at all times. Type in the following changes to Example 8.2:

```
change ''I=1'' to ''I=2''
20  shift 2,2:curs off:rem start from colour 2
195 ink 1:locate 10,0:centre ''Hi there''
```

8.1.4 The FADE instruction

FADE allows you to progressively fade the entire colour palette from one set of values to another. The most common use of this instruction is to fade out the background during your game's initialisation phase. Normally, all the colours on the screen are faded to black, whilst the new game screen is being drawn. The colour palette can then restored again as the game commences, producing a highly professional fading effect. But FADE is not just limited to your loading screens.

It's actually an extremely versatile command, capable of smoothly scrolling any set of colours through several intermediate shades. Try entering the statement:

```
FADE 10,$700
```

This fades the background colour down to red. The speed of the fade indicates the interval in 50th's of a second between each step, and can vary between 1 and 999. All fades are performed in exactly seven steps. So the maximum time to completion is about 140 seconds. (999*7/50).

With a little inventiveness, you can utilise FADE to create a range of startling animations, from sunsets to explosions. Here's an example of a simple sunset:

Example 8.3 The FADE instruction

```
10 mode 0:colour 4,$770:rem Yellow
20 cls physic:cls back:rem clear screen
30 circle 80,60,60:rem Yellow sun
40 fade 999,,,,,$700:rem Fade down to red
50 wait key
```

Notice the commas between the 999 and $700. These indicate that the colours between 0 and 3 and 5-15 are not to be faded by the instruction.

The FADE at line 40 fades the sun from yellow to red using the slowest available speed setting. Another potential use of the FADE command, is for teleport effects. These are especially useful for adventures/RPGs as they can be used to generate eerie ghost-like disappearances.

Since the STOS Basic sprites use the exactly the same colour registers as the screen, it's also possible to fade out any particular sprite. Providing you keep the colours used by your sprites completely separate from those required by the screen backgrounds, you can teleport them away with just a single FADE instruction.

8.2 The ANIM command

ANIM is probably the most widely used of all the STOS Basic animation commands. Since the ANIM command has already been covered in considerable detail in the STOS Basic manual, I'll limit myself to a discussion of some of the more practical considerations.

Whilst ANIM is ideal for the many applications, it's unwise to over-use the instruction. The first point to recognise, is that the quality of the animation does tend to decrease slightly as the sprites get larger. So if you try to animate several really large objects on the screen at once, an annoying flicker will begin to intrude into the game. This is especially true if you are subsequently intending to move the sprites with a MOVE instruction.

It's probably safest to keep your sprites down to sizes of around 32x32 for the best results. If your objects are much larger than this limit, you would often be wiser to forget about sprites completely, and manipulate the graphics directly with SCREEN$.

This was the approach used to animate the massive MAGEDON in the game Zoltar, and as you can appreciate, it works extremely well.

There's also the problem of synchronisation. Because of the interrupt system used by the ANIM command, you can never be absolutely sure about precisely which image is being displayed on the screen at any one time. Normally this doesn't really matter, but in some programs, such as platform games or RPGs, it can be of vital importance.

Let's assume you had animated the closing of a door using ANIM. The effect of the player who attempted to enter while the door was closing, would be completely different to that of someone who tried to walk through a fully closed door. It would be crucial to know the exact status of the door at the precise moment the character passed through. The solution is to bypass ANIM completely, and animate the door directly using the SPRITE instruction.

Example 8.4 Using the SPRITE instruction

```
load "animals1.mbk":rem from STOS Games disk
load "backgrnd.mbk":rem Background screen
10 cls : flash off
20 unpack 11,back : screen copy back to physic
30 for I=5 to 10
40 sprite 1,x mouse,y mouse,I : rem Move the sprite with
mouse
50 wait 10
60 next I
70 goto 30
```

It would be misleading to imply from this discussion that the ANIM command is rather inadequate. On the contrary, providing you use it with a little care, you can produce some wonderful effects. ANIM can be successfully exploited in anything from an Adventure game to a simulation.

One possibility is to incorporate a simple animation sequence to your background screens. Clocks can be made to "tick", and windmills can be seen turning away in the distance. With a little imagination, you can transform a boring static background into something which looks impressively realistic.

8.3 Screen animation

If you want to animate objects larger than around 48 by 50 pixels, you will need to make use of either SCREEN COPY or SCREEN$. Both of these commands allow you to copy large areas of the screen from one place to another. But, although the two commands are roughly equivalent, SCREEN$ is by far the most suitable for the purposes of animation. This is because it's much easier to manipulate an array of strings than an isolated block of screen segments.

8.3.1 SCREEN$

SCREEN$ allows you to capture each frame of the animation sequence in one element of a string array. It's then possible to quickly display successive parts of the sequence in turn using a simple loop.

Example 8.5 Animation with the SCREEN$ function

```
10  rem Generate a growing disk
15  hide on
20  mode 0 : flash off : cls physic : cls back
25  colour 3,0
30  dim FRAME$(5)
40  for I=1 to 5
50  R=I*16 : ink 3 : circle 160,100,R
55  rem Grab disk into string
60  FRAME$(I)=screen$(physic,160-R,100-R to 160+R,100+R)
70  next I
80  cls physic : cls back : colour 3,$770
90  for I=1 to 5
95  rem Redraw disk
100 screen$(physic,160-I*16,100-I*16)=FRAME$(I)
110 next I
120 wait key
```

Example 8.5 draws five disks on the ST's screen and loads them into the array FRAME$. The loop at 90 then displays each frame in quick succession, producing the impression of an energy bolt hurtling from the centre of the screen.

Notice how the disk vanishes after you press [RETURN]. Whenever a STOS Basic program terminates correctly, the "physical screen" being displayed is automatically over-written by the background screen used by the sprites. Since the program only copied the data to the physical screen, the background display is left completely blank. This would lead to serious difficulties if you wanted to use the routine alongside the STOS Basic sprites. In this case, you would need to copy all your graphics to both the physical and the background screens. You can add this by modifying Example 8.5 using the line:

```
115 screen$(back,160,50)=frame$(i)
```

Another factor to remember when using the SCREEN$ function is the screen synchronisation problem. This is covered in detail on pages 151-152 of the original STOS Basic manual.

The difficulty arises because of the unpredictable nature of the sprite movements. If a sprite is drawn between instructions 110 and 115, it's possible that the images will get corrupted slightly. The solution, is to use the SYNCHRO command to control the sprite updates within your own program.

8.3.2 Screen flipping

Screen flipping is an invaluable technique which can substantially improve the smoothness of your animation effects. The problem with the normal screen commands, is that they allow you to see the drawing operations while they are taking place on the screen. Although most of these operations perform remarkably quickly, there's still a noticeable flicker to your animated graphics.

The solution is to draw the object onto a separate logical screen which is invisible to the user. After the drawing has been completed, this screen can swapped with the physical screen to produce a smooth, flicker-free animation. The old physical screen is now hidden away from view, and this can be used for the new logical screen. The whole process works in a simple loop. This can be seen from the following piece of pseudo-code:

```
reserve logical screen
repeat
    draw graphics
    switch physical and logical screens
until game over
```

Since the location of the screen is held in a special register in the ST's graphic's chip, it is possible to perform this switching practically instantaneously. The only penalty to your program, is the extra 32k of memory needed by the logical screen. This is normally a fairly small price to pay for the improvement in the quality of your graphics.

If you wanted to add screen flipping to Example 8.5, you would need to generate a separate logical screen using the RESERVE command. You would then switch between the physical screen and the logical screen using as soon as the updates have been completed.

STOS Basic includes two useful facilities which allow you to simplify this screen switching. These are summarised in Table 8.1 below.

Table 8.1 The STOS Basic Screen switching commands

SCREEN SWAP	Swaps the logical and physical screens.
LOGIC	Always holds the current address of the logical screen. This can be changed at any time using a normal assignment statement, e.g. logic=6:rem set the logical screen to memory bank 6
DEFAULT LOGIC	Contains the address of the original logical screen. This can be used in the following way: logic=default logic

Table 8.1 The STOS Basic Screen switching commands(continued)

PHYSIC	Holds the address of the screen memory which is currently being displayed. Like LOGIC it can be changed at any time using a simple assignment statement: physic=8:rem set the physical screen to the start of memory bank 8
DEFAULT PHYSIC	This resets the physical screen to it's initial value which is loaded when the ST is turned on.

Finally, here's an example which exploits the animation techniques I've been discussing to generate a bouncing block.

Example 8.6 A bouncing block

```
10 cls physic : cls back
11 hide on : auto back off
20 ink 5 : bar 100,100 to 150,150
30 ink 6 : polygon 100,100 to 125,75 to 175,75 to 150,100
40 ink 7 : polygon 175,125 to 150,150 to 150,100 to 175,75
50 BLOCK$=screen$(physic,100,75 to 176,175)
55 cls physic : cls back
60 reserve as screen 10 : logic=10 : cls logic
70 X=0 : Y=0 : DX=16 : DY=8
85 rem Control horizontal movements
90 X=X+DX : if X>200 or X<16 then DX=DX*-1 : X=X+DX : TURN=1
100 Y=Y+DY : if Y>92 or Y<8 then DY=DY*-1 : Y=Y+DY : TURN=1
110 screen$(logic,X,Y)=BLOCK$
120 screen swap : wait vbl : wait 2
130 if TURN then cls logic : TURN=0 : goto 90 else cls
logic,0,X-DX,Y-DY to X+110-DX,Y+100-DY : goto 90
```

See Chapter 10 section 10.5 for a further example of this technique.

8.4 Conclusion

Used properly, animation can add a real feeling of excitement to even the most mundane game idea. STOS Basic is supremely good at this type of animation, and it's senseless to let all that power go to waste. Once you've seen what can be achieved, try introducing a little animation into your own games. I'm sure you will be amazed at the results.

9

Sampled sound

9.1 Introduction

A few years ago any sound effects found in computer games were restricted to the occasional beeps. The fact is that even the best machines of the early eighties were limited to producing only crude explosions or simple tones. So most programmers placed sound very low on their list of priorities, and concentrated their efforts on the graphical elements of a game instead.

As computers became more sophisticated, it slowly started to become practicable to incorporate rather more impressive sounds into a game. But all these effects were limited by the programmer's ability to generate the original sound synthetically. It was therefore extremely difficult to produce authentic impressions of real sounds without complex and expensive additional hardware.

The breakthrough came with the development of techniques to digitally encode natural sounds in a form which could be subsequently reproduced by a computer. The basic idea was very simple indeed. Samples of a sound were taken thousands of times per second, and converted into a list of numbers which could be held in the computer's memory. Each sample contained enough information to reproduce a fraction of a second of the recorded sound.

These samples could then be successively replayed through the computer's sound chip to generate an excellent approximation of the original sound.

Unfortunately, this approach consumes enormous amounts of memory. A couple of seconds of digitised speech can easily take up over 32k of memory. So although the technology first appeared in the heyday of the Commodore 64, it has only been the advent of really powerful computers such as the ST and the Amiga, that it has become genuinely feasible to add sampled sound to a computer game.

Since its initial introduction, sampled sound has quickly penetrated most areas of the computer games industry. Rather than being just an afterthought, sound effects are now widely recognised as a vital component of any well-written computer game. So it's almost impossible for an game to get a rave review from one of the top computer magazines, unless it contains literally mind-blowing sound effects. Sampled sound provides even the most inexperienced programmer with the ability to generate sound effects which would make a Spectrum user gasp in amazement.

But how do you actually incorporate some of these samples into your own STOS Basic programs? Well, it is important to realise that your requirements will vary depending on whether you wish to create a sample yourself, or just play back an existing sample.

If you want to record your own samples, you will need to buy a piece of special hardware known as a sampler cartridge. This will cost you around £50, and will plug into your ST's cartridge port. All the currently available packages contain software which allows them to be used in conjunction with the majority of programming systems. There is, however, only one package which allows you to exploit the full power of the STOS Basic system directly: the STOS MAESTRO system.

9.2 The STOS MAESTRO system

The STOS MAESTRO utility from Mandarin software comes in two forms currently priced at £25 and £70 respectively. The cheaper version includes software which allows you to play back previously generated samples within STOS Basic. These samples can be created using most of the sound samplers currently available for the ST. So if you've already bought one of these cartridges, you almost certainly won't need to replace it especially for use with STOS Basic.

This package also includes a whole disk full of sound samples, which are ready to use straight from the box. These samples can be added to your STOS Basic programs using a powerful set of extension commands. Furthermore, all samples are replayed using interrupts. You can therefore easily combine sampled sound with arcade games such as Zoltar, without affecting the speed of any of the action.

The second, more expensive package, supplies you with a purpose built STOS MAESTRO sampling cartridge. This is able to recreate any sound which can be entered from an external source such as a cassette recorder.

Since I was actively involved in the production of the Maestro documentation, it's hard to free myself completely from any possible accusations of bias. But I honestly feel that one or other of the STOS MAESTRO packages is an essential purchase for anyone who seriously wishes to add sampled sounds to a STOS Basic game. During my experience of using the system, I'm still amazed at the sheer simplicity of Jon Wheatman's sampler extensions. I was for instance, able to add sampled sound to a large STOS Basic program such as Zoltar in well under an hour. The only drawback I've so far been able to discover, is that Maestro is not fully compatible with the ST's music system. I don't think this is an actual deficiency, since given the limitations of the ST's (mono) sound chip, some restrictions are inevitable.

On the other hand, when I removed the music and added sampled explosions to Zoltar, I noticed a significant improvement in the animation speed. So there are certainly some compensations.

9.3 Special effects

9.3.1 Choosing the recording speed

In order to achieve the best results from the STOS Maestro package, you need to understand a little about the possible sample speeds. The choice of sample speed is a major factor in the quality of the eventual sound. So a full appreciation of the available effects is vital.

All sample speeds are measured in Kilohertz (kHz). These correspond to the number of samples which are taken from the sound in a single second. A speed of one kHz means that a thousand samples will be entered every second. Each individual sample uses up one byte of the ST's memory. The total length of a sample can therefore be calculated from the following simple formula:

```
LENGTH=SPEED*TIME
```

If, for instance, you had created a sample 10 seconds long using a speed setting of 5 kHz, the total sample size would be:

```
5000*10 bytes or 50k
```

Alternatively, if you recorded the same sample at 20 kHz, it would now occupy an astonishing 200k of memory. It should be obvious from the above calculation that the slower you can keep the sample speed, the more samples you will be able to pack into your programs. But there's also the question of the accuracy of the recording.

The apparent quality of a sound increases in direct proportion to the rate at which it was sampled. This is because the higher speeds generate a much more detailed representation of the original sound. The slowest samples do sound rather choppy and incoherent by comparison to the fastest. There is therefore a trade-off between the quality of the sample, and the amount memory it uses.

The key to the successful application of sampled sound, is to manage this trade-off in your own favour. You have to find a way of keeping the sample speed down to an absolute minimum, whilst still providing enough information to enable the sampler extensions to reproduce the sound realistically.

The STOS MAESTRO system allows you to record samples using a range of speeds between 5 and 32 kHz. Because the samples are played back using interrupts however, the maximum playback speed from within STOS Basic is limited to 22 kHz. This restriction was necessary to allow the rest of the STOS system enough time to perform the various other interrupt routines such as those controlling the sprite movements. There's only so much time to go round, and the more power you reserve for the MAESTRO extensions, the less will be available for the rest of the STOS system. So the slower the playback speed, the faster your Basic programs will run.

The only reliable way of selecting the correct recording speed in any particular case, is by careful experiment. Here are a number of guidelines which may prove helpful.

9.3.2 Getting the most out of your sampler

1 Record special effects such as explosions and ray-guns using a sample speed of between 5 and 12 kHz. The quality of these effects is often perfectly acceptable at even the lowest speeds. Furthermore, due to the way STOS MAESTRO's play-back routines are implemented, choosing the slowest sample speed will guarantee the maximum performance out of your Basic programs.

2 Speech requires a minimum sampling rate of about 8 kHz to be understandable. In practice, the desirable speed will be closer to 10 or 12 kHz. This was the speed which was used in the samples contained in the STOS MAESTRO demonstration disk.

3 If your sample needs to be of really high quality, you should make the recording at 32 kHz and then compress it to 16 kHz using the PACK option from the MAESTRO program. When the sample is played back, there will be a noticeable improvement over sound which had been originally recorded at a rate 16 kHz.

4 Whenever you are using an existing sample from a PD disk, remember that the PACK option can compress these samples as well. This allows you to reduce the speed of samples to a slower and more efficient rate. As an experiment, pack down some of the samples from the STOS samples disk. Most of the effects in the SOUND folder will compress nicely, without any appreciable loss in sound quality.

9.4 Potential sound sources

I'll now discuss a number of potential sources for your samples.

9.4.1 The MAESTRO samples disk

The STOS MAESTRO package provides a disk containing around 300k of professionally produced samples. These cover most of the more common requirements for your games such as a explosions and guns. There's also a number of stranger sounds, including a full range of musical instruments. In practice, you'll probably find that the samples held on this disk will be more than sufficient for the majority of your programming needs. So when you need a sample, the samples disk should always be your first port of call.

Even if the exact effect you want isn't available, you may be able to modify one of the existing samples to your current requirements. By carefully changing the play-back speed and adding reverberations and echoes, you can transform a simple play-back speed and adding reverberations and echoes, you can transform a simple sound out of all recognition.

Take the sample "EEARR.SAM" from the VOICE folder. When this is played back at around 7 kHz, the result sounds like a charging elephant. So the next time you need to a charging elephant in your game, you know where to look. It's also possible to change the direction of a sound, or mix several unconnected sounds together. If you use this technique, you can vastly increase the range of sounds obtainable from the samples disk with just a little extra work.

9.4.2 The public domain

As sound samplers have become increasingly popular, a number of discs have appeared in the public domain. Since the MAESTRO package is compatible with the majority of current sampling systems, it's usually possible to incorporate these samples directly into your STOS Basic programs. You can also load them into the STOS MAESTRO package and manipulate them from within the MAESTRO program in the normal way. A single disk could contain a large number of potentially useful effects. But beware of samples recorded at odd speeds like 7.5 kHz. These will sound *very* odd when played back from STOS Basic.

9.4.3 Films and Tapes

If you have access to a sampler cartridge, you may be tempted to "borrow" effects from your favourite records or video tapes. Whilst you are unlikely to encounter any problems with samples used in games you written for your own amusement, you will almost certainly need to get permission from the original producers if you wish to distribute your game commercially.

The situation regarding special effects like explosions and "Phasers" is rather more complex. This is because, after you have manipulated one of these sounds, it can prove almost impossible to recognise the original source. It's rather like trying to reconstruct an egg once you have made it into an omelette.

At the present time, the precise legalities of this situation have yet to be fully resolved. So it's advisable to make a note of all your original sources in your program documentation before submitting your work to a commercial software house. After all, if you are lucky enough to get your game accepted, the sound effects will probably need to be remixed anyway.

9.4.4 Television

If your TV set has a earphone socket, you will be able to enter samples into directly from a television program. Alternatively, you can record the sounds from the loudspeaker.

Although some of the sounds will be subject to copyright, there will be plenty of others which can be used in your games without any problems. These include a vast range of real sounds from an aeroplane landing at Heathrow, to the thundering of a Formula II motor race. Providing you use a little imagination, you can capture a variety of sounds which would otherwise be impossible, all from the comfort of your own living room.

9.4.5 Other sources

It's a well known fact that the best things in life are free. The world around you contains a vast spectrum of potentially useful sounds, from bird calls to car engines. By carefully using the MAESTRO sampler program, you can transform even the most mundane sound, like a door bell, or a dog bark, to a something strange and possibly even sinister.

In the earliest days of radio, it was commonplace for the various sound effects to be generated by hand during transmission. These clever people were capable of generating marvellous results from just couple of coconut shells or a few small bits of wood.

Even the original effects from the amazing ''Hitch-hiker's Guide to the Galaxy'' were created using equipment which would now appear laughably primitive compared to the facilities provided by a modern recording studio.

With a little ingenuity and a lot of experimentation, it's possible to produce almost any sound imaginable. Once you've entered this into the computer, you can then sculpt the sound into something incredible. Don't underestimate the power of your own voice. The range of sounds the human vocal cords are capable of producing directly is truly remarkable!

9.4.6 Creating an alien

Many games, such as ''Captain Blood'' incorporate interactive alien speech effects. If you've listened to some of these sounds in admiration, you will be delighted to hear that it's quite possible to create a convincing impression of alien speech using the STOS MAESTRO system.

Begin by taking the cassette recorder you are using to enter your samples, and preparing for a recording session.

Now start the recording and try to talk in gibberish for several minutes. (I found this especially easy!). If you attempt this feat with several people, you'll probably fall into hysterics at some point. This is perfectly natural, and nothing to be ashamed of. The resulting sounds might even be rather useful.

After you've made your recording, you will be left with a tape containing some extremely silly noises. Connect your tape recorder to your sampler cartridge and create a sample in the normal way using a speed setting of 16 kHz.

You should now gradually increase the play-back speed up to the maximum of 32 kHz, noting the results. Your original noise will quickly change into something quite alien. Reverse the process using speeds from 16 kHz down to 5 kHz. Again make a note of any effects with you find pleasing. You should then choose the results you particularly like, and save the samples to the disk. This allows you to manipulate your sounds without any fear of losing anything permanent.

You are now ready to enter the FX menu, and add some special effects. In practice, I've found that the best results are obtained with ECHO, REVERB, and HALL. It is important to note that the effects of these commands are cumulative. So if you repeatedly add reverberations to one of your samples, the quality of the sound will be progressively changed.

Hopefully, you will eventually have produced an interesting set of alien sound effects for use with your game. These can now be saved on the disk, and replayed at the appropriate points in your program.

9.4.7 Direct synthesis

If you're feeling really adventurous, you might attempt to synthesise a sample directly. Since each sample is represented by just a single number, it's possible to produce a range of effects by generating your own numbers straight out of the computer. Here is a simple example of this technique:

Example 9.1 A square wave

```
10  input "Frequency (1 to 1000)";F
20  fill start(5) to start(5)+10232,0
30  print "Please wait"
40  for I=1 to 10000/F
50  SND=32
60  for J=1 to F
70  if J=F/2 then SND=-32
80  poke start(5)+I*F+J,SND
90  next J
100 next I
110 click off : sound init
120 if F<1 or F>1000 then 10
130 samraw start(5),start(5)+length(5)
```

This produces a crude square wave which can be played using the SAMRAW command. It's only really intended as a demonstration, and is hardly impressive. In fact, a rather better effect could have been produced in a couple of seconds using the standard STOS sound commands. Despite this, synthetic sounds do have their uses. They are ideal for generating raw clicks and buzzes which can be combined together to create a background track. This can be subsequently merged with your main sample to produce a range of interesting sound effects.

9.5 Possible applications

I'll now discuss a number possible ways in which sampled sounds can be exploited in your games.

9.5.1 Arcade games

In my experience, adding realistic sound effects such as explosions to an arcade game, can produce a massive improvement in the game's overall quality. Often, these effects can be taken straight out of the samples disk included with the STOS MAESTRO package. A full explanation of the required programming technique can be found in the Chapter 3 of the *STOS MAESTRO manual.*

9.5.2 Simulations

The use of sampled sound in a simulation will often vary depending on the nature of the game. If you are simulating a real situation, it's often possible to generate the samples directly from the source. Take a game like golf, for instance. In this case, you can capture the *thwack* of a golf club as it hits the ball with just a simple visit to your municipal golf course with your tape recorder.

9.5.3 RPGs

One of the most impressive uses of sampled sound that I've so far encountered, was contained in FTL's excellent Dungeon Master. This included a host of realistic sounds for everything from a door opening to the shrieks of the monsters. Many of these sounds were of extremely short duration, and could be sampled at quite low speeds without any appreciable loss of quality.

Here a few ideas of how the various effects could be produced:

1 The sound of a door opening might be created by simply ringing a small bell.

2 The swish and the thud of the blades can be produced using some of the samples supplied with STOS MAESTRO.

3 The screeches can be sampled directly from your own voice. You may need to modify the sounds a little with REVERB or ECHO to get the desired effect.

9.5.4 Adventures

Adventures are traditionally extremely memory hungry. So although graphics have now become commonplace, I've yet to see a successful use of sound samples in an adventure game. I do however, firmly believe that there is immense potential for sampled sound in one of these games. I'm certain that as memory becomes cheaper, sampled sound will become a familiar part of many adventures.

The scope for sampled sound in an adventure game is enormous. By adding the appropriate effects as the adventure progresses, you can enhance the illusion of reality considerably. Supposing you are playing an adventure is set in a dungeon. (Just for a change.) As you progress through the caverns, you encounter a number of doors. Imagine how you would feel when you listened at a door, and heard a horrible scream! Even the most mundane sounds, such as the strike of a match, or a telephone ringing, can have a dramatic effect if the player isn't expecting them.

In order to conserve memory, it's advisable to store samples in separate files on this disk. When required, they can be entered into memory with LOAD, and played using the SAMRAW extension. If you record your samples at 10 kHz or less, you can pack up to 15 samples on a single sided disk, whilst still leaving enough room for another ten compacted pictures. This means that you don't necessarily have to sacrifice graphics to make the space for your sound effects.

9.6 Conclusion

Hopefully, you'll now be buzzing with ideas for using sampled sound in your STOS Basic programs. Sampled sound won't make a bad computer game a success. Nothing can do that, other than a major rewrite. But it will add a final gloss to an already enjoyable game. This might make all the difference if you try to sell it commercially. So add a little sound to your programs and make your players jump off their seats!

10

Scrolling techniques

10.1 Introduction

The ability to set the action against a moving background has now become a familiar part of everything from an arcade game to an RPG. Paradoxically, scrolling is one of those activities which has become increasingly difficult as computers have advanced. The stunning graphics which can be produced by the ST require a hefty 32K of memory. This compares badly with the maximum of 8K needed by the original Atari 800.

One unwelcome side-effect is that an ST program has to work very hard to generate scrolling effects which have would been trivial to one of its predecessors. In order to scroll the ST's screen by a single line, it's necessary to copy over thirty thousand pieces of information in memory. These scrolling operations will usually need to be performed several times a second. This is a severe challenge for even the fastest computer. The above problem is not restricted to the Atari ST incidentally; it applies equally well to all modern computers. The only feasible solution is to use a special piece of graphics hardware known as a Blitter. Unfortunately, the ST was originally designed as a business machine, and the expensive blitter chip was omitted for reasons of economy.

At the time of writing, blitter chips are slowly starting to percolate into the larger ST systems such as the Mega ST. For the time being, these machines are much too expensive for the majority of home users. Hopefully, it won't be long before all ST's have a blitter chip fitted as standard. Until then, I'm afraid we'll have to live with this problem.

Until recently, the only way of generating a smooth scrolling effect on an Atari ST, was to write the entire game in machine code, so screen scrolling games were restricted to expert machine code programmers with a detailed knowledge of the inner workings of the ST.

Although STOS Basic cannot escape the inherent limitations of the ST's hardware, it is still capable of generating some superb effects which come impressively close to the best commercial software. But if you're really serious about writing a screen scrolling game, it's still worth investing in a copy of the STOS Basic compiler. Screen scrolling games need every scrap of computer power you can give them, and the STOS compiler can certainly lead to a real improvement in the speed of your game.

You don't, however, have to take my word for it. After all, I did write the manual for the package, so maybe I'm a little biased. Get hold of a compiled copy of Bullet train, and compare it with the interpreted version provided on the STOS games disk. I think you'll agree that the difference in speed is remarkable.

I'll now discuss some of the basic techniques which can be used to add scrolling effects to one of your games. In order to make my discussion as general as possible, I will intentionally avoid going into too much detail about any individual game genre. So although I'll be concentrating on vertical scrolling, the same ideas can be applied equally well to a producing a horizontal scroller like Bullet. They can also be used to generate the more complex scrolling systems required by some RPGs.

You may be wondering slightly as to this strange treatment of Bullet. After all, I did give you a full breakdown of the other STOS games. Is there something wrong with this program? Well there's actually one important fact about Bullet which you are probably not aware of.

Bullet train was originally written for the French version of the STOS Basic package. (STOS v1.0). But the screen scrolling commands such as SCROLL or SCREEN$ were only incorporated into the STOS system for version two. The Bullet program was therefore forced to perform all scrolling operations entirely using SCREEN COPY! This must have been tremendously difficult, and I'm filled with admiration for programmer who managed to produce such an impressive game using such limited tools.

Fortunately, we English users have been spared all this complication with the introduction of the STOS Basic SCROLL commands. So we don't need to be a programming genius like Francois Lionet in order to write effective screen scrolling games in STOS Basic.

10.2 Basic principles

All the ST's graphics are stored in a set of thirty two thousand memory locations collectively referred to as the screen memory. Scrolling involves copying the data describing one part of the screen over the area used by another. Look at the picture in Figure 10.1a on the next page. The area (A) is the section of the screen which to be scrolled. If you were to copy (A) into the space above it (B), the entire screen would appear to scroll upwards. This can be seen from Figure 10.1b, also on the next page.

It is vital to realize that screen memory itself hasn't moved anywhere. The only change has been in the contents of the locations holding the image. Any graphics you

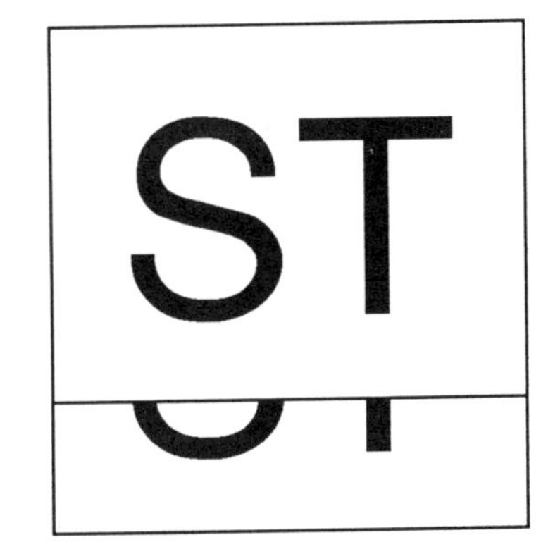

Figure 10.1a Before a vertical scroll

Figure 10.1b After a vertical scroll

have drawn at the top of the screen will of course be completely obliterated by the scrolling operation. Also, since the scroll didn't alter the lower portion of the data, the bottom edge of the screen will be totally unaffected.

So there will now be two copies of this section on the ST's screen. As you can see, from Figure 10.1b, the part of the original image which wasn't scrolled is interfering with the display. This useless "fringe" needs to be removed directly using the CLS command.

Here's an equivalent version of this diagram for a horizontal scroll. The only difference is that you are now moving your screen data either left or right.

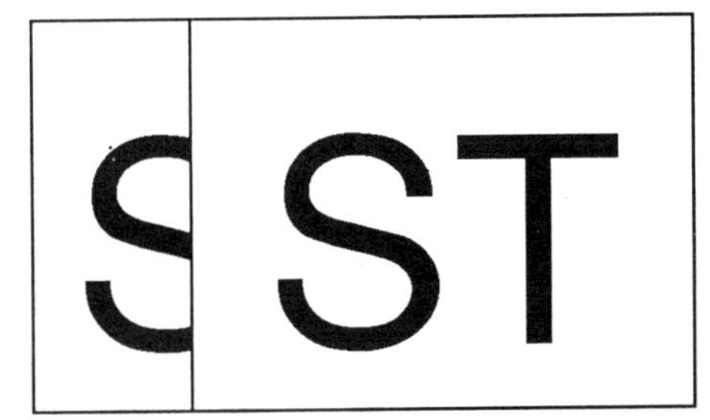

Figure 10.2a Before a horizontal scroll

Figure 10.2b After a horizontal scroll

The scrolling speed will depend entirely on the amount of data which is to be copied in each operation. The smaller the zone you wish to scroll, the faster the scroll will be performed. In practice, most games limit the scrolling area to about two-thirds of a screen. The rest of the screen is normally reserved for the high score table or the copyright notices.

The solution to incorporating scrolling effects successfully into your own games, is to keep the size of the scrolling zone to as small as possible. Any reduction in size will lead to a proportional increase in the scrolling speed. It is therefore possible to scroll half a screen, twice as quickly as the entire screen.

10.3 The SCROLL Command

STOS Basic provides you with a special instruction called SCROLL which enables you to scroll sections of the screen in every conceivable direction. Before using this instruction, you first need to define the size and position of the scrolling zone with

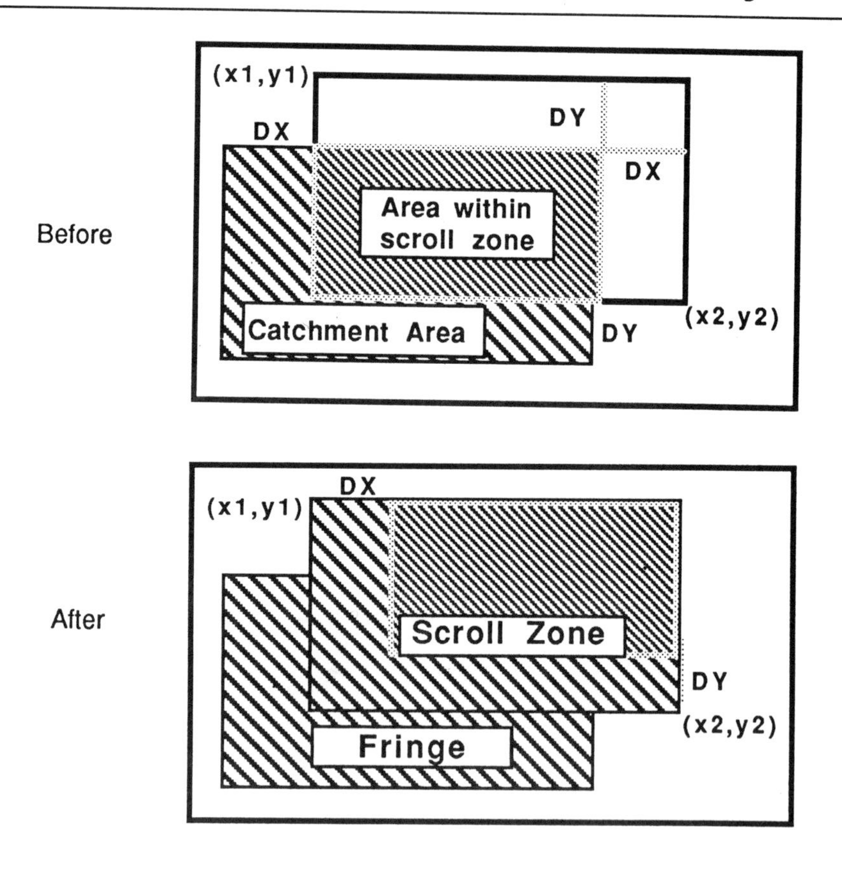

Figure 10.3 The Action of the SCROLL command.

DEF SCROLL. It's possible to use this feature to create sixteen independent scrolling zones on the screen at a time. This will be more than sufficient for the vast majority of your games.

The format of DEF SCROLL is:

```
DEF SCROLL Z,X1,Y1 to X2,Y2,DX,DY
```

Z is just the number of the scrolling zone from 1 to 16. The other values are slightly less obvious. Look at the diagram in Figure 10.3 on the previous page.

The coordinates X1,Y1 and X2,Y2 enclose a rectangular zone in which the scrolling takes place. Anything on the screen which lies outside this area will be completely

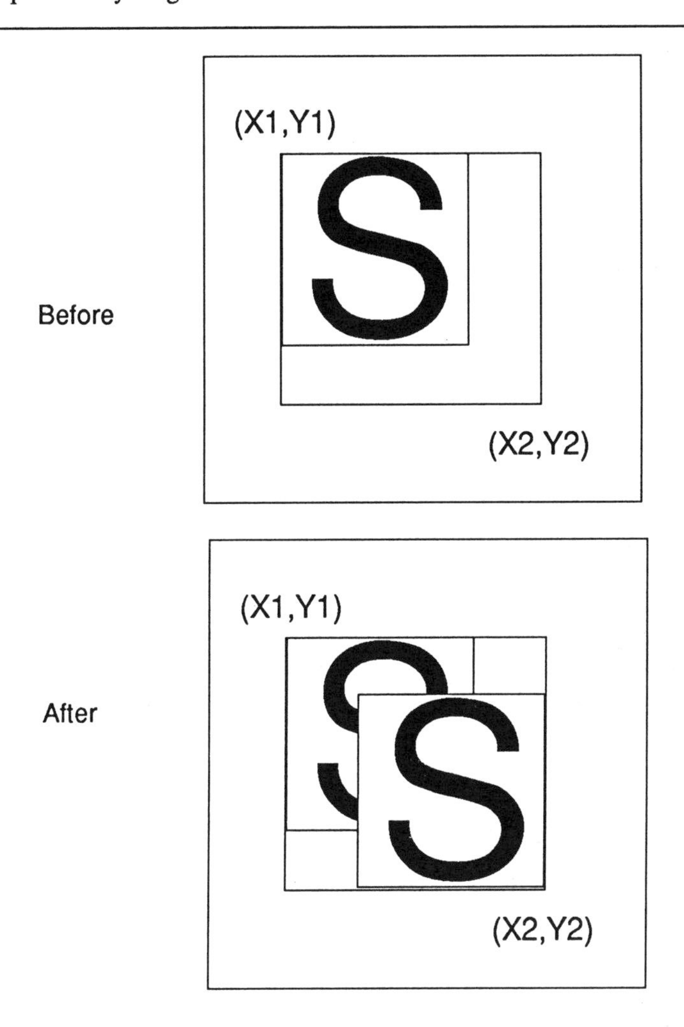

Figure 10.4 Scrolling a real image

unaffected by the scrolling operations. DX and DY specify the horizontal and vertical distances by which the area is to be scrolled.

As I mentioned earlier, the standard scrolling operation does not remove the existing parts of the image from the corner of this area. This L-shaped fringe, shown in Figure 10.4 on the previous page, needs to be removed by your program immediately after the scroll has finished.

Note that the diagram in Figure 10.3 only strictly applies if both DX and DY are positive. There are actually four main possibilities for the position of the scrolling area as shown in Figure 10.5 below.

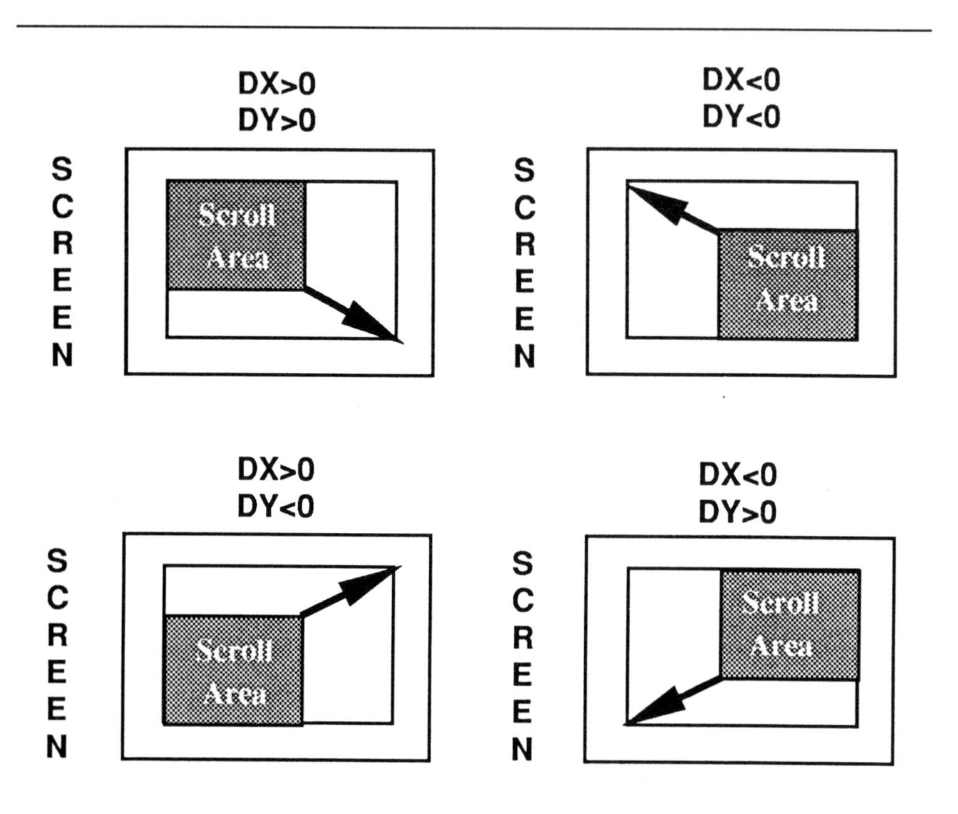

Figure 10.5 Possible scrolling directions

Additionally, there are the situations when either DX or DY is zero. In these circumstances the scrolling is in one direction only, and the scrolling zone is similar to that shown in Figures 10.1 and 10.2.

Warning! At the time of writing, the STOS Basic SCROLL command has a small bug. This may lead to some slight confusion when you are adding scrolling effects to your programs. (It certainly confused the heck out of me!). If you try to set values for DX and DY which are not exact multiples of sixteen, the scrolling zone tends to expand outside the limits you originally specified by DEF SCROLL. There's no guaranteed way of calculating the screen area in advance, but in all my tests the new zone always lies within the coordinates:

```
X1-abs(DX),Y1-abs(DY) to X2+abs(DX),Y2+abs(DY)
```

You therefore need to indulge in a little experimentation to determine the precise dimensions of the scrolling area. It's then just a simple matter of expanding your graphics to fit into the new area. Here's an experimenter program to help you along.

```
10 cls physic : cls back
20 input "dx =";DX : input "dy =";DY
30 def scroll 1,48,50 to 272,150,DX,DY
40 rbar 128,75 to 176,125
45 rem change for medium or high res
50 box 0,0 to 319,199 : box 47,49 to 273,151
60 wait key
70 scroll 1
80 wait key : goto 70
```

This program draws a rectangular bar inside two boxes. The dimensions of inner box shows you the current scrolling area, whilst the outer box simply highlights the borders of the screen.

On startup, you will be prompted for your values of DX and DY. You can then test the scrolling action by repeatedly pressing return. Try running the program with values of -10 and -10. This gives a good demonstration of the type of problem you a likely to encounter in your scrolling operations.

The easiest way of discovering the limits of the scrolling area, is to move the mouse pointer around on the screen. Since the program operates on the physical screen, the mouse pointer is scrolled along with it.

When you move your mouse outside the scrolling zone, this effect will stop. You can then hit <CONTROL><C> and print out the coordinates of the scroll boundary:

```
print x mouse,y mouse
```

Once you've defined your scrolling zone, you can now perform a scrolling operation using the SCROLL command. The format of this instruction is simply:

```
SCROLL n
```

Where:

n is the number of the scrolling zone you specified with DEF SCROLL.

Example 10.1 Horizontal and vertical scrolling

```
10  rem define a vertical screen scrolling zone
20  def scroll 1,0,0 to 160,200,0,16
30  rem define a horizontal scrolling zone
40  def scroll 2,0,0 to 320,100,16,0
50  cls physic:cls back
60  ellipse 80,100,60,80:rem draw an ellipse
70  for i=1 to 200
80  scroll i:rem Scroll the ellipse downwards
90  next i
100 cls physic:cls back
110 ellipse 160,50,150,40:rem draw an ellipse
120 for i=1 to 320
130 scroll 2:rem scroll ellipse to right
140 next i
```

10.4 A window to the world

So far I've neglected to remove the annoying fringe effects from the screen. Real programs, such as Bullet, incorporate the clever ability replace these useless sections with new parts of the game map.

These games treat the ST's screen as a sort of window, looking down on a much larger world. As the window moves up through this game world, the image on the screen moves accordingly. The fringe at the bottom is continuously updated to reveal the parts of the world which were previously hidden from sight. This generates a convincing illusion that the player is moving across a vast imaginary landscape.

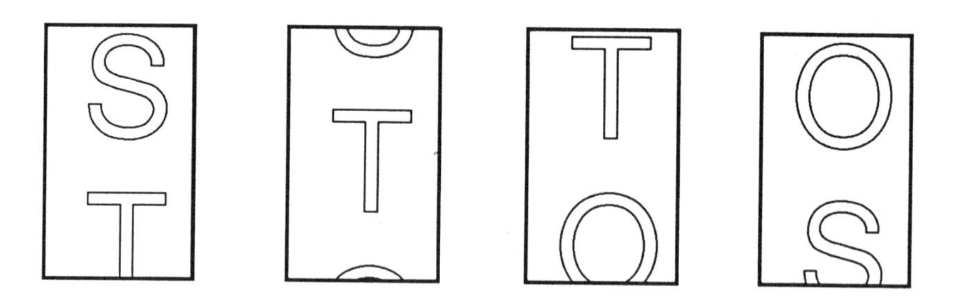

Figure 10.6 Illusion of movement

10.4.1 The game map

It's usual to implement this effect by storing the entire world view in a single large map. Every section of the map is built up out of a fixed number of components. The game map will contain nothing more than simple list of the identification numbers.

This reduces the amount of memory needed by the map by an extremely large factor, because the same components can be used to create a practically infinite number of screens. It's typically possible to compact all the information for a screen into a couple of hundred bytes. So you can cram literally hundreds of screens into your game without running out of memory on a standard 520 ST.

At this point, you might have realized that I'm actually making an oblique reference to the STOS Basic MAP Definer.

Since I actually wrote this program, I'm naturally interested in seeing it put to good use. Looking back, I can appreciate that the output routines could certainly do with a major injection of speed.

Fortunately, it's easy to adapt the same data to a whole range of other, faster drawing systems. I included an example of such a routine in Chapter 3, and I'll be exploiting this system in the scrolling programs towards the end of this chapter.

10.4.2 The MAP definer

Before I show you how you can use some of these techniques, it's worth saying a few words about the map definer itself. You will probably find that the definer works best if the height of the sprite divides evenly into the maximum height of the screen. So sizes of 16x20 are easier to handle than the 16x16 sprite included in the "BACK" file.

You'll also discover that the map definer performs fastest with sprites around 32x20 in size. This is because the program makes heavy use of the PUT SPRITE command, which is quite inefficient when dealing with large numbers of small sprites. I would probably have spotted this problem during the development process, but most of my example files used sprites with sizes of 32x20!

Thankfully, the drawing speed can be radically improved using the SCREEN$ system from Chapter 3. This works equally well for all STOS Basic sprites.

When you're creating your scrolling zones, set the scrolling dimensions sensibly according to the sizes of your sprites. Ideally, there should be a integral number of sprites in each line, and a whole number of lines per game screen. Don't bother drawing the areas of the map which lie outside your chosen scrolling zone. These can be safely ignored, and will lead to a small, but irrelevant, waste of memory in the finished map.

It is essential to keep the numbering system for your game screens as consistent as possible. If you are scrolling in a single direction, it's trivial to number your screens in the order they will be encountered by the player. But if you wish to scroll in several directions, you will need to devise a coherent pattern. An example of such a pattern can be seen in Chapter 5. (RPGs).

10.4.3 Storing the map

The way you will store your game map varies depending on the type of scrolling operations you will be performing. If you are writing a vertical scrolling arcade game, you are strongly advised to split the map into horizontal lines as follows:

```
dim MAP(row,col)
```

This format allows you to find the components of each line using a single FOR/NEXT loop, e.g.

```
for i=1 to col:component=MAP(line,i):gosub 1000:next i
```

I'm assuming that the routine at 1000 would be defined separately in your program to print out a component of your map. I'll be showing you a definition of this routine a little later.

The same storage strategy is also applicable to more complex scrolling systems. But in the case of pure horizontal scrolling, you will need to divide the screen into vertical strips. So the MAP array would be defined as:

```
dim MAP(col,row)
```

If you wished display the contents of a particular strip, you would need to modify the FOR/NEXT LOOP to:

```
for i=1 to row:component=MAP(col,i):gosub 1000:next i
```

10.4.5 Scrolling through a map

I'll now demonstrate how you can use one of these game maps in an actual program. The scrolling process is really incredibly easy. This can be seen from the pseudo-code description in Figure 10.7 on the next page.

Note that this code is only intended to illustrate the general principles of the scrolling system. If your game was limited to a single movement direction, you could simplify the pseudo-code considerably.

```
initialise game map
draw first screen
repeat
     play game
     if down selected and row>0 then scroll up
     if up chosen and row<max_row then scroll down
     if right and column>0 then scroll left
     if left and column<max_columns then scroll right
     redraw fringe
     redraw sprites
until game over
```

Figure 10.7 Pseudo-code description of a scrolling game

10.4.6 Initialising the game map

During the initialisation phase, the data produced from the map definer will should be loaded into one of the MAP arrays I mentioned earlier. Oddly enough, the format of the map data was originally set up for horizontal scrolling. I'm sure that I had an extremely good reason for this at the time, but can't for the life of me remember it!

I'll now provide you with a couple of routines which will perform this procedure automatically for you. Don't hesitate to use them in any of your own programs.

Example 10.2 Loading the map array for horizontal scrolling

```
10 dim MAP(100,100)
100 rem Initialization routine for horizontal scrolling
110 read LS,NSCR
115 rem LS= number of data lines per screen
116 rem NSCR=Number of screens defined
120 for S=0 to NSCR-1
130 restore 50010+S*LS
135 read W,H : ROWS=199/H : COLS=319/W : rem get unit size
140 for C=0 to COLS
150 for R=0 to ROWS
160 read MAP(S*NSCR+C,R)
170 next R : next C : input A$ : next S
```

Example 10.3 Loading the map array for vertical scrolling

```
100 rem Load a map for vertical scrolling
105 rem read data lines per screen and no of screens
110 read LS,NSCR
120 for s=0 to NSCR-1
```

```
130 rem get sizes of sprites
140 read W,H:cols=199/h:rows=319/w
150 d=200-cols*h:rem do the sprites divide evenly into
screen
160 for c=1 to cols+1
170 for r=1 to rows
180 read MAP(s*rows+r,c)
190 next r
200 if d then read DUMMY:rem if last row not used, ignore it
210 next c:next s:return
```

10.4.7 Redrawing the fringe

This subroutine forms the heart of your scrolling routine. Its action is to redraw the parts of the game map which have just been revealed at the edge of the screen.

Your program begins by creating a list of the location of the screen segments which make up the fringe. The sizes of these segments will obviously depend on the sizes of the sprites you used when designing the screen using the map definer.

If your game requires the screen to scroll in several directions, it is sensible to define one set of positions for each possibility.

Supposing you wished to produce a simple vertical scroll. The fringe area would look something like the one shown in Figure 10.8:

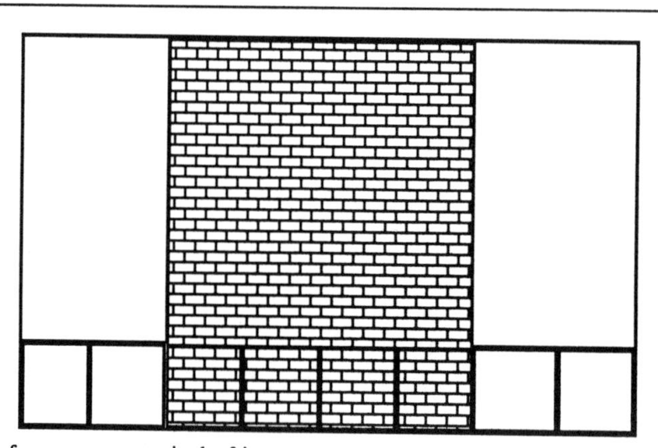

Figure 10.8 List of screen segments in the fringe

The program stores one set of coordinates for each component of the fringe. If you had ten sprites making up each horizontal line, then you could initialise the fringe array using the following code:

```
100 dim SLOT(10):rem dimension array for position of fringe
110 for SL=1 to 10 : SLOT(SL)=(SL-1)*32 : next SL
```

Note that for a purely vertical scroll, it's only necessary to store the X coordinate of the component. But in the case of a more complex scroll, the fringe will be L-shaped, and you will therefore need to store both the X and Y coordinates of the segments to completely specify their position.

After you've stored this data, you are ready to redraw the fringe using the data stored in the map array. The fastest way of achieving this in practice, is to load each sprite image into a string using SCREEN$. You can then output the entire line at high speed using the following code:

Example 10.4 redrawing the fringe

```
220 for c=1 to cols
225 rem YROW=Y coordinate of fringe
226 rem SEG$ array holds block images
227 rem MAP holds world map
228 rem CL holds number of current line
230 if MAP(CL,SP)>0 then
screen$(physic,SLOT(c),YROW)=SEG$(MAP(CL,c))
240 next c
```

seg$ is an array containing the sprite images used for your segments. These images would be loaded into the seg$ array using a routine such as:

```
420 rem Enter sprite images in SEG$ array
430 cls physic : cls back
435 rem no_of_blocks holds number of sprites to be grabbed
440 for I=0 to no_of_blocks
450 cls physic,0,0,0 to 16,16
460 sprite 1,0,0,I+1 : put sprite 1 : wait vbl
470 SEG$(I+1)=screen$(physic,0,0 to 16,16) : next I
480 sprite 1,-100,-100,1
490 return
```

Here's a complete example which demonstrates these techniques to scroll a large spaceship through the screen. Before you can run this program, you will need to load the background sprites supplied on the STOS Basic accessory disk.

```
load "back.mbk"
```

Note that it's also possible to use this routine directly with your own map definitions. This will avoid typing in all those boring data statements at the end of the program. Create your maps in the normal way using the Map definer, and save them using the S.ASC function. Now load them into memory, and delete the old output program with:

```
load "map.asc":rem Or whatever you called your maps
delete 50000-50003
```

You may now enter the program in Example 10.5, ignoring the data statements at 600 onwards.

Example 10.5 Vertical Screen scroller version 1

```
10  rem Vertical screen scroller
20  rem Screen generation using mapper
25  dim SEG$(40):rem define segment array
30  mode 0 : cls physic : cls back : flash off
40  gosub 420:rem load sprite images into SEG$ using SCREEN$
50  ROOM=1 : gosub 500 : rem draw first screen
60  def scroll 1,0,0 to 320,192,0,-16 : rem define scrolling
70  def scroll 2,0,0 to 320,176,0,16 : rem define scrolling
80  dim MAP(100,20),SLOT(20) : rem dimension MAP and SLOT
90  rem load slots
100 for SL=1 to 20 : SLOT(SL)=(SL-1)*16 : next SL
110 rem initialise game map
120 restore 600
130 read LS : rem read number of lines per screen
140 read NSCR : rem read number of screens
150 for S=0 to NSCR-1
160 rem get sizes of sprites
170 read W,H : ROWS=199/H : COLS=319/W
180 D=200-COLS*H : rem do sprites divide evenly into screen
190 for C=1 to COLS+1
200 for R=1 to ROWS
210 read MAP(S*(ROWS)+R,C)
220 next R
230 if D then read DUMMY : rem if last row not used, ignore it
240 next C : next S
250 rem Main scrolling loop
260 CL=12:rem start line
265 rem main loop
270 repeat
280 rem Scroll screen up
290 if jup and CL>13 then dec CL : gosub 360
300 if jdown and CL<ROWS*NSCR then inc CL : gosub 320
310 until fire
315 stop
316 rem Scroll the screen down
320 scroll 1 : cls physic,0,0,176 to 320,192 : rem erase
fringe
330 rem redraw fringe
```

```
340 for C=1 to COLS+1 : if MAP(CL,C)>0 then
screen$(physic,SLOT(C),176)=SEG$(MAP(CL,C))
350 next C : return
360 rem scroll the screen up
370 scroll 2 : cls physic,0,0,0 to 320,16 : rem erase fringe
375 rem redraw fringe
380 for C=1 to COLS+1 : if MAP(CL-12,C)>0 then
screen$(physic,SLOT(C),1)=SEG$(MAP(CL-12,C))
390 next C : return
400 default
410 stop
420 rem Enter sprite images in SEG$ array
430 cls physic : cls back
440 for I=0 to 30
450 cls physic,0,0,0 to 16,16
460 sprite 1,0,0,I+1 : put sprite 1 : wait vbl
470 SEG$(I+1)=screen$(physic,0,0 to 16,16) : next I
480 sprite 1,-100,-100,1
490 return
495 rem New version of Map output program
496 rem Rewritten using SCREEN$ for extra speed
500 restore 600 : read NL,NROOM
505 if ROOM>NROOM or ROOM<=0 then return
510 restore 610+(ROOM-1)*NL : read GRIDW,GRIDH : cls physic
520 for I=0 to 319/GRIDW
530 for J=0 to 199/GRIDH
540 read S
550 if S>0 then screen$(physic,I*GRIDW+1,J*GRIDH)=SEG$(S)
560 next J : next I : return
570 rem Distance between screens, number of screens
580 rem The distance may need changing after you have
590 rem renumbered these lines from 50000+
600 data 13,2
605 rem Screen 1
610 data 16,16,0,0,0,0,0,0,17,17,17,17,17,0,0,0,0,0,0,
0,17,17
620 data17,17,17,17,17,0,0,0,0,0,17,17,1,1,1,1,17,17,0,0
630 data0,0,17,17,1,1,1,1,1,1,17,0,0,0,17,17,17,1,1,1
640 data1,1,1,17,0,0,17,17,17,17,17,17,17,17,17,17,17,0,
17,17
650 data17,22,20,20,22,17,17,17,17,17,0,17,17,17,23,18,
18,23,17,17
660 data17,17,17,0,17,17,17,23,18,18,23,17,17,17,17,17,
0,17,17,17
670 data23,18,18,20,20,20,20,20,20,0,17,17,17,23,18,18,
20,20,20,20
```

```
680 data 20,20,0,17,17,17,23,18,18,23,17,17,17,17,17,0,
17,17,17,23
690 data 18,18,23,17,17,17,17,17,0,17,17,17,24,20,20,24,
17,17,17,17
700 data 17,0,0,17,17,17,17,17,17,17,17,17,17,17,0,0,0,
17,17,17
710 data 1,1,1,1,1,1,17,0,0,0,0,17,17,1,1,1,1,1,1,17
720 data 0,0,0,0,0,17,17,1,1,1,1,17,17,0,0,0,0,0,0,17
730 data 17,17,17,17,17,17,0,0,0,0,0,0,17,17,17,17,17,
0,0
735 rem screen 2
740 data 16,16,0,0,0,0,0,0,0,0,0,0,0,0,17,17,0,0,0,0,0
750 data 0,0,0,0,0,0,17,17,17,0,0,0,0,0,0,0,17,0,17
760 data 17,17,0,0,0,0,0,0,17,17,0,17,17,17,17,0,0,0,0
770 data 0,0,17,17,0,17,17,17,17,17,0,0,0,0,17,17,17,0,
17,17
780 data 17,17,17,0,0,0,0,17,17,0,0,17,17,17,17,17,0,0,0,
17
790 data 17,17,0,0,17,17,17,17,17,17,17,17,17,17,0,0,0,
20,20,20
800 data 20,20,20,20,20,20,20,20,20,0,20,20,20,20,20,20,
20,20,20,20
810 data 20,20,0,17,17,17,17,17,17,17,17,17,17,0,0,0,17,
17,17,17
820 data 17,0,0,0,17,17,17,0,0,17,17,17,17,17,0,0,0,0,17,
17
830 data 0,0,17,17,17,17,17,0,0,0,0,17,17,17,0,17,17,17,
17,17
840 data 0,0,0,0,0,17,17,0,17,17,17,17,0,0,0,0,0,0,17,17
850 data 0,17,17,17,0,0,0,0,0,0,0,0,17,0,17,17,0,0,0,0
860 data 0,0,0,0,0,0,0,0,0,0,0,0,0,0,0,0,0,0,0
```

Most of this program should be fairly familiar, since I've already discussed the major components in some detail. Variable CL holds the number of the current line. At the start of the program it is set to twelve, which is the bottom line of the screen.

The routines from 320 and 370 scroll the screen and replace the fringes with the hidden data from the MAP array. Also note that I have set the direction of scrolling to be opposite to the direction you moved the joystick. This is because when you are walking across the ground, the ground seems to scroll away in the beneath you, in the opposite direction to your motion. It therefore makes sense to pull the joystick to scroll up, and push the stick to move down.

10.5 Screen flipping

Although the program in Example 10.5 works quite well, especially when compiled, it does suffer from a slight jerkiness. This is caused by the fact that you can see the image currently under construction. The solution is to use a separate logical screen for the image your are generating. This can be interchanged with the current physical screen using the SCREEN SWAP instruction.

If you want to exploit this idea, you need to remember that as the two screens are only displayed on alternate scrolling operations, each scroll must be twice the normal size. This needs to be executed with a little finesse, because the physical and logical screens have to be carefully kept in step with each other.

You should also take care that the sprite background always contains an exact copy of the physical screen for use by the STOS Basic sprites. If you omit to update the background screen, the sprites will start to interfere with your scrolling operations.

The ideal solution is to scroll the background screen directly, and then copy over the results into the physical screen. There are however a number of complications. You can't just swap the background screen with the physical screen, as this would corrupt the various sprite operations. You therefore need to keep a separate copy of the logical screen somewhere in memory, and copy the background screen into this. I'll clarify the technique with a little pseudo-code.

```
reserve screen

draw first image

copy image to sprite background

repeat
      scroll background
      copy background to logical screen
      screen swap

Until game over
```

Figure 10.9 Scrolling the screen using screen flipping

This technique can be incorporated into the program from Example 10.5 by adding the following lines:

```
35  reserve as screen 6
320 OLD=logic : logic=back
330 scroll 1 : cls logic,0,0,176 to 320,192 : rem erase
fringe
340 for C=1 to COLS+1
345 if MAP(CL,C)>0 then
screen$(logic,SLOT(C),176)=SEG$(MAP(CL,C))
```

```
350 next C : logic=OLD : screen copy back to logic
355 wait vbl : screen swap : return
360 OLD=logic : logic=back
375 scroll 2 : cls logic,0,0,0 to 320,16 : rem erase fringe
380 for C=1 to COLS+1
385 if MAP(CL-12,C)>0 then screen$(logic,SLOT(C),1)=
SEG$(MAP(CL-12,C))
390 next C : logic=OLD : screen copy back to logic
395 wait vbl : screen swap : return
550 if S>0 then screen$(physic,I*GRIDW+1,J*GRIDH)=SEG$(S)
: screen$(back,I*GRIDW+1,J*GRIDH)=SEG$(S)
```

10.6 Using sprites with a screen scrolling game

The vast majority of screen scrolling games also make heavy use of the STOS Basic sprites. If you try to use the normal sprite operations for this purpose, you will quickly discover that the sprites clash with the scrolling operations. Normally, all the sprites are redrawn automatically by STOS Basic. It is this redrawing process which generates the interference. The solution is to take control of the sprite updates yourself. This can be achieved using either the UPDATE or SYNCHRO commands

10.6.1 Difference between UPDATE and SYNCHRO

The actions of these two commands are broadly similar. Both instructions redraw any sprites which have moved on the screen since he last update. The difference between them is subtle but important.

As you probably know, the coordinates of the STOS Basic sprites are usually updated every 50th of a second using an interrupt routine. It is however, impossible to update the actual positions of the sprites on the screen within the interrupt. There simply isn't the time. Instead, STOS Basic automatically calls the redrawing operations directly within your program between successive Basic instructions.

UPDATE OFF turns off this redrawing process but has no effect on the interrupt which actually changes the sprites screen coordinates. So the sprites are still moving around in memory, even when they are not being displayed on the ST's screen. You can force the redrawing process at any convenient point in your program using UPDATE. The SYNCHRO command is rather different, because it disables the sprite interrupt completely. The coordinates of the sprite are now only updated when it is redrawn using SYNCHRO.

Both commands have their own advantages and their disadvantages. If your sprites need to move independently of the background, then UPDATE will produce the smoother effect. But if you want to move your sprites along with the background, you will need to control every aspect of the sprite movements in your program. This will force you to use the SYNCHRO instruction instead.

10.7 Conclusion

The STOS Basic scroll commands make smooth scrolling effects an achievable reality rather than just an impossible dream. With a little work, you should be able to add scrolling backgrounds to any of your own games, without having to resort of any complicated programming tricks or optimization strategies. But don't try to be over-ambitious. Even STOS Basic has to live on the ST, and unless you restrict the sizes of your scrolling zones ruthlessly, you'll need to work quite hard to produce true commercial quality arcade games using this system. On the other hand, if Bullet had been written today using the SCROLL command, it would probably have been much more effective. So there's certainly nothing stopping you from incorporating some marvellous scrolling effects in your games!

11

Assembly language programming techniques

11.1 Why program in assembly language?

Throughout this book, I've been emphasising the fact that you can write commercial quality games without the need to involve yourself in complicated 68000 assembly language programming. So why have I felt the need to include a section on assembly language programming at all?

Well, I do have an excuse. I am after all an enthusiastic assembly language programmer myself. Like many such people, I often find it very hard to restrain myself from hacking out a quick 68000 routine to optimise one of my STOS Basic programs. You may not NEED to use assembler from STOS Basic but if you already understand it, there's absolutely nothing stopping you from combining your favourite assembly language routines directly into a STOS Basic program.

A few years ago, it was common practice to generate a commercial quality game using a hybrid of Basic and assembler. This allowed the skilled programmer to write the critical parts of a game in machine code, whilst controlling the simpler sections using Basic. Even on a Atari 800 XL this technique was capable of producing some mind-blowing results. Imagine what you could achieve with STOS Basic!

Since STOS Basic is already very powerful, it wouldn't take a lot of assembly language to transform even the most sluggish STOS Basic game into a machine code masterpiece. That's why several major software houses are now starting to use STOS Basic in a big way. I'll now provide you with a complete explanation of the STOS Basic assembly language interface. This will include a detailed examination of the various extension formats you can use to add whole libraries of new commands to your STOS Basic system.

In order to make the most of this section, you'll already require a basic grasp of 68000 assembly language. If you are unfamiliar this subject, you should refer to one of the 68000 tutorials listed in the bibliography before preceding any further. The only hard part of 68000 programming is the learning process. Once you've got the knack, you will be astonished at how easy it really is. So don't be afraid to persevere for a while until you have passed the initial confusion. Everyone has to struggle at the beginning, and the longer you work at 68000 assembler the simpler it becomes.

11.2 Choosing an assembler

11.2.1 The STOS Basic assembler

As you know, STOS Basic comes complete with its own 68000 assembler utility. If you've experimented with this program, you will have realized that it has a number of annoying limitations.

The fact is, the STOS Basic assembler was originally created for use with the French version of the package. It was included with the English system as an after-thought, and was never really intended as a serious development tool. So although the STOS assembler is fine for simple programs, it's not really very useful. I would therefore strongly advise you to treat yourself to one of the many alternative assemblers available on the market.

Luckily, STOS Basic is compatible with most 68000 assemblers, so the choice of package is entirely up to you. Here are a few suggestions.

11.2.2 Other assemblers

K-SEKA

K-SEKA is notable because it was used by Francois Lionet and C.Sotiropoulos during the development of the original STOS Basic package. K-Seka may not be the most advanced assembler on the market, but it's incredibly small, and impressively fast.

Francois was therefore able to assemble the complete 600k or so of STOS Basic source code in a matter of minutes using an unexpanded 1040 ST. Overall, K-SEKA is definitely worth thinking about if you want to write large programs on a standard 520 ST.

Supplier: Kuma

DevpakST (Version 2)

In my opinion DevpakST 2 is the best assembler currently available for the ST series of computers. At £59.95, it's not exactly cheap, but if you are serious about using 68000 assembly language on the ST, you'll quickly regard it as money well spent.

One feature which is especially useful for STOS programmers, is the AMONGST program. This can be placed in the AUTO folder of your working copy of STOS

Basic, and will load automatically along with the rest of the system. Whenever a processor error occurs, the MONST monitor is entered immediately from memory. You can now debug your program by placing an illegal instruction such as a TRAP #10 at the problem points in your assembly language routine.

Supplier: Hisoft

Devpack 1 ST

This an earlier version of the DEVPAK assembler which justly earned a rave review from yours truly in Atari ST User. It's nowhere near as good as the latest system, but it does include everything you need to generate useful assembly langugage programs.

The really interesting thing about DEVPAK 1 is that you may be able to obtain it quite cheaply. It did after all, form the centre piece for one of the ST/AMIGA FORMAT cover disks. (Issue 10). So if you're lucky, you might still be able to get hold of a back issue from Future publishing. (If you're really fortunate, you may already have a copy lying around in your disk box waiting to be used.)

Supplier: Hisoft

Don't panic, by the way, if you already own an assembler which I haven't mentioned. You almost certainly won't need to replace it especially for use with STOS Basic.

11.3 Free standing assembly language programs

The easiest method of adding some assembly language into a STOS Basic program is to place your routines directly into a memory bank. You can then execute these procedures using the CALL command as follows:

```
CALL Bank no
```

Any of the registers A0-A6 and D0-D7 can be accessed directly from Basic using the AREG and DREG functions.

Another approach, is to load your machine code routines into a string variable. In this case, you will need to ensure that all your routines are fully relocatable, as STOS Basic strings can move around in memory. You should also remember that STOS Basic strings are limited to 32k.

Supposing you had previously placed some machine code into the string CODE$. You could now execute this routine with a line like:

```
CALL VARPTR(CODE$)
```

Your assembly language programs can make free use of any of the DOS, BIOS, and XBIOS traps allowable under the TOS operating system. You can also call the WINDOW, SPRITE, and MUSIC functions detailed on pages 257 to 265 of the STOS Basic manual. You should however, steer well clear of the TRAP #4 and TRAP #6 functions. These have been omitted in the later versions of STOS Basic for reasons of space. So any attempt to call them will, I'm afraid, be doomed to failure.

11.4 STOS Basic extensions

One of the most exciting features of STOS Basic, is the ability to add whole new instructions to the standard system. These can be incorporated directly into your Basic programs and can be executed like any other STOS Basic instructions. With a little extra work, it's also possible to compile these new instructions using the COMPILER accessory.

STOS Basic extensions provide you with the perfect way of expanding the language to your own individual requirements.

So in the unlikely event that there's anything you really hate about STOS Basic, you'll probably be able to change it using an extension.

Whenever STOS Basic is run, the BASIC.PRG program searches the STOS folder for any files with the extension .EXn, where n can be any of the letters from A to Z (except B). These files are then loaded into memory, and the appropriate extension commands are installed automatically. Similarly, the STOS Basic compiler checks the COMPILER folder for compiler extensions in the form ".ECn" .

It's likely that you've already been using some of these extension commands for some time without actually realising it. The STOS Basic package includes a powerful set of screen compression extensions in the file COMPACT.EXA. These provide you with the two extra instructions PACK and UNPACK. Neither instruction is native to STOS Basic. If you've purchased the STOS MAESTRO package, you will also be familiar with the various sampler extensions.

I'll now show you how you can create one of these extensions for use in your own programs. All extensions are written in assembly language, using a special format. Although this format looks rather daunting at first, it's well worth persevering. After all, when you've successfully mastered the art of extension programming, you will be able to incorporate fast machine code into your games using your very own STOS Basic instructions.

Different techniques are required to produce the extension files needed for the STOS Basic interpreter and the compiler. I'll begin with the interpreter extensions because they are easier to understand.

11.5 Interpreter extensions

11.5.1 The header

At the start of every extension there is a list of information which details of the number and type of the extension commands defined in the file. Since this header data is not directly executable by the ST, the first instruction should always be a jump to an initialisation routine. e.g.

```
bra INIT
```

Each STOS Basic command is assigned a unique number known as a token. Even tokens refer to Basic instructions, and odd tokens are used for the functions. STOS Basic allocates 128 tokens for use by your extension. These range from 128 to 255.

The header commences with the number of the first token in your list. This value should always be set to 128.

```
even
dc.b 128
```

Note that these token numbers are automatically combined with the number of the extension during initialisation. So it's perfectly legal to use the same numbers in several different extension files.

The header now contains a detailed list of all the Basic instructions which will be provided by your extension. This list consists of the names of your instructions (in lower case), followed by their respective token numbers. The entire token list is terminated by a chr$(0).

Here is an example of one of these lists in Table 11.1.

Table 11.1 Example of a token list

tokens:	
dc.b "at",128	Instructions have EVEN tokens
dc.b "vers",129	Functions are ODD
dc.b "code$",130	Commands can contain almost any character including spaces
dc.b "test",132	Tokens may be out of sequence
dc.b "test on",134	All the characters in a name are significant
dc.b "test off",136	So "test","test on" and "test off" are DIFFERENT instructions
dc.b 0	The end of the token list is indicated with a ZERO
even	

The names of your instructions can be practically anything you like. But you can't include the names of any existing STOS Basic instructions in your new commands, because these are processed before your extensions.

So a command like DECODE, would be illegal, and would be interpreted by STOS Basic as:

```
dec ODE
```

You should also note that you are not allowed to use tokens with the numbers 160 or 184, as these are reserved for STOS Basic's internal use.

The next part of your extension informs the STOS system of the addresses of your new commands in memory. These are specified in the form of a "jump table", with the first word containing the number of jumps, and the succeeding words holding the actual addresses of your routines. The number of jumps in the list will often be the same as the number of new commands. If however, you are using tokens out of sequence, you need to include "dummy" values for any of the positions you will not be requiring.

So although there were only 6 instructions in the example in Table 11.1, you would actually be forced to include 9 addresses in your jump table.

The number of jumps required can be calculated by the formula:

number of jumps = last token - first token + 1
= 136 - 128 + 1
= 9

Here is a jump table for the example in Table 11.1

Table 11.2 The jump table for an extension

```
jumps:    dc.w 9
          dc.l AT          128
          dc.l VERS        129
          dc.l CODE        130
          dc.l DUMMY       131
          dc.l TEST        132
          dc.l DUMMY       133
          dc.l TESTON      134
          dc.l DUMMY       135
          dc.l TESTOFF     136
```

The labels AT, VERS, CODE, etc. refer to the addresses of the start of your extension routines. I'll be showing you the definition of DUMMY slightly later.

The final step is to add the messages which will be printed out after the extension has loaded. Two messages are needed, one in English and one in French. Each message is terminated by a chr$(0), as follows:

```
welcome: dc.b "Tiny extension",0
        dc.b "Extention Tiny!",0
```

If you don't speak French, you can place any message you like in the second position; you cannot omit the message altogether. In practice, it's well worth taking the trouble to translate your welcome into French, using a dictionary.

This keeps the system tidy, and recognizes the French origin of the STOS Basic package.

You should now reserve some space for two variables which will be required by the extension.

```
SYSTEM:dc.l 0              Address of system routines
RETURN:dc.l 0              Used to return back to Basic
                           (See later)
```

SYSTEM holds the address of a table containing the location of some of STOS Basic's internal subroutines. These can be called at any time from your extension. Features available include the conversion of a number from floating point to an integer, and the ability to exit back to Basic with a specified error condition.

RETURN is used to keep a copy of Basic's return address. This will be needed to allow your extension to safely returns to STOS Basic when it has finished.

11.5.2 Initialisation section

This is the first thing which is executed after the extension has been successfully loaded. Its action is to place the address of the end of the extensions into register A0, and the address of the COLD start routine in A1. e.g.

```
 INIT:      lea EXIT,a0         EXIT is a label at the END of
                                your program
            lea COLDST,a1
            rts
```

After this initialisation has been performed, the cold start routine at COLDST is immediately executed.

On entry, a pointer to the system routines is placed into register A0. This should be immediately saved in the SYSTEM variable you defined in the header. You must now inform the STOS Basic system of the location of the various bits of header information you created earlier, in the following way:

```
COLDST:    move.l a0,SYSTEM       Copy address of system table
                                  into memory

           lea WELCOME,a0         Address of welcome message
           lea WARMST,a1          Address of Warm start routine
           lea TOKENS,a2          Address of the TOKEN table
           lea JUMP,a3            Address of the JUMP table
```

The warm start routine is entered whenever STOS Basic is reset with <UNDO>. It's possible to exploit this feature to redefine any important variables used by your program to their default values after a reset. As the vast majority of extensions don't need this type of initialisation, it's common practice to substitute a single RTS instruction in this position:

```
WARMST:    rts
```

11.5.3 Syntax checking

Once you've completed your header definition, and set up the initialisation section, you are finally ready to implement your actual extension commands.

Whenever you call an instruction from Basic, you normally include a number of parameters. A parameter is just a fancy name for a value you provide to a Basic instruction. Take, for instance, the STOS Basic BOX command:

```
     BOX 10,15 to 200,100
```

This has the four parameters: 10, 15, 200, and 100. In the same way, a line like x=max(17,Z) has parameters of 17 and Z.

Any parameters which have been input to your commands will need to be accessed one at a time from within your extension routine. Fortunately, most of the really complicated stuff is performed automatically by STOS Basic. By the time your extension has been reached, the number, type, and even the values of the parameters are already known.

When your new instruction is executed, the number of parameters will be placed in register D0. The parameters themselves are pushed onto the A7 stack in the order they were typed, from left to right. Since Basic calls your extension using a JSR instruction, the first item on the stack will be the return address of the extension handler. The first action of your extension routine should therefore be to load this address in the RETURN variable you defined earlier. This will allow your extension to return back to Basic after it has completed. e.g

```
EXT:       move.l (a7)+,RETURN  Save return value
               :      :
               do extension
               :      :
```

```
          move.l RETURN,a0      Load return address into A0
          jmp (a0)              Jump back to STOS Basic
```

Your routine should now check the number of parameters supplied by the user against the number which is required by the instruction. Some instructions are capable of being successfully called in several different formats. In this case, each allowable format needs to be tested individually. If the wrong number of parameters has been input, your extension should immediately jump back to Basic using an error routine found in the SYSTEM table. This can been called using the following code:

```
SYNTAX    moveq #12,d0          Error number 12
          bra.s ERROR

TYPEMIS   moveq #19,d0          Error number 19
          bra.s ERROR

ILLEGAL   moveq #13,d0          Error number 13

* Load start of SYSTEM table into A0

ERROR:    move.l SYSTEM,A0
          move.l $14(A0),A0     Get address of error handler
          jsr (a0)              Jump to error handler
```

Note that the error numbers used by this function correspond precisely to the normal STOS Basic error messages. See pages 233-238 of the *STOS Basic manual.*

Providing the user has entered the correct number of parameters, your extension can now pull them directly off the A7 stack in REVERSE order. Each parameter is stored in four parts, and these are normally loaded into the registers D2-D4 using an instruction like MOVEM.L (a7)+,D2-D4.

The contents of these registers will vary depending on the type of the parameters you are using. I'll now provide you with a list of the possible formats, along with a sample set of syntax checking utilities to get you started:

```
INTEGER:

D2.B = 0
D3.L = Number
D4.L = 0

* Get integer from stack and check for syntax error
* INPUTS: none
* OUTPUTS: D3 = integer

GETINT:   move.l (a7)+,a0       Save return address
```

```
            movem.l (a7)+,d2-d4 Get parameter
            tst.b d2            Is the argument an integer?
            bne TYPEMIS         No! Signal an error
            jmp (a0)            Return from subroutine

TYPEMIS:    moveq #19,d0        Error number 19
            bra.s ERROR         Jump to error routine defined
                                previously.
```

Another useful subroutine allows you to convert an floating point number into an integer. This can be incorporated directly into the GETINT routine above:

```
* Convert an a floating point number into an integer
* INPUTS    D3/D4=Floating point number
* OUTPUTS   D3=Integer

INTFL:      movem.l d0/d1/d5/d6/d7/a0-a2,-(a7)
            move.l SYSTEM,a0    Get address of system routines
            move.l 4(a0),a0     Get address of FLTOINT routine
            jsr (a0)            Call FLTOINT
            movem.l (a7)+,d0/d1/d5/d6/d7/a0-a2
            rts

FLOATING POINT:

D2.B = $40
D3.L = Top half of number
D4.L = Bottom half of number

* Check for the presence of a floating point parameter
* Assumes the existence of the TYPEMIS routine shown earlier
* INPUTS: none
* OUTPUTS: D3/D4 hold number in floating point format

GETFLOAT:   move.l (a7)+,a0     Save return address
            movem.l (a7)+,d2-d4
            tst.b d2            Is the argument in floating
                                point?
            ble TYPEMIS         No! Signal an error
            jmp (a0)            Return from subroutine
```

There's also a routine to convert an integer into a floating point number. This can be called using the system table in the following way:

```
* Convert an integer into a floating point number
*INPUTS     D3=Integer
*OUTPUTS    D3/D4=Floating point number
```

```
FLINT:      movem.l d0/d1/d5/d6/d7/a0-a2,-(a7)
            move.l SYSTEM,a0      Get address of system routines
            move.l 8(a0),a0       Get address of FLTOINT routine
            jsr (a0)              Call FLTOINT
            movem.l (a7)+,d0/d1/d5/d6/d7/a0-a2
            rts
```

Incidentally, during the changeover from STOS Basic V2.3 to the latest version 2.4 the format of floating point numbers has changed. This has NO effect on the workings of your extensions.

```
STRING:
D2.B = $80
D3.L = Address of string
D4.L = 0

* Get a string from the stack and check syntax
* INPUTS: none
* OUTPUTS: D2 holds length of string, D3 contains address
* Note this routine destroys the contents of A1

GETSTR:     move.l (a7)+,a0       Save return address
            movem.l (a7)+,d2-d4   Get parameters
            tst.b d2              Is the argument a string?
            bge TYPEMIS           No!
            move.l d3,a1
            move.w (a1)+,d2       Get length of string
            jmp (a0)              Return from subroutine
```

The first two bytes of the string hold its length, and there is NO chr$(0) at the end. You therefore need to reformat the string for use by the various TOS routines.

```
* Routine to convert a string from STOS to GEMDOS format
* INPUTS:  D3=Address of string
* OUTPUTS: D1=Length of string
* Corrupts D2

STRFIX:     movem.l a1-a2,-(a7)   Save registers
            move.l d3,a1
            move.w (a1)+,d2       Get length of string
            move.w d2,d1          Save in d1
            move.l d3,a2
STRL1:      move.b (a1)+,(a2)+    Create space for chr$(0)
            dbra d2,STRL1         Loop through string
            move.w #0,(a2)+       Copy zero at end of string
            movem.l (a7)+,a1-a2   Restore registers
            rts
```

After you've called the STRFIX routine you can print out the string using the various GEMDOS commands. Before returning to STOS Basic, you should always take the trouble to reconvert the string back to its original format. Otherwise an error will occur whenever you try to use that string again from STOS Basic.

```
* Converts a string for TOS format back to STOS
* INPUTS: D1= Length of string, D3= Address of string
* OUTPUTS: none
*

STOSSTR:   movem.l d0/a1/a2,-(a7)Save registers
           move.l d3,a1          Save address of string
           move.l d3,a2          Save destination address
           add.l #2,a2           Add 2 for length
           move.w d1,d0          Set counter in D0
STRL2:     move.b (a1)+,(a2)+    Make room for length
           dbra d0,STRL2         Loop through string
           move.l d3,a1
           move.w d1,(a1)+       Replace length at start
           movem.l (a7)+,d0/a1/a2
           rts
```

You can use these syntax checking routines by simply calling them from your program with a JSR. Supposing you had an instruction called TEST which had three parameters in the format:

```
TEST string,float,integer
```

A typical call to this function might be:

```
TEST "Hi",3.141,42
```

You could now retrieve the parameters using the following fragment of assembly language:

```
TEST:      move.l (a7)+,RETURN Save return address for Basic
           cmp #3,d0           Check for THREE values
           bne ILLEGAL         Signal an error
           jsr GETINT          Get an integer
                               (Parameters in REVERSE order)
           move.l d3,d5        Save integer in D5
           jsr GETFLOAT        Get a floating point number
           move.l d3,d6        Save top half of number
           move.l d4,d7        Bottom half
           jsr GETSTR          Get a string
           move.l d3,a0        Save address of string in A0
```

```
         .
         .                      Body of TEST routine
         move.l RETURN,a0       Get return address for Basic
         jmp (a0)               Return to Basic

ILLEGAL: moveq #13,d0           Illegal instruction
         bra ERROR              Jump to error routine
```

Note that the body of your extension program should always save the registers A3/A5/A6 before changing them. These are reserved for STOS Basic's internal use and should be restored to their original values at the end of your routine. The best way of achieving this is to define a data area at the end of your extension and save the registers using something like:

```
leas averegs,a0          where saveregs is the address
                         of the end of your data area
movem.l D5-D6/A1-A6,-(a0)
```

At the end of your routine (just before the MOVE.L RETURN,a0), you can then reset these registers to their starting values with:

```
lea loadregs, a0         loadregs = Address of the
                         start of your data area
movem,l (a0)+,D5-D6/A1-A6
```

The space for the registers should be defined in the form:

```
loadregs ds.l 8
saveregs:
```

11.5.4 Function definitions

Any functions included in your extension will need to be able to return a value back to STOS Basic. This can be done by simply setting the registers D2-D4 using exactly the same format.:

Type	*Registers*
Integer	D3 = Integer returned
	D2 = 0
Floating point	D3/D4 = Floating point number
	D2 = $40
String	D3 = Address of string
	D2 = $80

11.5.5 System support routines

I've already mentioned that the SYSTEM table contains the addresses of a number of important routines. The full list runs to several pages, so I'll limit myself to a summary of more interesting ones:

```
* Check whether a value is an address or a bank number
* INPUTS: D3.L=Value
* OUTPUTS:
* If D3 contains the number of a reserved memory bank
* then D3 is loaded with the start address of the bank
* If the bank is not reserved, an error is generated

 GETBANK:  movem.l a0-a2,-(a7) Save registers
           move.l SYSTEM,a0    Get address of SYSTEM table
           move.l $88(a0),a0   Get ADORBANK address
           jsr (a0)            Call routine
           movem.l (a7)+,a0-a2 Restore register
           rts

* Check whether an address or a bank number is a screen
* INPUTS: D3.L=Value
* OUTPUTS:
* If successful, D3 contains the start address of the screen
* Otherwise an error is generated

 GETSCR:   movem.l a0-a2,-(a7) Save registers
           move.l SYSTEM,a0    Get address of SYSTEM table
           move.l $80(a0),a0   Get ADORSCRN address
           jsr (a0)            Call routine
           movem.l (a7)+,a0-a2 Restore register
           rts

* Generate a user defined error condition
* INPUTS: A0 = The address of a string containing the error
*                 messages in TWO languages!
*            D0 = The number of the error message to output
* OUTPUTS: NONE

 MYERROR:  movem.l a0-a2,-(a7) Save registers
           move.l SYSTEM,a0
           move.l $18(a0),(a0) routine number $18
           jmp (a0)
           rts

* Get space for a new string
```

```
* INPUTS D3.L = Length of new string
* OUTPUTS A0 = Address of allocated string
            A1 = Another copy of the address in A0
            move.l SYSTEM,a0
            move.l $1C(a0),(a0) routine number $1C
            jsr (a0)
            rts
```

Another very useful routine is the DUMMY command I mentioned earlier.

```
DUMMY:      move.l (a7)+,return  Remove return address
            bra SYNTAX           Generate a syntax error
```

Now for a full blown extension for you to type in:

Example 11.1 The Tiny extension

```
* Tiny Extension By Stephen Hill
* Adds three (trivial) new commands to STOS Basic

* caps on
* turns on caps lock within a program
* caps on
* ALL INPUT TEXT IS IN UPPER CASE

* x$=code(a$,n)

* encodes a string by adding an integer n to each character
* useful for adventure games
* eg c$="ATTACK":print code$(c$,2) gives
* CVVCEM

* caps off
* now you're back in lower case

* Extension Header
            even
            bra INIT              Jump to initialization
                                  routine
            dc.b 128              Starting at token number 128

* Token list

TOKENS      dc.b "caps on",128    Instructions are even
            dc.b "code$",129      Functions are odd
            dc.b "caps off",130
            dc.b 0                End of new instructions
```

```
* Jump table

            even
 JUMPS      dc.w 3                  Number of extension commands
            dc.l CAPSON             Addresses of extensions
            dc.l CODE
            dc.l CAPSOFF

* Welcome messages in TWO languages

 WELCOME    dc.b 10,"Tiny extension",0
            dc.b 10,"Extension tiny",0
            dc.b 0
            even

* Reserve space to hold address of Basic variables

 SYSTEM     dc.l 0

* Reserve space to hold return address from Basic

 RETURN     dc.l 0

* Load a0 with offset to end of extensions in memory

 INIT       lea EXIT,a0
            lea COLDST,a1           Address of cold start routine
            rts

 COLDST     move.l a0,SYSTEM        Copy address of variables
                                    into A0
            lea WELCOME,a0          Address of welcome message
            lea WARMST,a1           Address of Warm Start routine
            lea TOKENS,a2           Address of token list
            lea JUMPS,a3            Address of jump table
            rts

 WARMST     rts                     Currently does nothing

* Support routines for a STOS Basic extension

* Get an integer argument

 GETINT     move.l (a7)+,a0         Save return address
            movem.l (a7)+,d2-d4     Get a parameter
            tst.b d2                Is the argument an integer?
            bne TYPEMIS             No!
```

```
          jmp (a0)              Return from subroutine

* Get a string argument

 GETSTR   move.l (a7)+,a0       Save return address
          movem.l (a7)+,d2-d4   Get parameter
          tst.b d2              Is the argument a string?
          bpl ILLEGAL           No!
          jmp (a0)              Return from subroutine


* Ask STOS nicely for some string space
* Thanks Francois!

 ASK      move.l SYSTEM(pc),a0
          move.l $1c(a0),a0
          jsr (a0)
          rts

* Syntax errors

 SYNTAX   moveq #12,d0          Error number 12
          bra.s ERROR

 TYPEMIS  moveq #19,d0          Error number 19
          bra.s ERROR

 ILLEGAL  moveq #13,d0          Error number 13

 ERROR    move.l SYSTEM(pc),a0Get address of Basic routines
          move.l $14(a0),a0     Get address of error routine
          jmp (a0)              Jump back to basic

* caps on
* sets capslock on

 CAPSON   move.l (a7)+,RETURN   Save return address
          movem.l A0-A6,-(a7)   Be paranoid!
          move.w #16,-(a7)      Set bit 4 for kbshift
          bra SETCAPS           Jump to BIOS Call

* caps off command
* Turns off CAPS Lock

 CAPSOFF  move.l (a7)+,RETURN
          movem.l A0-A6,-(a7)   Be paranoid!
```

```
            move.w #0,-(a7)      Resets keyboard completely

SETCAPS     move.w #11,-(a7)     Call kbshift
            trap #13             BIOS trap
            addq.l #4,a7
            movem.l (a7)+,a0-a6  restore registers
            move.l RETURN,a0     Jump back to basic
            jmp (a0)

* x$=code$(s$,n)

CODE        move.l (A7)+,RETURN  Save return address
            cmp #2,d0            Two parameters?
            bne SYNTAX           Syntax error
            bsr GETINT           Get an integer
            move.w d3,d1         Store in D1
            bsr GETSTR           Get a string
            move.l d3,a2         Save address of string in A2
            moveq #0,d3          Zero D3
            move.w (a2)+,d3      Get length of string
            jsr ASK              Get some space for result
            move.w d3,(a0)+      Save length in new string
            subq #1,d3

ADSTR       move.b (a2)+,d2      Get first byte
            add.b d1,d2          Code byte
            move.b d2,(a0)+      Save in new string
            dbra d3,ADSTR        Loop through string
            move.l a1,d3         Save address of string
            move.w #$80,d2       Tell STOS to expect a string
            move.l RETURN,a0     Jump back to basic
            jmp (a0)
            dc.l 0
EXIT                             End of routines
```

This program should be assembled into PC Relative code and placed in a file such as TINY.EXE inside the STOS folder on your BACKUP of the STOS Basic system disk. The new commands will be loaded automatically when you next run STOS, and can be used straight from the editor. Try typing in the following small program:

```
10 caps on
20 input "Please input some text to encode";C$
30 input "Please enter the code number (1 to 255);C
40 print code$(c$,c)
50 caps off:goto 20
```

11.5.6 Interpreter extension checklist

1 Add a jump past the header information to the main initialisation routine.

2 Produce the token table for the extensions, starting with a token number of 128. Each new instruction will need its own definition in this table. End the token table with a CHR$(0).

3 Create the jump table. This specifies the addresses of the various extension commands included in your file. One entry is needed for each token. Don't forget to add the dummy entries for any tokens you aren't using in the sequence.

4 Add welcome messages terminated by a CHR$(0) in TWO languages.

5 Reserve space for RETURN and SYSTEM variables.

6 Initialisation. Set up the addresses of the end of the extension and the cold start routine. Feel free to use the code directly from my examples.

7 Cold start routine. Defines the addresses of the header information for use by the Basic interpreter.

8 Warm start routine. This called every time STOS Basic is reset using the <UNDO> command. The warmstart can be anything from a simple RTS to a complex piece of initialisation code.

9 Start your extension instructions. These should begin by saving the return address with "move.l (a7)+,RETURN"

10 Check the number and type of parameters entered by the user. Abort with an error if there has been an input mistake otherwise load the parameters.

11 Perform the main body of your extension routine.

12 Exit back to STOS Basic with something like:

```
move.l RETURN,a0
jmp (a0)
```

11.5.7 B is for BUG!

When STOS Basic was first produced, a couple of minor bugs were left in the extension commands. These have been corrected in version 2.4 of STOS Basic, but they are still well worth knowing about if you are intending to sell your extensions commercially.

1 You can't use an extension file with the letter B. So TINY.EXB would be illegal. This is not a major problem, as there are 24 other letters to choose from.

2 This is the big one. The original STOS source allocated the space for the extension instructions with DC.L 26 instead of DS.L 26. This means that the

addresses of the extensions are actually loaded into the stack used for the FOR NEXT loops! Fortunately, this is not as bad as it sounds. As a default you are allowed to use nest ten of these loops inside each other. You would therefore be able to type a horrendous program such as:

```
100    FOR A=1 to 100
110      FOR B=1 to 200
120        FOR C=1 to 300
130          FOR D=1 to 400
140            FOR E=1 to 500
150              FOR F=1 to 600
160                FOR G=1 TO 700
170                  FOR H=1 TO 800
180                    FOR I=1 TO 900
190                      FOR J=1 TO 1000
200                        PRINT A+B+C+D+E+F+G+H+I+J
210                    NEXT J
220                  NEXT I
230                NEXT H
.                  .
.                  .
.                  .
etc...
```

In practice, few Basic programs actually need this level of nesting. Every extension file you use in STOS V2.3, reduces the number of nested FOR/NEXT loops by one. This means that there is a practical limit of around six or seven extensions in version 2.3. At the present time there are only two extensions available to the general public. One of these, the compiler extension, includes a copy of STOS version 2.4 which fixes the problem completely. So there's nothing to be unduly worried about.

3 If you are defining a function with no parameters, you will be unable to use it in a normal Basic expression. e.g.

`B=TESTEXT*5` Doesn't work

Where TESTEXT was your new extension. The solution is simply to add a dummy parameter in your extension definition. This can then be manipulated in the standard way.

`B=TESTEXT(0)*5` Is legal

Don't forget to remove the parameter from the stack inside your extension. Otherwise the useless parameters will lurk dangerously on the stack.

11.6 The compiler extensions

The STOS Basic compiler expects to find full details of all the current extensions in the \COMPILER folder. The format of these extension files is effectively split into two sections.

One section gives a complete description of the syntax of the new instructions. This information is needed during compilation to allow the compiler to detect any possible errors in a program before converting it into machine code.

The second, and rather longer part, contains a set of library routines which will be selectively incorporated into the final machine code program. Since there's no way of knowing where these routines will be situated in the ST's memory, it's vital to remember to generate them using PC RELATIVE code.

11.6.1 The header for a compiler extension

The compiler header starts off with a list of three relative addresses.

```
START:     dc.l PARA-START     Offset to the parameter list
           dc.l INIT-START     Offset to the Initialisation
                               section
           dc.l LIB1-START     Offset to the start of the
                               library routines.
```

Next comes the library catalogue. This holds the lengths of all the library routines which you are defining in your extensions. In the case of the TINY extension I showed you previously, this catalogue would look like this:

```
* LIB1 is label referring to the address of the CAPSON

* LIB2 is a label holding the address of start of the CODE
routine

* LIB3 is a label indicating the position of the CAPSOFF
extension.

* LIBEX is a label denoting the address of the end of library
```

```
CATALOG    dc.w LIB2-LIB1      length of routine 1
           dc.w LIB3-LIB2      length of routine 2
           dc.w LIBEX-LIB3     length of routine 3
```

The header now contains the parameter definitions needed by the compiler's syntax checker:

```
    PARA: dc.w 2,2
```

The first number corresponds to the total number of library routines in the file, and the second value to the number of new instructions. Normally, both numbers will be exactly the same, but it's theoretically possible to create internal library routines which are common to several instructions.

You now enter the offset to the parameter definitions needed by each extension instruction:

```
dc.w     PCAPS-PARA     Offset to parameter set for CAPS ON
dc.w     PCODE-PARA     Offset to parameters for CODE
dc.w     PLOW-PARA      Offset to parameters for CAPS OFF
```

The order of these definitions is exactly the same as the order you used in your EX file when you created your interpreter extensions. As before, if you are using instructions out of sequence you will need to include dummy definitions for all the tokens which are not required.

You are now ready to specify the parameters for each new extension command. If your command has several possible formats, you will need to include all allowable forms in this definition.

The parameters are defined using the following coding scheme:

0 = Integer parameter
$40= Floating point number
$80= String
1 = End of one set of parameters for the instruction.
1,0= End of entire parameter definition for a specific instruction.
"," indicates that the parameters are to be separated by a comma.

The format of the definition is the same for both instructions and functions. The first byte in the definition holds the type of value which is returned by the command. If your command is an instruction, this value will be set the zero.

One useful trick is to define a constant for each of the different types of data. This enables to read the definitions at a glance, without having to refer back to the table, for example:

```
I EQU 0
F EQU $40
S EQU $80
```

Now for a set of example definitions for you to examine.

```
* CODE x$,n
P1: dc.b 0,S,",",I,1,1,0

* X$=UNCODE(C$,N)
```

```
P2: dc.b S,S,",",I,1,1,0

* Parameter definition for the STOS Basic MAX function.

* x=MAX(a,b)

MAX:   dc.b I,I,",",I,1       First set of parameters
       dc.b F,F,",",F,1       x#=max(a#,b#)
       dc.b S,S,",",S,1       x$=max(a$,b$)
       dc.b 1,0               End of parameters for max

DUMMY:     dc.b 0,1,1,0       Dummy parameters. Needed for
                              unused tokens.
```

The next part of the extension definition is the initialisation routine. This section is always incorporated into the compiled machine code program. It performs any essential set-up procedures, and includes all the data needed by your extensions. Generally the data areas are reserved at the beginning of the segment. So the first instruction is usually a jump to the cold start routine itself, e.g.

```
INIT       bra COLDST         Jump to cold start routine

DATA
* Place any data values needed by your extension here
* (Optional)
* e.g.

BUFFER:    dc.l 0             Typical variable
           .
           .
           .
```

On entry to the cold start routine, A0 is loaded with the address of the memory available for your use, and A1 to end of this area. Additionally A5 points to the start of Basic's variable table. There's also a special EXIT routine which is called when the extension has finished. The address of this routine should always be placed in A2 at the start of the initialisation section.

Here is a really simple set up for you to look at:

```
COLDST:    lea END(pc),a2
           rts
END:       rts                No termination routines
                              needed
```

Incidentally, if a problem occurs during the installation process, you can signal an error condition by placing a POSITIVE value in D0.

Also, if you manipulate the value in A0, you can reserve some memory for your extensions exclusive use.

Reserving memory for a compiler extension:

```
* Reserve 1000 bytes for internal use

COLDST:
     lea   BUFFER-INIT(pc),a2 Get address of your variable
     move.la0,(a2)            Save start of memory block in
                              variable BUFFER
     lea   1000(a0),a0        Reserve memory
     cmp.la1,a0               Is there enough memory free?
     bcc   OUTOFMEM           No
     clr.wd0                  D0 is set to zero if no error
     lea   END(PC),a2         load address of end routine
     rts

OUTOFMEM:
     moveq#1,d0               Signal an error condition
     rts
```

11.6.2 The compiler library

The library system supported by the compiler is "smart". This means that only the library routines which are actually used by your program will be inserted in the machine code produced by the compiler. You can call a library function from the main compiler library using an instruction like:

```
     jsr LIB
```

LIB is simply the number of the library routine. Here are a couple of functions which are especially useful for your extensions:

```
GETBANK    EQU 214               Gets address of a bank
           INPUTS:               Bank number .L. This is placed
                                 on the A6 stack e.g.
                                 movem.l #No,-(a6)
           OUTPUTS:              D3.L = Address of bank
           REGISTERS CHANGED: D0-D3:A0-A3

GETSCR     EQU 234               Checks whether an address in
                                 D0 points to a screen.
           INPUTS:               Bank number .L. Place on A6
                                 stack
           OUTPUTS:              D3.L = Address of screen
           REGISTERS CHANGED: D0-D3:A0-A3
```

```
ASK          EQU 70              Asks STOS Basic to allocate
                                 you some space for a string
             INPUTS:             D3.L = No of bytes of string
                                 space in reserve.
             OUTPUTS:            D3.L = Address of allocated
                                 string
```

It's also possible to define your own library routines for use in your extension file. In practice, however, these routines can be a nightmare to actually implement. Since the benefits of an internal library are pretty marginal, I would therefore strongly advise you to avoid these routines completely. But if you enjoy a challenge, here's the format:

```
jsr number+$80000000
```

where number is the number of the library routine relative to the start of the catalogue.

11.6.3 Creating a compiler library

Each new instruction in your extension requires an appropriate library routine to be produced. Whenever an attempt is made to compile your instruction, a call to this code will be generated by the compiler. If you are accessing any internal library routines in your extension, you need to place a list of addresses at the start of your code. This list contains the relative positions of all the places in your routine where you are calling one of these functions. The list is terminated by a zero word. The reason for this list is that the final addresses of the various internal libraries are only known during the compilation process. So it is vital that the compiler is able to replace your "jsr number" statements with the correct jump to an absolute address in your program. For example:

```
L1:          dc.w L1a-L1,0       Tell compiler that there is a
                                 library call at L1a
             .
             .                   Rest of extension code
             .

L1a          jsr GETBANK         Call GETBANK routine
             .
             .
             rts
```

The extension itself is just a simplified version of the instruction you created in the ".EX" file. Since all the syntax checking is performed by the compiler, there is no need to perform any complicated error handling. You can exit from your extension routine at any time using a simple RTS instruction.

Note that the end of your extension lists should always be terminated by a zero word,e.g.

```
ENDEXT      dc.w 0                  End of your extensions
```

11.6.4 Retrieving the parameters entered by the user

On entry to the extension, D0 is loaded with the number of the parameter list which has been entered by the user. This is NOT the number of the parameters. A6 contains the address of a stack containing of these parameters.

You can now access each parameter in reverse order using an instruction in the following format:

```
move.l (a6)+,d0        Pull an integer from the stack D0=INTEGER
                       input by the user
move.l (a6)+,a0        Pull a string from the a6 stack A0=Address
                       of the string in STOS format. (First
                       word=length)
move.l (a6)+,d0        Removes top half
move.l (a6)+,d1        and bottom half of floating point number.
```

Similarly functions need to push their results on the A6 stack after the function has been completed, e.g.

```
move.l d1,-(a6)        Return an integer
movem.l d1-d2,-(a6)    Return a floating point
move.l a0,-(a6)        Return a string. Always request space for
                       this string using ASK before returning.
```

11.6.5 Using a data area

I'll now briefly explain how you can manage the data area if you reserved one earlier. Although this gets a little technical, it is important to realise that none of the information below is essential for the creation of an extension. It is only relevant if you are writing large programs which need to reserve their own private work spaces. Every time one of your extensions is incorporated into a compiled program, the data area you included in the initialisation section (between INIT and the start of your extensions) is automatically included into the final machine code. The address of the data area can be retrieved using a special system variable called DEBUT. This is normally contained in a large INCLUDE file called "EQUATES.S" which is not currently available to the general public. I have however, assembled this file and retrieved the number you need directly, e.g.

```
DEBUT EQU $92c
```

You can now get the address of your data array by adding the following lines at the start of your extensions:

```
move.l debut(a5),a3    get address of DEBUT variable
move.l 0(a3,d1.w),a3   get address of data area
```

Let's assume you had defined a list of your variables in this area as follows:

```
data:                          Start of data area
var1       dc.w 10
var2       ds.l 5
var3       dc.b "Hello"
```

You could now access these variables using the following instructions:

```
move.l var1-data(a3),d0 D0 is loaded with ten
lea.l var2-data(a3),a0  A0 is loaded with the start of
                        the long words you defined at
                        var2
lea.l var3-data(a3),a1  A1 points to the string
                        "Hello"
```

11.6.6 System variables

The variable table from 11.6.5 contains two useful addresses which can be accessed by your extension.

```
FLAGEM EQU  $9a0   Set to one if compiled program is running
                   from the GEM desktop, otherwise zero
ERROR  EQU  $93c   Holds the address of the error handler
                   routine. Call using the following code:
                   moveq   #err_no,d0     STOS error no
                   move.l  error(a5),a0 Address of routine
                   jmp     (a0)           Signal an error
```

Example 11.2 A compiler extension for TINY

```
* Example Compiler library

* Set up system variables
Debut   EQU $92c
Error   EQU $93c
FlaGem  EQU $9a0

* Define extension addresses
```

```
START   dc.l PARA-START  Parameter definitions
        dc.l DATA-START  Reserve data area for program
        dc.l LIB1-START  Start of library

CATALOGdc.w LIB2-LIB1    length of routine 1
        dc.w LIB3-LIB2   length of routine 2
        dc.w LIBEX-LIB3  length of routine 3

PARA    dc.w 3           Number of Library routines
        dc.w 3           Number of extension commands
        dc.w PCAPS-PARA  Offset to first parameter set
        dc.  PCODE-PARA
        dc.w PLOW-PARA   Offset to parameters for UNCODE

* Parameter definitions
I       EQU 0
F       EQU $40
S       EQU $80
* "," Forces a comma between any commands
* 1   Indicates the end of one set of parameters for an in-
      struction
* 1,0 Indicates the end of the commands entire parameter
      definition

PCAPS       dc.b   0,1,1,0        Dummy for caps on

PCODE       dc.b   S              Function return value
                                  (optional)
            dc.b   S,",",I        Parameter definitions
            dc.b   1,1,0          End of definition
PLOW        dc.b   0,1,1,0        Dummy for caps off

* End of parameter definitions

            EVEN

*  Initialisation section
* This code is loaded into memory during initialisation
* It can be accessed using the address placed in the DEBUT
  variable

DATA        bra    INIT

INIT        lea    END(pc),a2     Load position of end into A2
            rts
```

```
END         rts

* Extension Library

* caps on
* set capslock on

LIB1        dc.w    0                   No library calls
            movem.l a0-a6,-(a7)         Be paranoid!
            move.w  #16,-(a7)
            move.w  #11,-(a7)           Call kbshift
            trap    #13                 BIOS trap
            addq.l  #4,a7
            movem.l (a7)+,a0-a6         restore registers
            rts

* X$=code$(x$,10)

ASK         equ 70

LIB2        dc.w    CALASK-LIB2,0       call ASK
            move.l  (a6)+,d1            Get n
            move.l  (a6)+,a2            Get code string
            moveq   #0,d3
            move.w  (a2)+,d3            Get length of string
CALASK      jsr     ASK                 Get a new string in A0
            move.w  d3,(a0)+            Move length to destination
            move.w  d3,d0
            subq    #1,d0               Adjust for DBRA
ADSTR       move.b  (a2),d2             Get a character
            add.b   d1,d2               Add in offset
            move.b  d2,(a0)+            Replace encoded character
            dbra    d0,ADSTR            Repeat for all characters
            move.l  a1,-(a6)
            rts

LIB3        dc.w    0                   No library calls
            movem.la0-a6,-(a7)          Be paranoid!
            move.w  #0,-(a7)            Resets keyboard completely
            move.w  #11,-(a7)           Call kbshift
            trap    #13                 BIOS trap
            addq.l  #4,a7
            movem.l (a7)+,a0-a6         restore registers
            rts

LIBEX       dc.w    0                   End of library
```

11.6.7 Compiler extension checklist

1 Start the extension header with a list of offsets to your parameter definitions, your initialisation section, and your extension instructions.

2 Create the library catalogue. This contains the lengths of all the library routines you are adding in your extension.

3 Produce the header for the parameter list. Begin with two words holding the total number of libraries created, and the number of new instructions in your extension. Then add a list of offsets to the appropriate parameter definitions.

4 Generate the parameter definitions in the same order they appear in your interpreter extension. Don't forget to cover all possible sets of parameters.

5 Write initialisation/data section. If you are not using an internal workspace, then this will be very simple.

6 Add your extension programs. These should commence with a list of the addresses in your routine where you call a library procedure. Library procedures may be internal (defined in your program) or external (built into the main compiler library).

7 Read the user's parameters off the A6 stack in REVERSE order.

8 Exit your instruction with an RTS.

9 Exit your extension with a dc.w 0 directive

11.7 Conclusions

The STOS Basic extension system provides you with the perfect opportunity to take a real part in the continuing development of the STOS Basic system. Given the undoubted talent of many users, I confidently expect to see some incredible results. But if you have any problems with these extensions, drop me a line via the STOS User club. I'll be happy to try and set you on the right track.

Well that's it for this book. I hope you've enjoyed reading it as much as I've enjoyed writing it. Writing a game in STOS Basic can be an extremely rewarding experience. So do have a go. The journey you will travel to reach your objective may be long and hard, but the feeling of satisfaction you will get from reaching it will repay you many times over. So what are you waiting for? Get out and write a computer game today!

Glossary of Terms

Acceleration (Simulation) Acceleration measures the rate of increase of an objects speed. It's commonly measured in (Meters Per Second)/ Per second

Attributes (Role-playing) Attributes provide a role playing game with a measure of the strengths and weaknesses of the various characters. Typical attributes are STRENGTH, DEXTERITY, and STAMINA

Axes (3D graphics) The axes of a coordinate system highlight the three directions from which the coordinates will be measured. These directions are given the labels X,Y, and Z

Background screen (Sprites) This is a separate screen used by STOS Basic to hold a copy of the area UNDERNEATH the sprites. The address of the screen is held in the reserved variable BACK.

Colour registers The Atari ST allows you to display up to sixteen different colours on the screen at a time. The precise shade of each colour is held in a set of 16 memory locations known as the colour registers.

Colour scrolling Colour scrolling is a simple technique which progressively changes the values held in the ST's colour registers to produce a range of interesting animation effects.

Connection list A list of the connections between the various rooms in an adventure. Usually held in an array such as: map(room_number,exit_number)

Coordinate systems These allow you to specify the exact location of a point in 3D space relative to an arbitrary starting point.

Data structure A list of connected information treated as a unit. Typical data structures include arrays and records.

Documentation A complete written description of the workings of a computer program. Often supplemented by the use of copious REM statements within the program.

Extensions Special assembly language programs which can add whole new instructions to the STOS Basic system.

Fringe (Scrolling) A useless region of the image which is left over from a scrolling operation. Usually removed using the CLS instruction (Extended version).

Fumble (Role playing) A random number generated during the combat calculations of an RPG which represents a disastrous mistake on the part of the players character.

Game map (Adventures) A complete map of the locations of each room, and the connections between them. The game map is usually drawn up on a piece of paper when you are designing your adventure. It often includes brief descriptions of the various puzzles and objects which are to be encountered by the players.

Game plan A complete plan of your game written as an aid to programming.

Game world The imaginary world created inside a computer game such as a simulation or an adventure.

Game time The time which is presumed to have passed inside the game world. Sometimes this can be very different from the actual time experienced by the player.

Garbage collection An automatic reorganisation of the ST's memory which releases any memory which is no longer needed by your STOS Basic program.

Implementation The process of converting a written specification (or game plan) into a STOS Basic program which can be entered directly into your computer.

Interrupt Interrupts are internal routines which are called automatically after a certain period of time. Used by STOS Basic to control the sprites and the music operations.

Level (Role playing) A single number which indicates the general level of abilities attained by a player's character. The level of a character usually increases with experience.

Logic error An error in the DESIGN of your program.

Logical screen The screen which is used by the ST for all drawing operations. If this is different from the physical screen, then the image under construction will not be displayed until your program specifically requests it. See SCREEN SWAPPING. STOS Basic stores the location of this screen is a special variable called LOGIC.

Look up table	A table of values calculated in advance. Look-up tables allow you to replace complex calculations with a direct read from an array, and can speed up many programs considerably.
Mêlée rounds (Role playing games)	Mêlée rounds split a combat situation into a number of phases which can be performed by a computer.
Mock-up	Mock-ups are simple sketches of the game screens produced during the planning process. They can be easily created with Neochrome or DEGAS for use as test screens while your game is being developed.
Movement table (Arcade games)	Movement tables contain a list of the successive positions of a sprite during an attack wave. They are used extensively in games such as Zoltar or Space Invaders.
Origin (3D Graphics)	The arbitrary starting point from which the coordinates are measured. The origin always has coordinates of (0,0,0)
Parabola	A smooth curve which is traced in the air by an projectile such as a golf ball.
Parry (RPG's)	An attempt by characters in an RPG to defend themselves from attack.
Parser (Adventures)	The section of an adventure program which reads the users commands and translates them into a form that can be interpreted by a computer.
Physical screen	The physical screen is an array of memory locations which hold the image which is currently being displayed on your TV. It is not necessarily the same as the screen used for the various drawing operations. See Logical screens. The location of the physical screen is always held in the STOS Basic variable PHYSIC.
Pixels	Short for PIcture ELements, pixels are the smallest individual points which can be manipulated on the ST's screen.
Prototyping	The process of testing possible ideas experimentally before including them in the final game plan.
Pseudo-code	A simplified form of English which allows you to concisely describe the action of a program without having to involve yourself with any messy implementation details.

Realtime	The time which is actually experienced by the players of a simulation. Separate from the time assumed to have passed in the Game world.
Rebound table (Rebound games)	A table containing the rebound directions for all the various obstacles in a rebound game.
Real RPGs	The original Role playing game played out on paper.
RPG	Short for Role playing game
Screen swapping	The art of updating a piece of graphics on an invisible logical screen and smoothly updating the actual display. This technique can be used to generate some delightful effects.
Scenario	The "plot" of an adventure game or an RPG.
Simulation	A mathematical "model" of a real world situation held inside a computer.
SIN and COS	Two mathematical equations which describe the ratios of the various sides of a right-angled triangle. Used in many 3D graphics programs.
Specification	A detailed plan of a computer program made out prior to its creation. Similar to a Game plan.
Sprite	Sprites are special pieces of graphics which can be manipulated independently from the rest of the screen. See Chapter 4 of the original STOS Basic manual for more details.
Stats	See Statistics
Statistics (RPGs)	These specify the abilities of a particular character in a role playing game. See Attributes.
Structured programming	The art of unravelling the detailed workings of a computer program from a simple pseudo-code description.
Synonyms (Adventures)	Words with an identical or similar meaning. ie GET and TAKE. Lists of common synonyms are held for each of the possible commands in an adventure to reduce the risk of ambiguity.
Syntax errors	Errors generated by typing mistakes made when you are entering your program into the ST. e.g prunt "This is a syntax error"

Systems analysis
The act of analysing a problem and generating a solution. This solution often takes the form of a computer program.

Thought experiments
A thought experiment describes the process of thinking through the various implications of an idea before committing yourself to actually using it in one of your games. This can save you hours of frustration trying to write a program which will never really work out in practice

Velocity
A measure of an objects speed in a specific direction. e.g. Ten miles per hour due North.

Zone
Zones are areas of the screen defined using the STOS Basic SET ZONE command. They can be used to recognise the collision between a sprite and a section of the screen.

Index

3D effects, 125, 171, 177, 181
    movements, 86
    rotation, 186
68000 programming, 242

A
acceleration, 78
AD&D, 99
adventure, game plan, 141
aliens, moving, 30, 32
ANIM, 205
ARKANOID, 48, 67
array, view, 184
asembly language programs,241 - 243
ASTEROIDS, 4
attack paths, 32
attributes, 101, 109

B
background, 41
    animation, 44
    screens, 12
ball, 54, 57
bat, 53, 54, 56, 62
Bullet, 228

C
call, 243
characters, 100, 110, 127
    classes, 101
    controlling, 125
    generation, 111
    creating, 109
    leading, 128
    player, 100
clipping, 184
collide, 21, 24, 39
collisions, 40, 56, 57, 58, 60
collision detection, 21, 39
Colossal Cave, 137, 138
colour registers, 201
    scrolling, 201
combat, 128
commands, dummy, 255
    movement, 169
compiler, 244
    extensions, 260, 269
    library, 264, 265
connection list, 159
control loop, 12, 42, 69
    panels, 90
controlling
    characters, 125
    guns, 37
coordinate systems, 171
coordinates, 172
    game world, 183
    object, 183
    transformation, 175
COS, 190
creating a character, 109
    map, 140
critical phases, 12
    routines, 48
current location, 162

D
data
    area, 266
    structures, 17
DEBUT, 266
DEC, 26
DEF SCROLL, 225, 227
defence factor, 131
definitions, function, 253
Degas, 12, 14, 152, 155
descriptions, 157
designing
    graphics, 12
    screen, 50
detect, 21, 59
DevpakST, 242
direct synthesis, 217
directions, rotation, 186
disk, samples, 214
displaying
    map from above, 115
    part of a map, 116
documentation, 22
drawing the map, 115
drop, 166
dummy, 246
dummy command, 255
Dungeons and Dragons, 99

E
economic simulation, 92
elevation, 87
Elite, 183
equations of motion, 77
errors, logic, 23
    syntax, 23

events, 142, 163
    local, 142
    priority of, 142
expanding the parser, 149
experience, 103
extensions, 244, 255
    compiler, 260, 269
    interpreter, 258

F

FADE, 204, 205
flags, 163
FLASH, 203
flight simulators, 88, 89, 197, 198
follow, 23
fringe, 226, 232, 233
fumble, 130
function definitions, 253

G

Galaxians, 28
game map, 106
game plan, 1, 3, 6, 9, 19, 48, 89
    adventure, 141
    role-playing, 108
    Shoot-em-up, 31
    using, 20
game world, 76
game world coordinates, 183
game-time, 77
garbage collection, 19
get, 166
global commands, 165
glueing (the ball to the bat), 54
graphics
    adventures, 153
    choosing, 152
    designing, 12
gun, controlling, 37

H

high priority event, 142, 164
hyperspace, 204

I

INC, 26
individual control, 128
initialisation, 12, 42, 67
initialising, 231
input, joystick, 126
INSTR, 147
interpreter extensions, 245, 258
inventory, 165, 163
irregular object, 58

J

joystick
    handler, 90
    input, 126
jump table, 246

K

K-SEKA, 242
keyboard, 125
kilohertz, 213
Kingdom, 9, 2, 93

L

laws of motion, 77 -78
leading character, 128
level, 103
library routines, 261
local, 164
    commands, 167
    events, 142, 167
logic, 208
logic errors, 23
LOOK, 167
look-up tables, 25
low priority, 164
low priority events, 142

M

machine code, 241
magic, 135
map
    creating, 140
    definer, 50, 52, 229
    displaying from above, 115
    displaying part of, 116
    drawing, 115
    scrolling through, 230
    storing, 230
    room, 116
mass, 81
mêlée, 131
mêlée rounds, 129
memory, 16, 18, 19
missile, 39, 40
mock-ups, 4, 14, 16
modular programming, 7
moon lander, 79, 84
motion in two dimensions, 82
mouse, 53, 127
move X, 33
move Y, 33
movement
    commands, 169
    directions (eight), 56
    directions, 55
    strings, 32, 33, 55
    tables, 34, 43
    3D, 86
moving
    between rooms, 116, 158
    aliens, 30, 32

N

Neochrome, 12, 14, 152, 155
Newtonian laws, 77
NPC, 100

O
objects, 161
  coordinates, 183
  scaling, 175
obstacles to the players, 107
optimization, 25, 27
Orbiter, 14, 26, 48, 51, 67
origin, 172, 174

P
parabola, 82
parameters, 248, 262, 265
parry, 130
parser, 144
  expanding, 149
  verb noun, 144, 147
perspective, 177
perspective factor, 179
picturing the scene, 152
planning a game, 1
player characters, 100
players, obstacles to, 107
prepositions, 149
programming, modular, 7
programs, assembly language, 243
pseudo-code, 7, 19

R
reading the <HELP> key, 126
reading the controls, 89
Real-RPG, 100
real-time, 77
rebound, 59, 62, 63, 66
  game plan, 49
  tables, 59, 61
  zones, 64
recording speed, 213
resolution, choosing, 13
rooms, 155
  description, 155, 156
  maps, 116
  moving between, 116, 158
rotation
  directions, 186
  formulae, 187
routines,
  critical, 48
  system support, 253
RPGs, 99, 100

S
sampler, making the most of, 214
sampler disk, 214
Save game, 163
scaling, 176
  an object, 175
scenarios, 104, 105, 139
SCREEN$, 205, 206, 207, 222
screen , 50
  animation, 206
screen
  background, 12
  compactor, 152
  coordinates, 184
  copy, 206
  designing, 50
  flipping, 208, 236, 237
  input system, 153
  scroll, 224
  swap, 208, 237
SCROLL, 227
scrolling
  through a map, 230
  zones, 225
SEG$52
separating words, 145
SHIFT, 203
Shoot-em-up, game plan, 30 - 31
simulation, 75, 92
  economic, 92
simulator, flight, 197 - 198
sines, 26
  tables, 199
SINH, 190
sound sources, 214
space invaders, 28
space simulations, 91
special effects, 213
specification, 3
sprites, 15, 238
STAC, 139
storing the map, 230
STOS Basic
  assembler, 242
  compiler, 27, 199, 222, 260
  MAP Definer, 229
STOS MAESTRO, 212
SYNCHRO, 238
synchro, 44, 207
syntax
  checking, 248
  errors, 23
system support routines, 253
system variables, 267
systems, coordinate, 171

T
tables, rebound, 59, 61
termination, 12
testing, 23, 24
text, understanding, 144
The Pawn, 13
token, 245
transformation of coordinates, 175
trap, 243, 244

U
Universal control panel 90, 153
Universal Control System 37
UPDATE, 238
using the game plan, 20

V

vanishing point, 178
velocity 78
verb noun parser, 144, 147
view array, 184
visibility, 121, 194
VPN, 165

W

weapon, 129
weight, 81

Z

Zoltar, 29, 30, 41, 206, 212
zone, 21, 24, 57, 58, 90, 153
zones, scrolling, 225
Zork, 137

BEST SELLERS AND NEW TITLES FROM SIGMA PRESS

Manage Your Business - Computerise your Accounts *Malcolm Briggs*
After word processing, most PC users need an accounting package. Although this book uses the *Sage Sterling* package as an illustration, the principles are sufficiently general for any other package to be used. It explains the principles of small business accountancy and how to transfer smoothly from a manual system. Contents include: simple accounting; setting up a computerised system; nominal ledger; sales (or debtors) ledger; stock control and order processing; benefits of integration.
Spring 1990 ISBN: 1-85058-147-9 250 pages £12.95

Timeworks Publisher Companion - DTP on a PC *Ray Morrissey*
This is a `hands on' approach to using the popular, low- cost Timeworks package. The package has been widely acclaimed as having many features only found on Ventura, Pagemaker and other high-cost packages. With Timeworks and a low-cost PC, you really can get started in desk-top publishing. Contents: Word Processing and DTP; Introduction to typography; Installing Timeworks; Designing the layout - using the `toolbox'; Text and graphics manipulation; Preparing single page and multi-page documents; Choosing printers; Advanced applications.
Summer 1989 ISBN: 1-85058-149-5 250 pages £12.95

Ventura Adventure - moving up to Version 2.0! *Philip Crookes*
This explains what the manual never told you - and it also shows the differences between version 1.1, 1.2 and the new, greatly enhanced version 2.0. See how to deal with the ordinary and extraordinary problems of desktop publishing, and how you can use Xerox's Ventura Publisher packages even on such a low-cost machine as the Amstrad PC1512. After an introduction to DTP and Ventura, you'll see how to: read in text from word processors, spreadsheets, and databases; how to edit and typeset on the screen; exploiting the full character set; creating graphics not just from Ventura, but also from GEM, from spreadsheets and from CAD programs; placing pictures in the text; letting the computer do the work of indexing, preparing contents pages, building tables
Winter 1988 1-85058-123-1 216 pages £12.95

Communications and Networks - a handbook for the first time user *Philip Croucher*
Many PC users want to transfer files from other computers, or to network their hardware so that expensive resources such as laser printers are shared between computers. Phil Croucher provides low cost solutions, in practical terms for the beginner, in an easy conversational style. The first part covers computer communications and includes:; ; Principles; Protocols; Communication packages (including Kermit); Hardware (modems, fax cards, telex cards) ; Troubleshooting. The second part describes networking: Advantages; Networking versus multi-user; Hardware and software; Packet switched systems; Security.
Spring 1989 1-85058-136-3 180 pages £11.95

Hypertext and HyperCard - Theory and Applications *Nigel Woodhead*
This book presents an overview of the theory, core Hypertext features, available applications and specific case studies. It will be of interest to those who need an introduction to the area and to those needing to see Hypertext in the context of database models, object-oriented and frame-based programming. Contents include: History of Hypertext; early models; innovations and methodological issues; Potential of Hypertext: identifying application areas; Case studies: the Stackware culture; financial and library management; real-time databases; Available packages. Companion tables of relative costs and features; bibliography and source addresses.
Spring 1990 ISBN: 1 85058 183 5 £12.95 250 pages

The Shareware Handbook *Odd de Presno*
Thousands of public domain and shareware programs are available for the cost of a telephone call from a bulletin board, or for a few pounds by mail. But how to select the best from the crowd? Published comparative evaluations of shareware is rare - and that's where this book comes in. It presents a selection of the best public domain and shareware products available. It guides the reader to choose the best and to judge whether it suits his or her needs. It highlights strengths, weaknesses and indicates applications. The book is supported with a library on a UK Bulletin Board.
Summer 1989 ISBN: 1 85058 157 6 220 pages £11.95

Moving Up To WordStar 5.5 *Tony Hollins*
This book, written in a friendly practical style, covers the latest releases of WordStar - enabling users of version 4 and earlier to move up to the newest versions. It covers: installation; upgrading; file management; mailmerge; DTP applications; short cuts; communications
Winter 1989 ISBN: 1 85058 184 3 £12.95: 250 pages

Amiga in Depth - the complete owner's guide *Patrick Hall*
Patrick Hall has the knack of explaining difficult concepts in an easy, relaxed manner. This is essential for Amiga owners struggling to do more than scrape the surface of this powerful machine's capabilities. Unlike other Amiga books, this is comprehensive and complete in one volume.
Spring 1990 ISBN: 1 85058 178 9 250 pages £12.95

Programmer's Technical Reference: MS-DOS and the IBM PC (to version 4.01)
Dave Williams
This book is intended for advanced PC users, programmers, system builders and others wishing to exploit the full power of MS-DOS.
Packed with tables of reference data, the *Technical Reference* has been developed and tested over a period of many years prior to publication. The Technical Reference includes copious detail on every aspect of the PC and its operating systems. Writing in a friendly style appreciated by other programmers, Dave Williams examines all technical features in depth. Numerous appendices are included for reference.
Winter 1989 ISBN: 1 85058 199 1 350 pages £14.95

The Comms Book - edited by *Dennis Jarrett*
Communications is now the most rapidly expanding area of computing but it is sometimes difficult for the newcomer to understand the terminology, or experienced users to keep up with the trends. The COMMS BOOK is a comprehensive and practical answer. Written by many of the well-known names in the computer industry, it offers a wide-ranging survey of the background and applications to computer communications.
Summer 1989 ISBN: 1 85058 179 7 300 pages £12.95

Mastering Protext *Jeremy Williams*
The book specifically covers versions 4.2 and 4.3, the most recent and enhanced versions of this popular and powerful word processing package. Protext is available for a wide range of computers, including the IBM PC, Atari ST, Amiga and Amstrad PCW. For PCW owners, who invariably start with LocoScript, there are great attractions in using the more powerful and standardised Protext which enables them to move easily to other machines.
Spring, 1990 ISBN: 1 85058 182 7 250 pages £11.95

Foxbase and Clipper Tools of the Trade *David M Bell*
Over several years, the author has developed software and databases using dBase III and similar languages. Great use has been made of Foxbase Plus and Clipper, and the wealth of tools associated with these products. Many of these powerful tools are little known in the UK, but they can help to make software development more productive and pleasurable.
The book is aimed at those who already know dBase and are considering Clipper or Foxbase. Also, regular users of these products will find the book to be an invaluable reference.
Spring 1990 ISBN: 1-85058-205-X 280 pages £12.95

Inside The Z88 *Dave Oborne*
The Z88 portable computer from Cambridge Computers retains a solid following despite the near-absence of in-depth books. This new book is not a re-write of the manual, but instead an exploration of how to get the best from the machine. For example, the word processor contains many functions and facilities to ease the programs use. Numerous examples and actual screen dumps illustrate the techniques used.
Spring 1990 ISBN: 1-85058-204-1 250 pages £12.95

A complete catalogue of all of our books is available. Order our books from your usual bookseller or, in case of difficulty, contact us direct:

Sigma Press, 1 South Oak Lane, Wilmslow, Cheshire, SK9 6AR. Phone 0625-531035; 24 hour tele-ordering and message service. Fax 0625-536800. Access and Visa orders are welcome.